IMAGES
of America

SAN ANGELO 1950s AND BEYOND

ON THE COVER: This photograph shows Hazel Neff operating the miniature locomotive at the Neff's Amusement Park. See page 42 for more information about the photograph. (Courtesy of Carolyn Kersten.)

IMAGES
of America

SAN ANGELO 1950s AND BEYOND

Gerron S. Hite

ARCADIA
PUBLISHING

ISBN 978-0-7385-9686-0

Published by Arcadia Publishing
Charleston, South Carolina

Printed in the United States of America

Library of Congress Control Number: 2012947002

For all general information, please contact Arcadia Publishing:
Telephone 843-853-2070
Fax 843-853-0044
E-mail sales@arcadiapublishing.com
For customer service and orders:
Toll-Free 1-888-313-2665

Visit us on the Internet at www.arcadiapublishing.com

This book is dedicated to my parents, especially my mother, who started teaching me about design and the built environment while pushing me around in a stroller.

Contents

ACKNOWLEDGMENTS

I want to thank Susan Campbell, head of the Dr. Ralph R. Chase West Texas Collection (WTC) at Angelo State University, for all her help in annotating the collection for my particular project. Shanon Sturm, university archivist, was always available to answer questions and scan photographs that citizens loaned for my book. Carol Mathews, support staff, as well as, Zacchary Dowdle and Ray Theiss, student assistants, were a great help. The other major collection I used was the archives at Fort Concho National Historic Landmark (FC). Bob Bluthardt, director, reviewed the draft text, and Evelyn Lemons, librarian/archivist, were very helpful in the pursuit of photographs and information. Dan Utley, historian and friend, made constructive comments throughout the writing process. Golda Foster, chair of the Tom Green County Historical Commission, provided a wealth of information. Many organizations and individuals freely provided information, photographs, architectural drawings, and scrapbooks to help tell of the recent past. These include the following: Bobby Abbott; Roger Allen, director, Chicken Farm Art Center; Loleta Barnhart; Earl Berry; CRS Center, College Station, Texas; Dale Chadwick, Myers Drug; Charles Ducote; Laura Ducote; Laura Gillis; Gary Goetz; Dr. John Garrett; Brenda and Ken Gunter; Barbara Hesse; Larry Justiss, director, Stephens Central Library; Mike Knittel, Kaiser Owners Association; Carolyn Kersten; Margaret Mallard; Ann and Ben McCulloch; J. Mark McLaughlin, Texas State Bank; Jack E. Meek, emeritus, American Institute of Architects (AIA); J.L. Mercer and Son; Pamela Miller, vice president of San Angelo Convention and Visitors Bureau; Dr. Pepper Museum & Free Enterprise Institute, Waco, Texas; Lee Pfluger; Barbara Rallo; Linda Rasor; Henry Schmidt, AIA; Rick Smith, *Standard-Times*; George K. Randall, Randall Motors; Howard Taylor, director of the San Angelo Museum of Fine Arts; Texas Department of Transportation; Sandy Whittley, executive secretary Texas Sheep & Goat Raisers Association; and Genora C. Young, executive director of Downtown San Angelo, Inc.

I want to also thank Lauren Hummer, Laura Bruns, and other staff at Arcadia Publishing for helping direct me through the various steps toward my first published book.

Introduction

This book explores the recent past in San Angelo, Texas. The term "recent past" is commonly used to describe historic resources or events less than 50 years old. In this case, though, we are defining it as the period from 1950 to the present. Many people are unwilling to accept the fact that events or changes in the built environment that happened in their lifetime could be historic. For example, several years ago, a county judge said to me, "I remember when our courthouse was built in 1939, so it could not be historic." This book will shed light on historic themes, people, and events that helped shape San Angelo during the recent past.

With the 1923 discovery of oil at the Santa Rita No. 1, located 85 miles west of San Angelo; the construction of the Goodfellow Air Force Base; and the establishment of ranches to raise sheep, goats, and cattle, San Angelo grew steadily as the largest trading center in the region after World War II.

In the years 1940 to 1950, the population doubled to 52,095. The larger city needed more schools, including Central High School (1958), which is nationally recognized for architectural innovation as the first campus-like high school in the United States, and Belaire Elementary School (1955), with its economically designed, pie-shaped classrooms and early use of air-conditioning. Excellence in education continued into the next decade with the construction of John Glenn Junior High (1967), which also received international attention for its space-age architectural design combined with an innovative curriculum.

San Angelo had its share of regional and national businesses, such as Woolworth, S.H. Kress & Co., Sears, J.C. Penney, and Safeway, and the booming economy influenced thriving local businesses. They included Just-A-Bite Café, Triangle Inn, West Texas Café, Lund's Drive-in, the Fair department store, Little Mexico Café, Cactus Grill, Liberty Café, Texas Drug Store, Goodwin Tavern, Blue Bonnet Steam Laundry, Texas Kreme Kone, Roosevelt Drug, Del-Tex Candy, Sam's Chicken House, Tony's Drive Inn, Log Cabin Steak House, Beaver Lodge Motel, M System grocery stores, Sherwood Lanes bowling alley, Neff's Amusement Park, Crystal Confectionery, Hudman's Drug Store, and drive-in theaters with names like Stardust, Twilight, Jet, and Rocket. Some businesses are still remembered, while others have quietly disappeared into the past.

Water has played a part in the history of San Angelo. The floods of 1881 and 1936 were devastating, but many other weather events have occurred here since 1950, including the drought of the mid-1950s that slowed growth in the area. The O.C. Fisher Reservoir was officially impounded in 1952 to provide flood control and secondary drinking water, but the 2011 drought claimed it as a victim. The 1950s drought was followed by torrential rains during the spring of 1957. In the 1960s, Twin Buttes Dam was built to provide water and recreational activities for the city. Hailstorms have also done tremendous damage, occurring in June 1954, April 1960, May 1993, and the worst in decades on May 28, 1995. In 1953, a tornado hit the Lake View neighborhood of San Angelo, killing 8, injuring 159, and resulting in property damage estimated at $3.25 million.

By the 1970s, San Angelo followed the national trend of its downtown businesses moving to the suburbs or completely ceasing operations.

In 1968, Victor Gruen, creator of the modern shopping mall concept, was hired to solve the downtown problems, but his downtown mall was never built. Growth occurred in the southwest and southeast sections of downtown with the construction of Sunset Mall (1979), but later, big box stores accelerated the exiting of downtown.

In 1986, the exhibit "Visions and Choices," which refers to the quality of life and built environment downtown, was held at the San Angelo Museum of Fine Arts, with a forum by AIA, R/UDAT (American Institute of Architects, Regional/Urban Design Assistance Team). In 1992, R/UDAT returned to develop a plan for the revitalization of downtown, titled "Connecting the Past to the Future." The construction of Celebration Bridge happened immediately after the plan was approved.

Since then, other landmark projects have included the construction of a new art museum, the restoration of historic buildings on Concho Avenue, the $12 million rehabilitation of the former Hemphill-Wells department store into the main county library, and the $11 million restoration of the 1928 Modern-style city hall, designed by Trost & Trost of El Paso. More work continues in the historic core by the city and private enterprises.

One

1950s

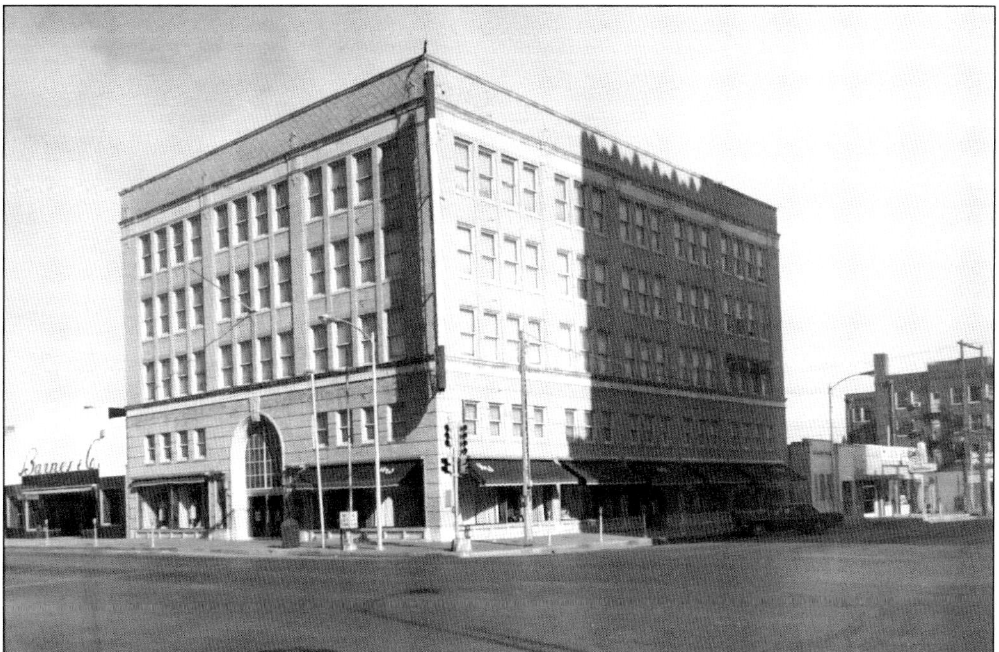

Hemphill-Wells Department Store. In 1929, Baker-Hemphill moved into the five-story building at Irving Street and Beauregard Avenue. The name changed in 1937 to Hemphill-Wells to reflect the new ownership. As tastes and markets changed, modern buildings were preferred, and the department store was torn down in June 1971. Temporary facilities were arranged at the Cox-Rushing-Greer Building at 213–215 South Chadbourne Street and the ground floor of the old San Angelo National Bank Building at 7 West Twohig Avenue. On February 12, 1973, the store moved into its new building at Irving Street and Beauregard Avenue. (WTC.)

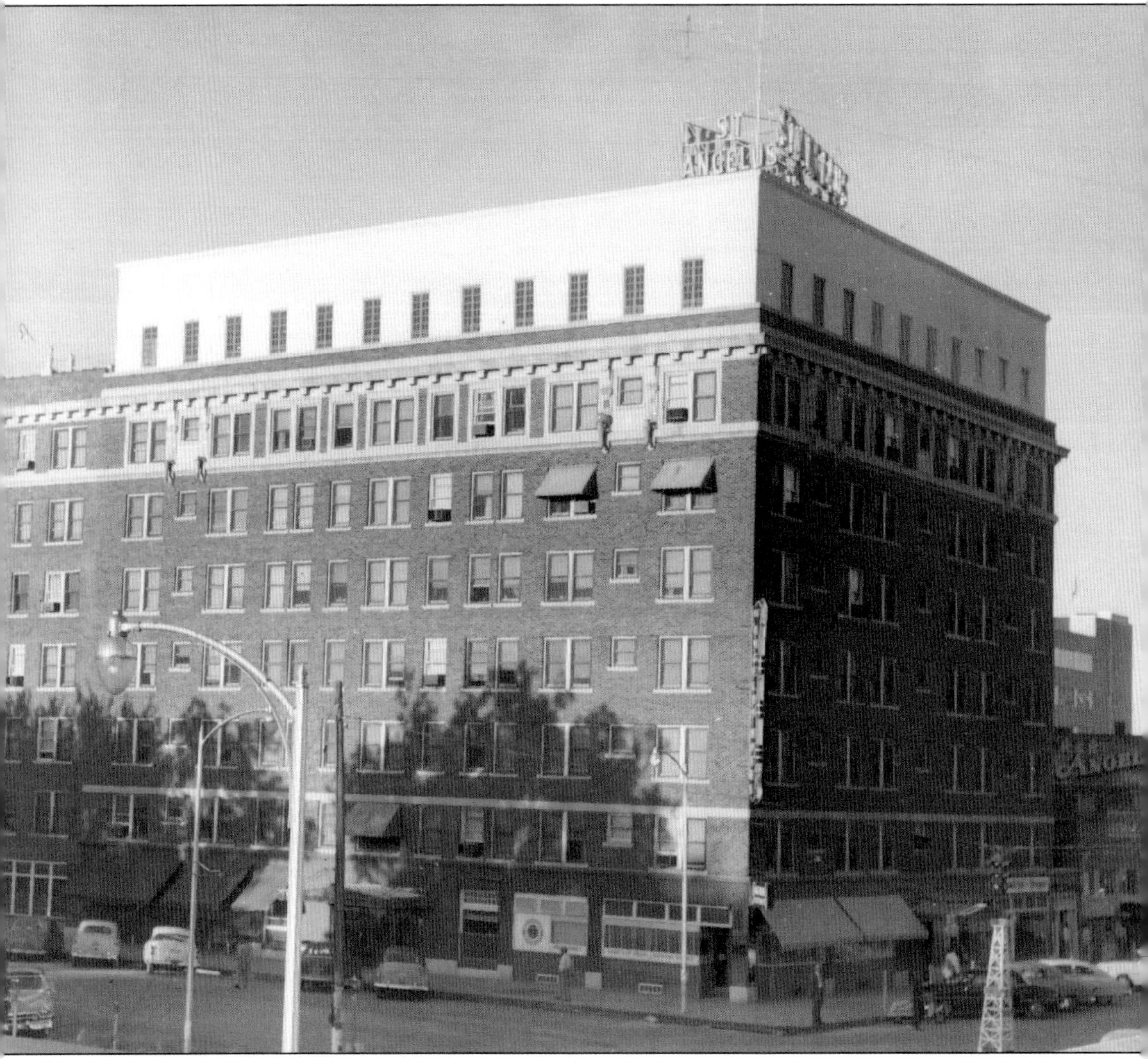

St. Angelus Hotel. The St. Angelus Hotel, located at Beauregard Avenue and Irving Street, was built in 1917, enlarged in 1926, and remodeled in 1958. On March 10, 1964, however, the owners turned off the lights and locked the doors for the last time. The last permanent guest was prominent West Texas rancher Lea Aldwell, who had made his home on the seventh floor of the hotel since it opened in 1917. He relocated to the Town House Hotel, where he continued to run his ranching operations. The St. Angelus Hotel Building was purchased and demolished along with five other buildings for the 1967 construction of the Central National Bank. See page 61 for a photograph of the bank. (WTC.)

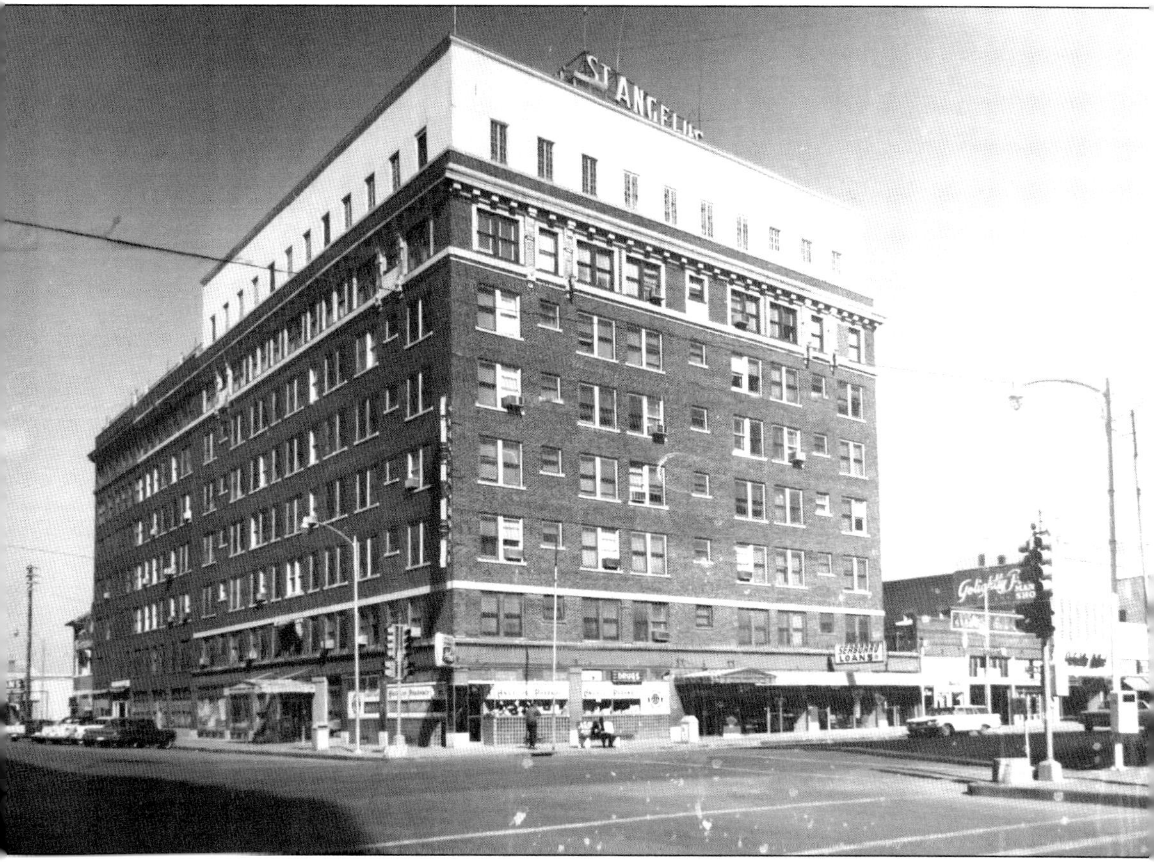

BEAUREGARD AVENUE AND IRVING STREET. This is a view of the St. Angelus Hotel, located across the street from the Hemphill-Wells department store, Tom Green County Courthouse, and the Western Reserve Building, later renamed the McBurnett Building. Three of the four buildings being constructed gave an impressive urban feeling. The hotel originally had elegant canopies over the sidewalk to denote the two main entrances; the Cactus Hotel has a similar feature, which can still be experienced today. Many gala parties and dances were hosted at the roof garden of the St. Angelus Hotel. (WTC.)

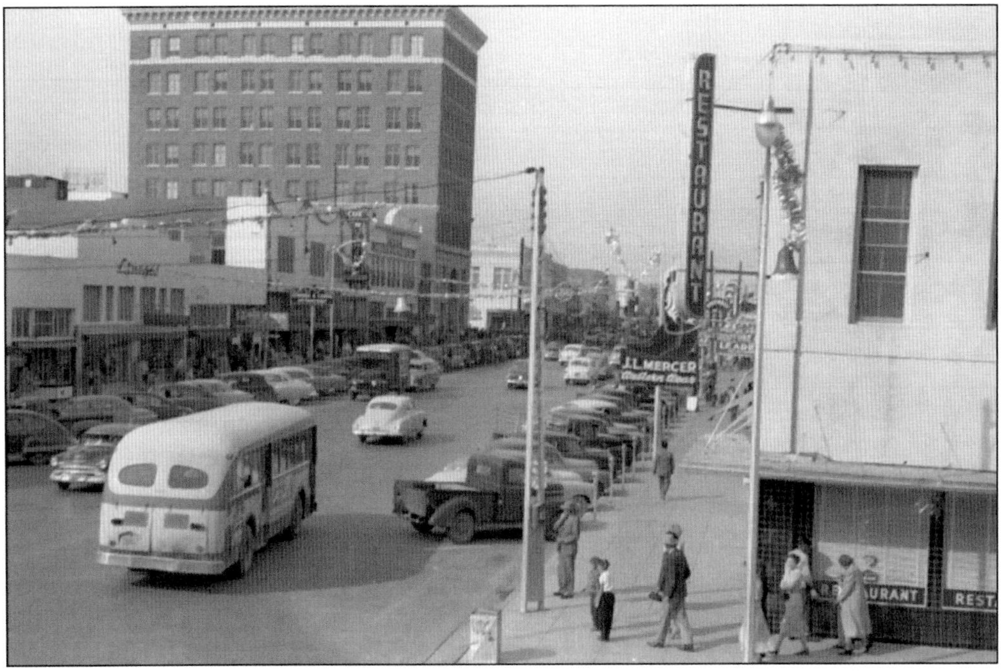

Chadbourne Street and Concho Avenue. Shown here is a 1950s view of Chadbourne Street and Concho Avenue, looking toward Twohig Avenue. (WTC.)

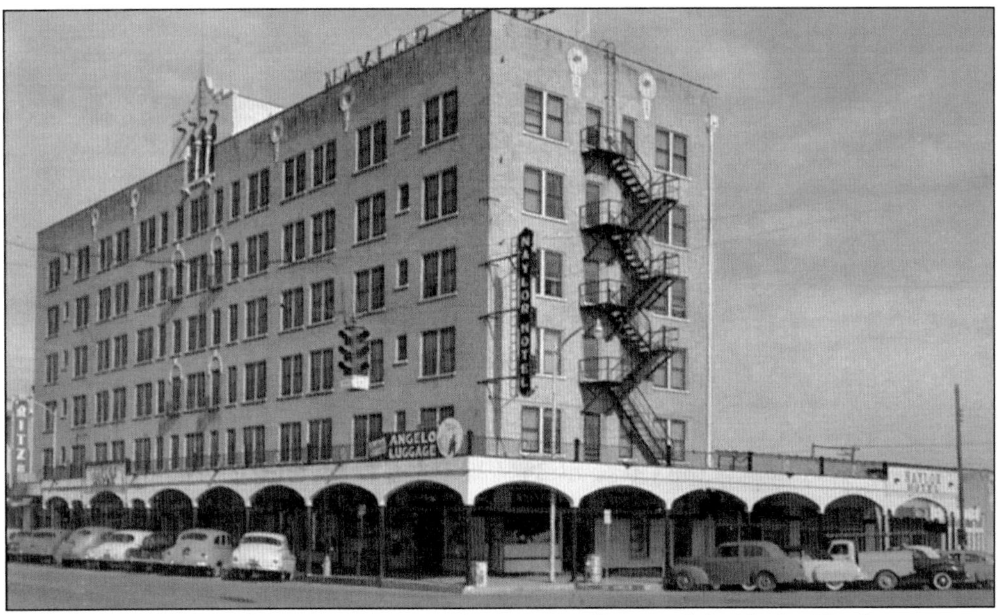

Town House Hotel. The Town House Hotel was originally named the Naylor Hotel, comprising 150 rooms, a coffee shop, a drugstore, and the Ritz Theatre. In 1955, as part of a major remodeling of the building, a contest was created to rename the hotel. The winning entry was Town House Hotel. The theater was converted into a ballroom, and other changes were made by the new owner. These changes were not successful in the long run, and the upper floors of the building are now vacant. Located on a main intersection, this is a historically important building that needs to be stabilized until a use can be developed and funding secured. (FC.)

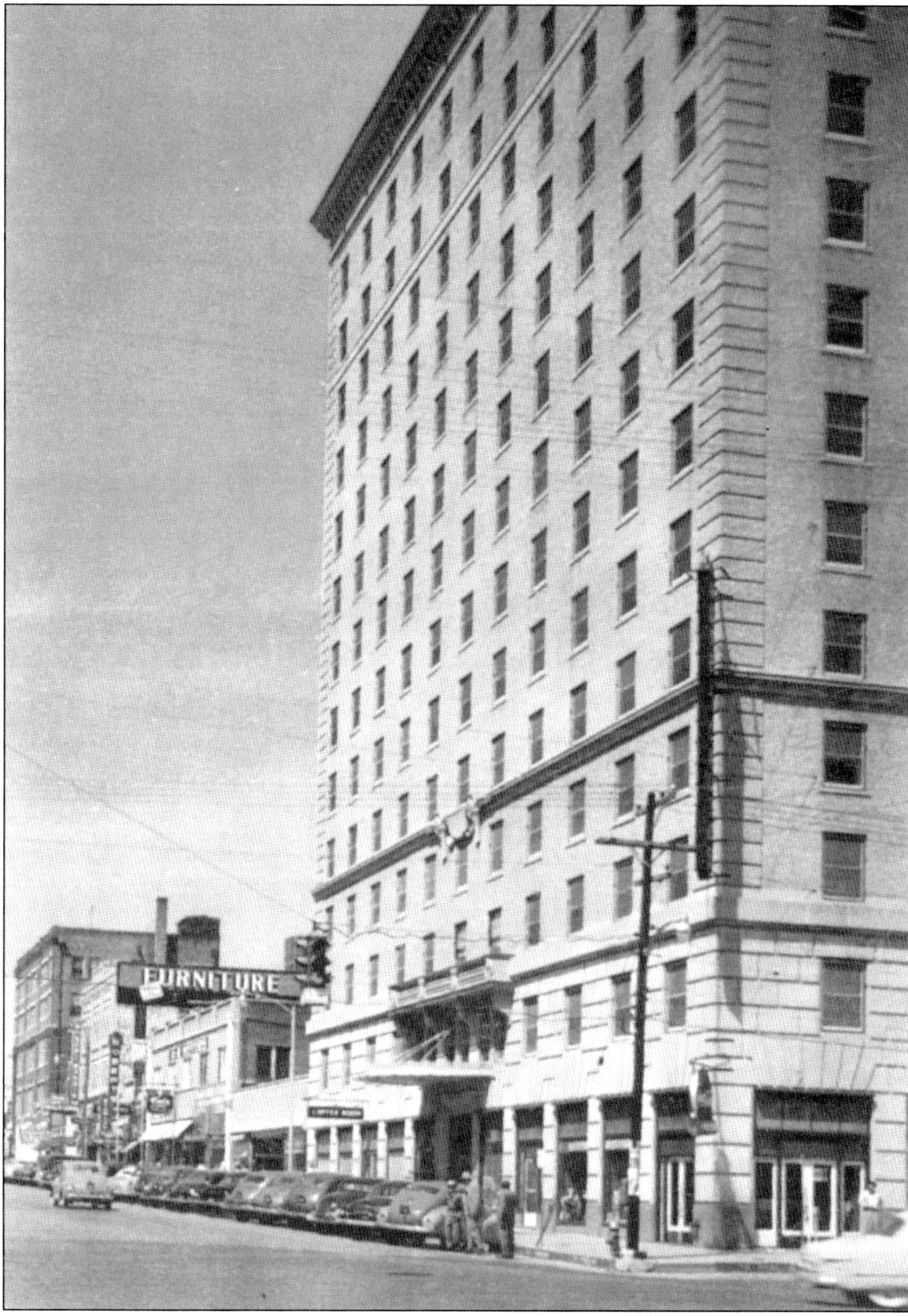

Cactus Hotel Streetscape. This is a view looking up East Twohig Avenue in front of the Cactus Hotel in the 1950s. The "Furniture" sign belongs to the Robert Massie Furniture Store, which was restored later by the Junior League of San Angelo. See page 123 for more information on that building. (FC.)

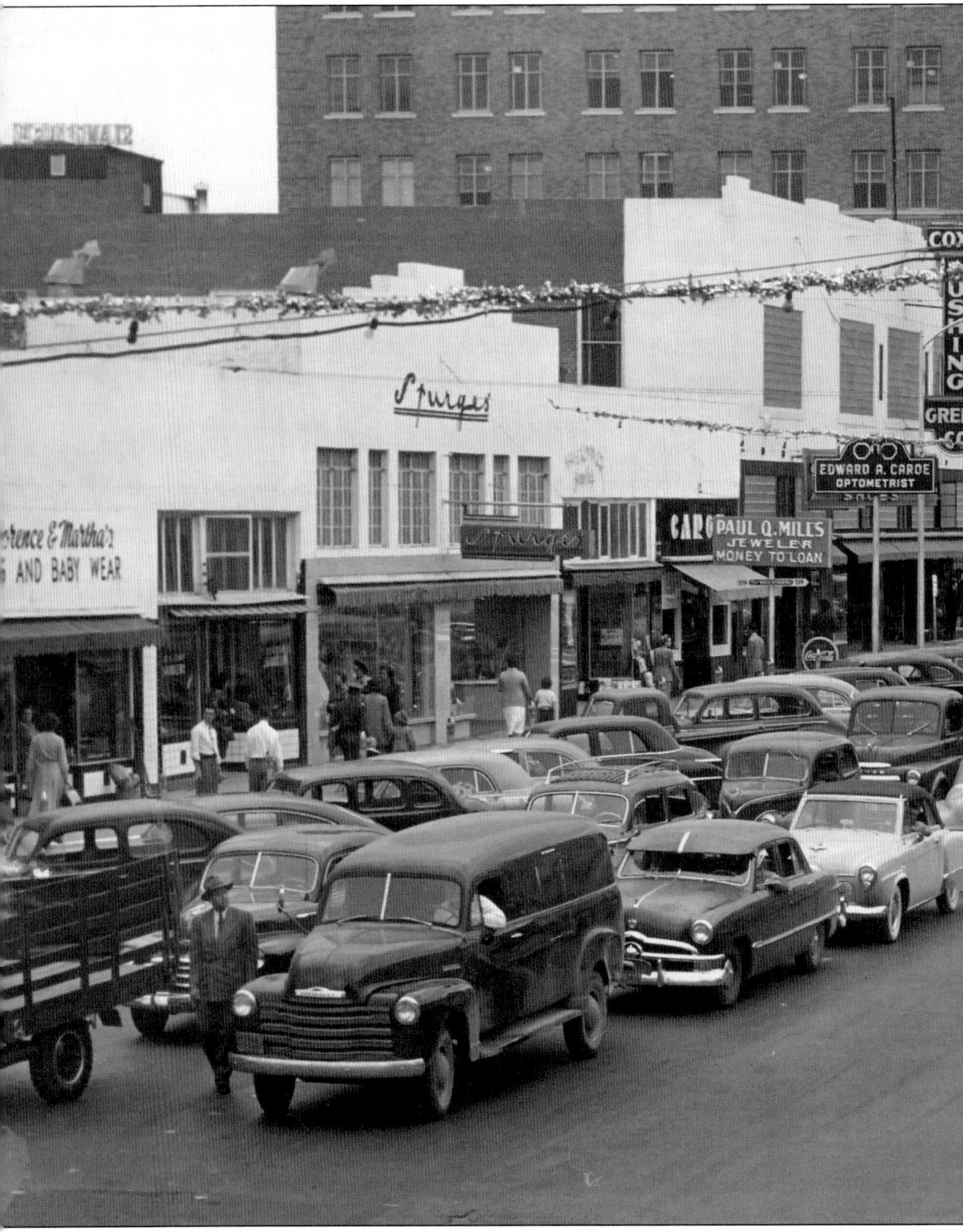

DOWNTOWN. This c. 1950 photograph of downtown shows Chadbourne Street, with Twohig Avenue in the distance. Note the J.L. Mercer neon sign on the right. An interior photograph of the boot shop is on page 36. The street decorations indicate that the photograph was taken at

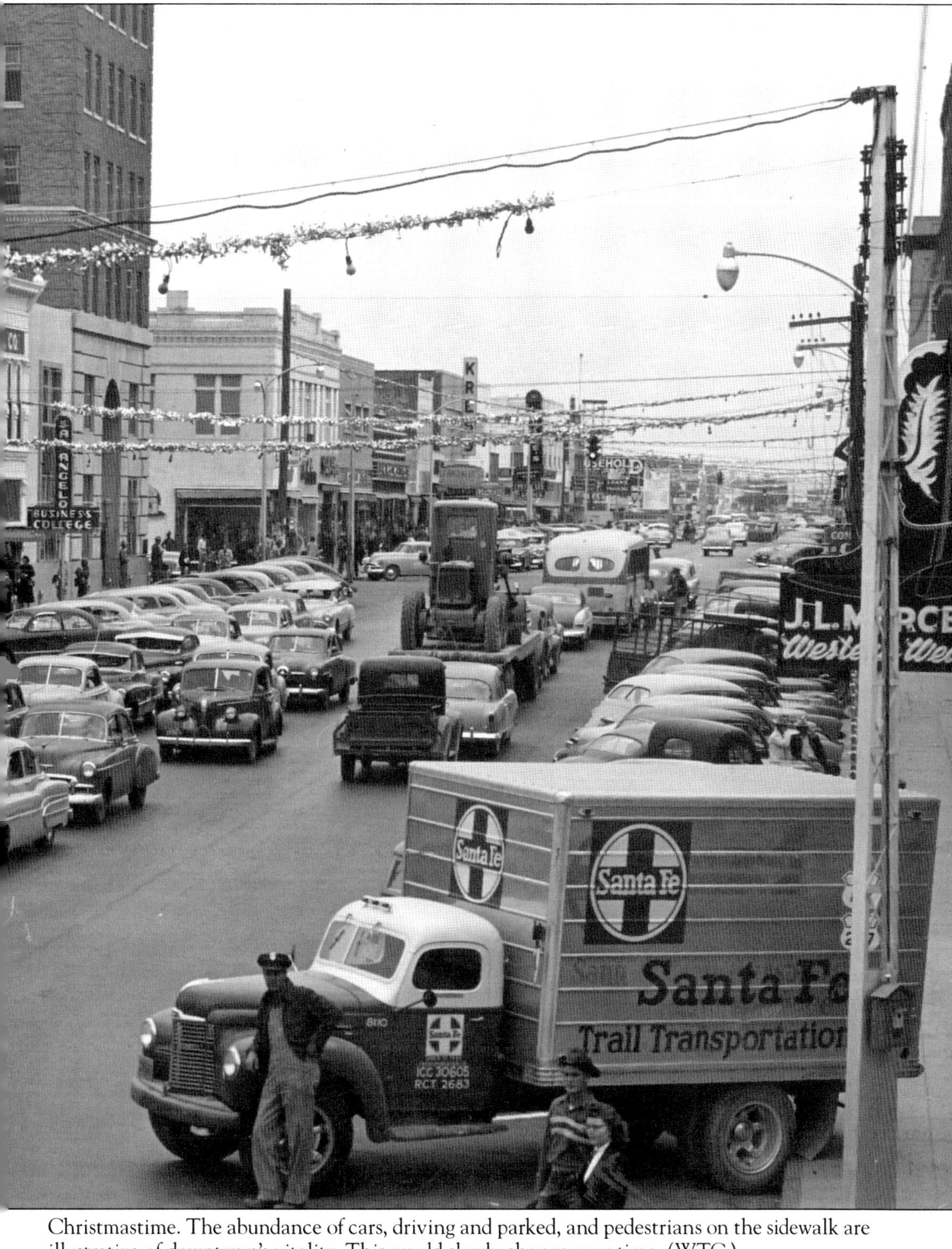

Christmastime. The abundance of cars, driving and parked, and pedestrians on the sidewalk are illustrative of downtown's vitality. This would slowly change over time. (WTC.)

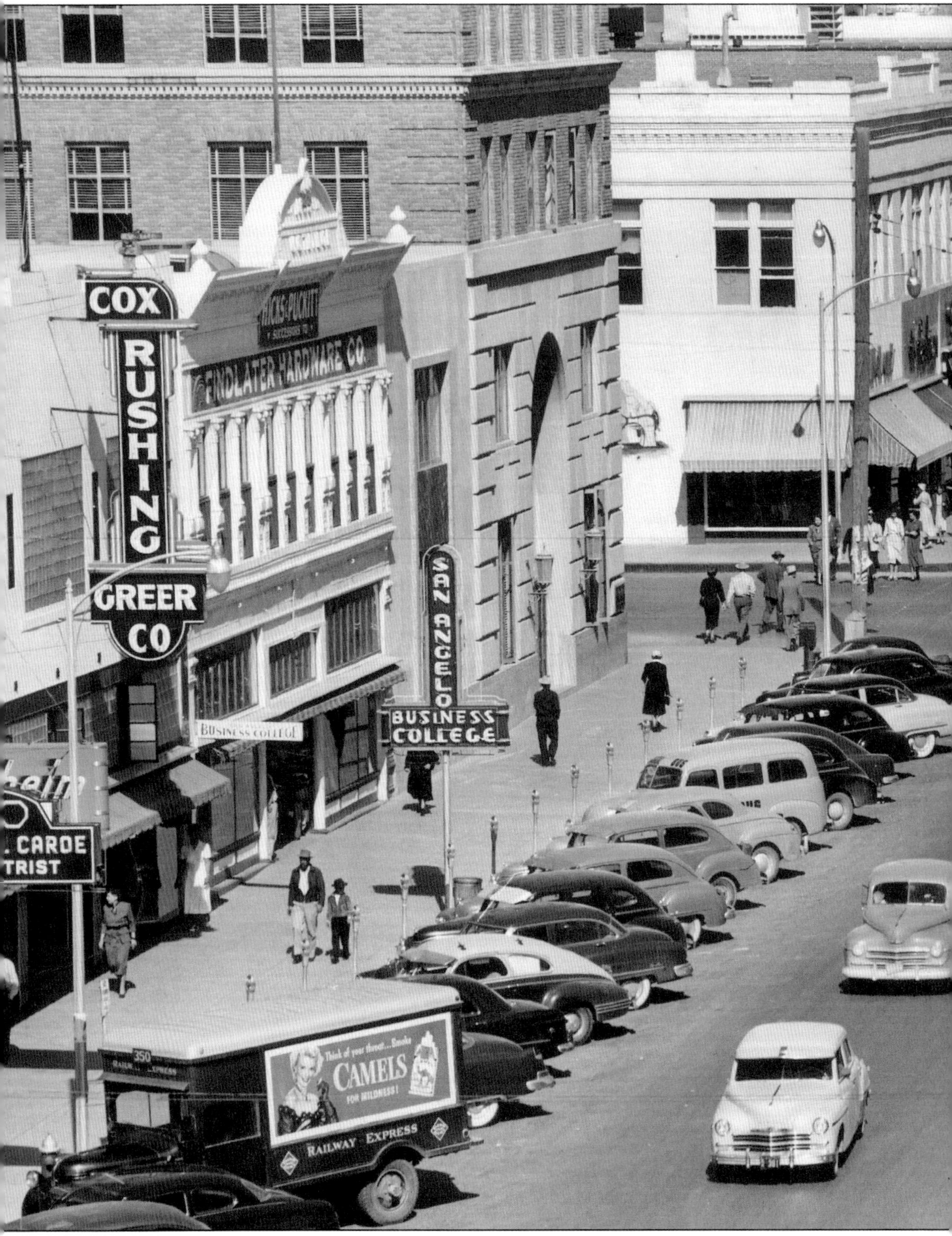

DOWNTOWN. Though taken at a different angle, this photograph shows a similar bird's-eye view to that on the previous pages. Note the national brands, such as Walgreen, Kress, and US Royal,

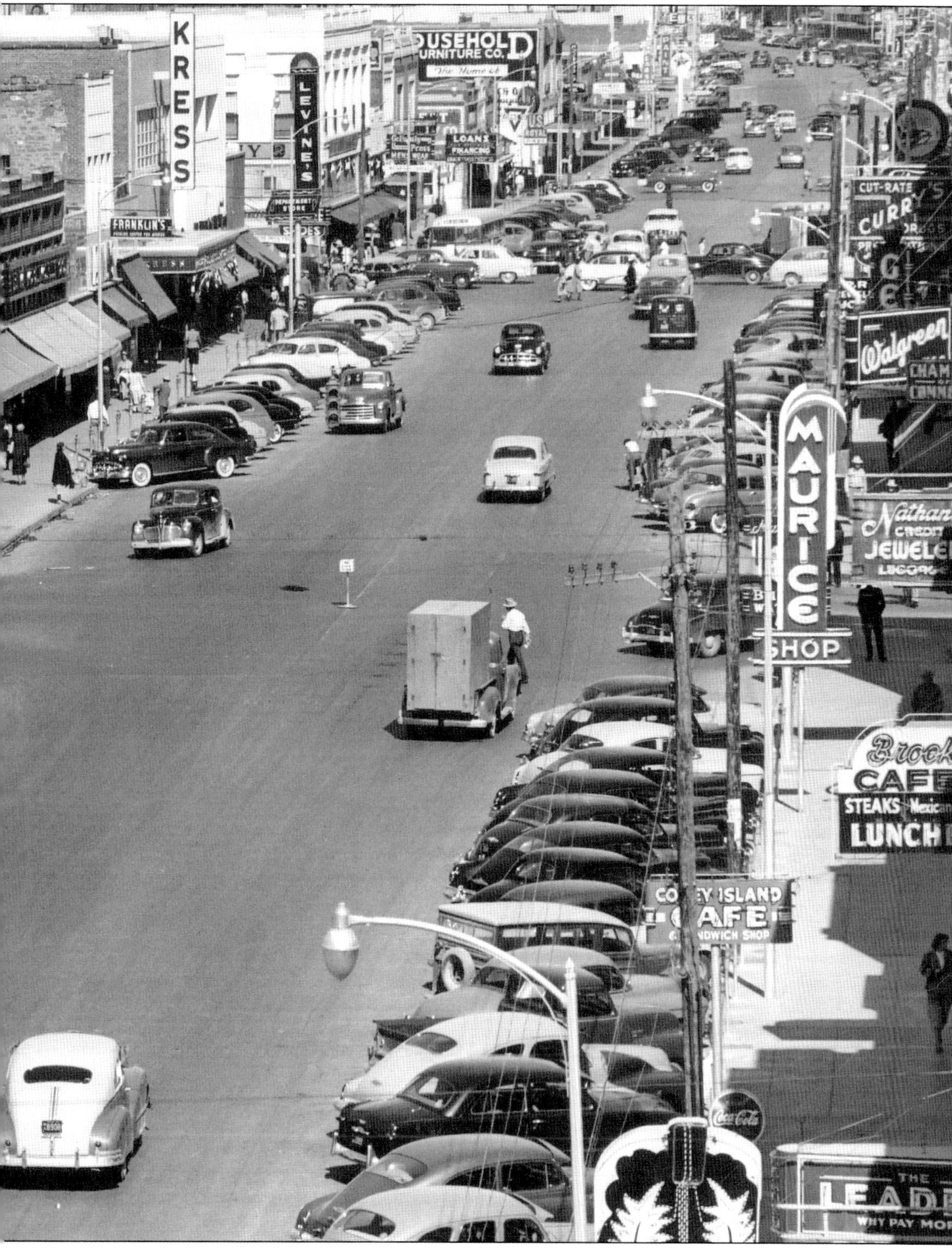

as well as local businesses, like Coney Island Café, Brooks Café, and Findlater Hardware Co. The projecting signs are very visible, along with numerous canvas awnings. (WTC.)

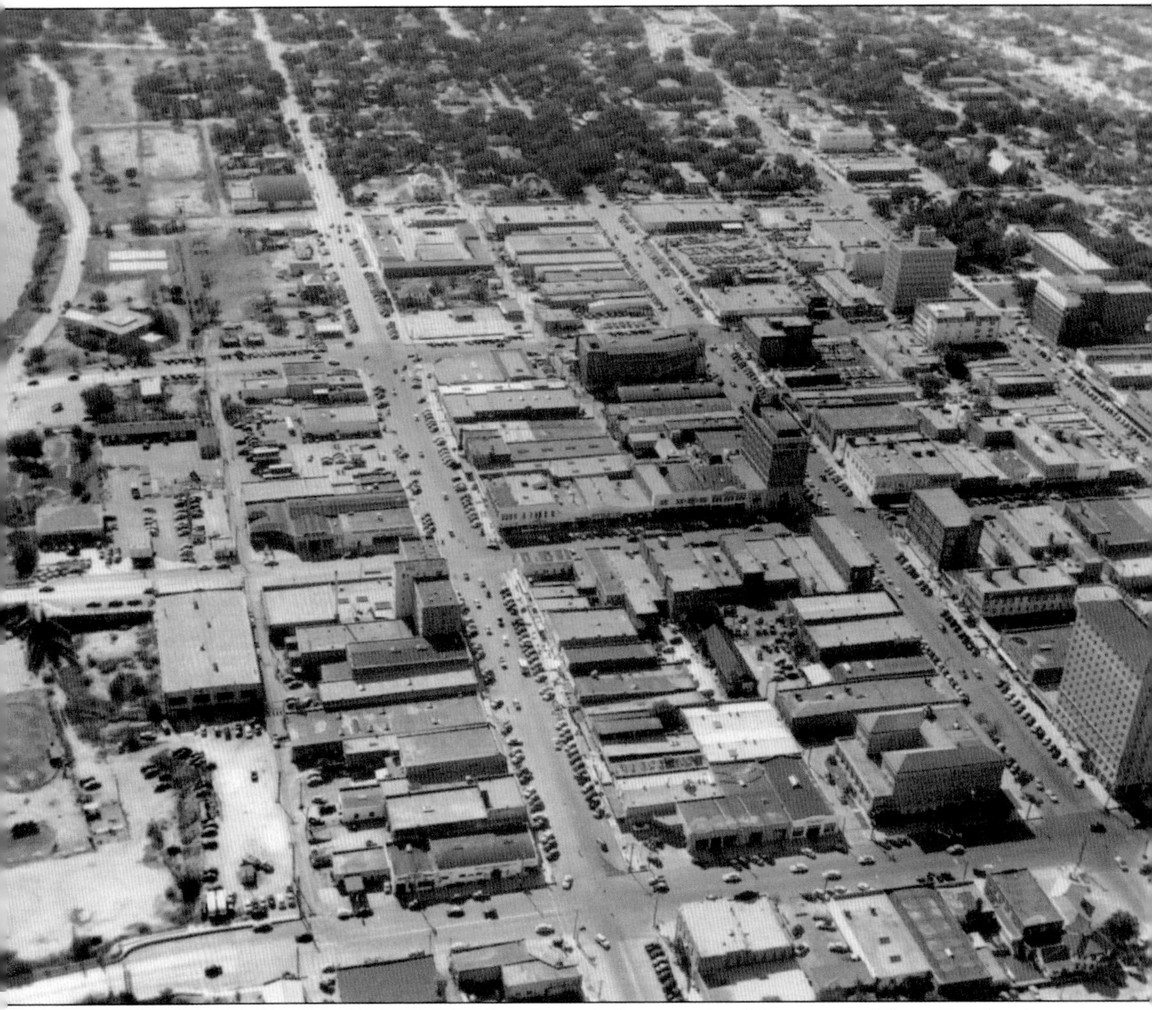

Aerial of Downtown. This is an undated aerial photograph of downtown. Note Concho Avenue in the middle of the picture, Cactus Hotel in the bottom right-hand corner, and Neff's Amusement Park in the bottom left-hand corner. (Courtesy of Barney's Studio.)

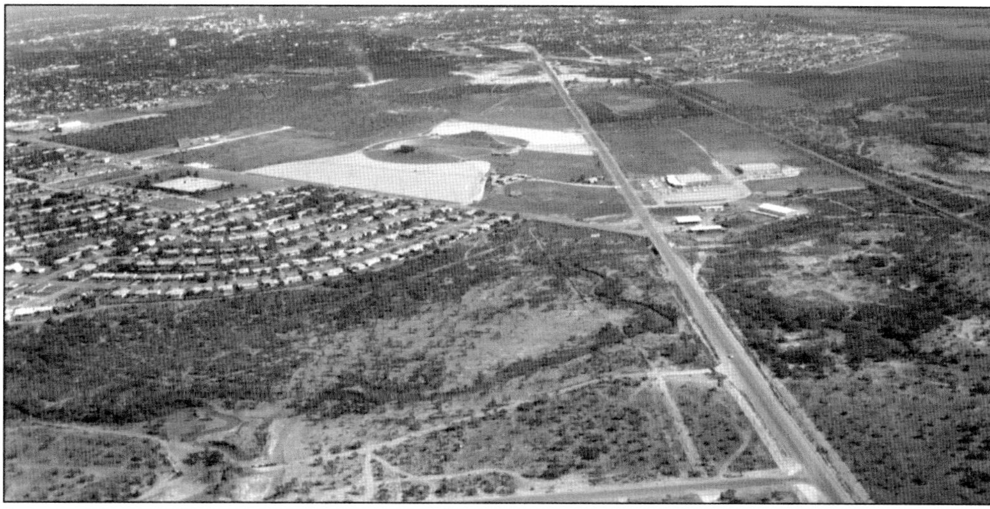

Aerial View of Knickerbocker Road. This aerial photograph of Knickerbocker Road, looking south, was taken sometime in the 1960s. Note Sunset Drive in the foreground, as well as South Johnson Street and College Hills subdivision. Also pictured is the large one-story General Telephone Building, constructed in 1954. San Angelo Stadium, built in 1956, is visible in the center of the photograph. Right of the stadium and across Knickerbocker Road is Stadium bowling alley (1963). (Courtesy of Barney's Studio.)

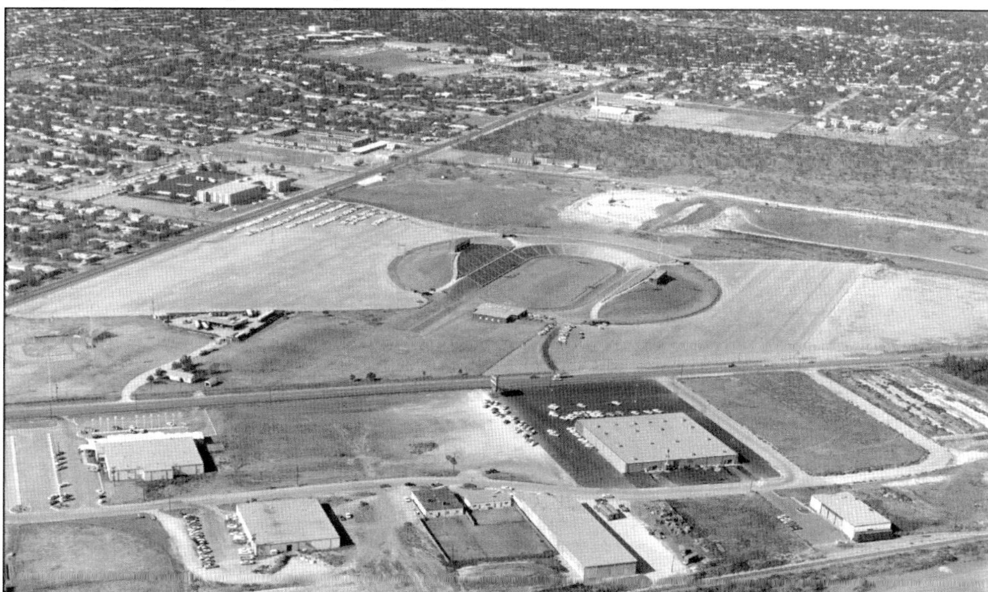

Stadium at Knickerbocker. Knickerbocker Road is in the center of this aerial photograph. San Angelo Stadium was built in 1956 and expanded in 1963. Photographs of the stadium were featured in an exhibition at the Museum of Modern Art in New York City as an outstanding example of modern engineering. The rear elevation of the Stadium bowling alley is visible on the left side of the photograph along with the start of Stadium Park Shopping Center. Above the stadium, the ground is being prepared for construction of John Glenn Junior High School. The General Telephone Building, with its 1965 addition, is visible in the upper left of the photograph. San Angelo College is at the top of the photograph with Rosemont Apartments to the left. (WTC.)

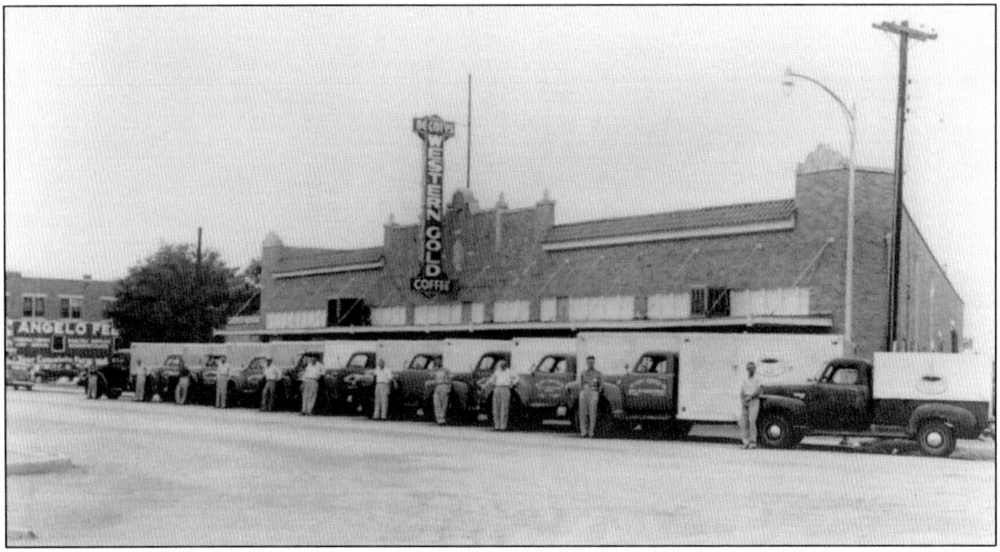

DeCoty's Coffee Headquarters. From 1937 to 1964, the 12,500-square-foot DeCoty's Coffee plant was located at 618 South Chadbourne Street. Approximately 80,000 pounds of coffee per month were being roasted at that location. The 11 trucks parked in front of the plant reflect the expanding business and customer demand for coffee, as well as for spices. Warehouses were built in Odessa in 1956 and Austin in 1958. The name of the business changed from Concho Coffee Company to DeCoty's Coffee when it moved to this location. Folks in West Texas had a bit of trouble properly pronouncing the Cajun-French surname Ducote, so the phonetic spelling "DeCoty" was adopted. Note the Angelo Feed Store, owned by F.E. Parker, father of Fess Parker, in the background. (Courtesy of Laura Ducote.)

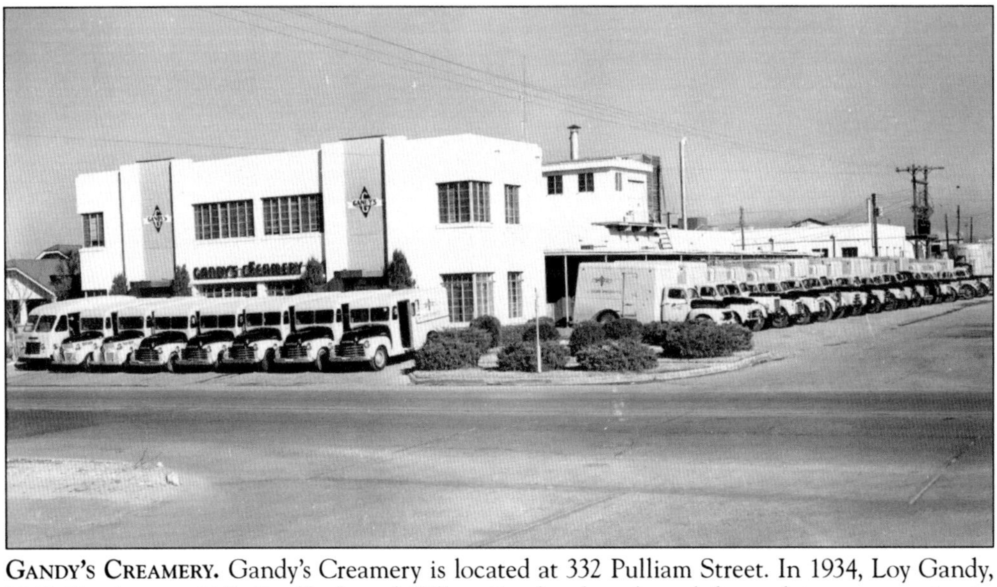

Gandy's Creamery. Gandy's Creamery is located at 332 Pulliam Street. In 1934, Loy Gandy, H.C. Vandervort, E.E. Bradford, and Gillert Sanders bought a defunct dairy cooperative in San Angelo. They remodeled it into a modern plant to serve West Texas. In the 1970s, it was purchased by Dean Foods and was consolidated in 1994 with Bell Creamery in Lubbock. The business continues to expand its operations in producing milk, buttermilk, ice cream, and butter. The plant on Pulliam Street is now used for sales and distribution. (WTC.)

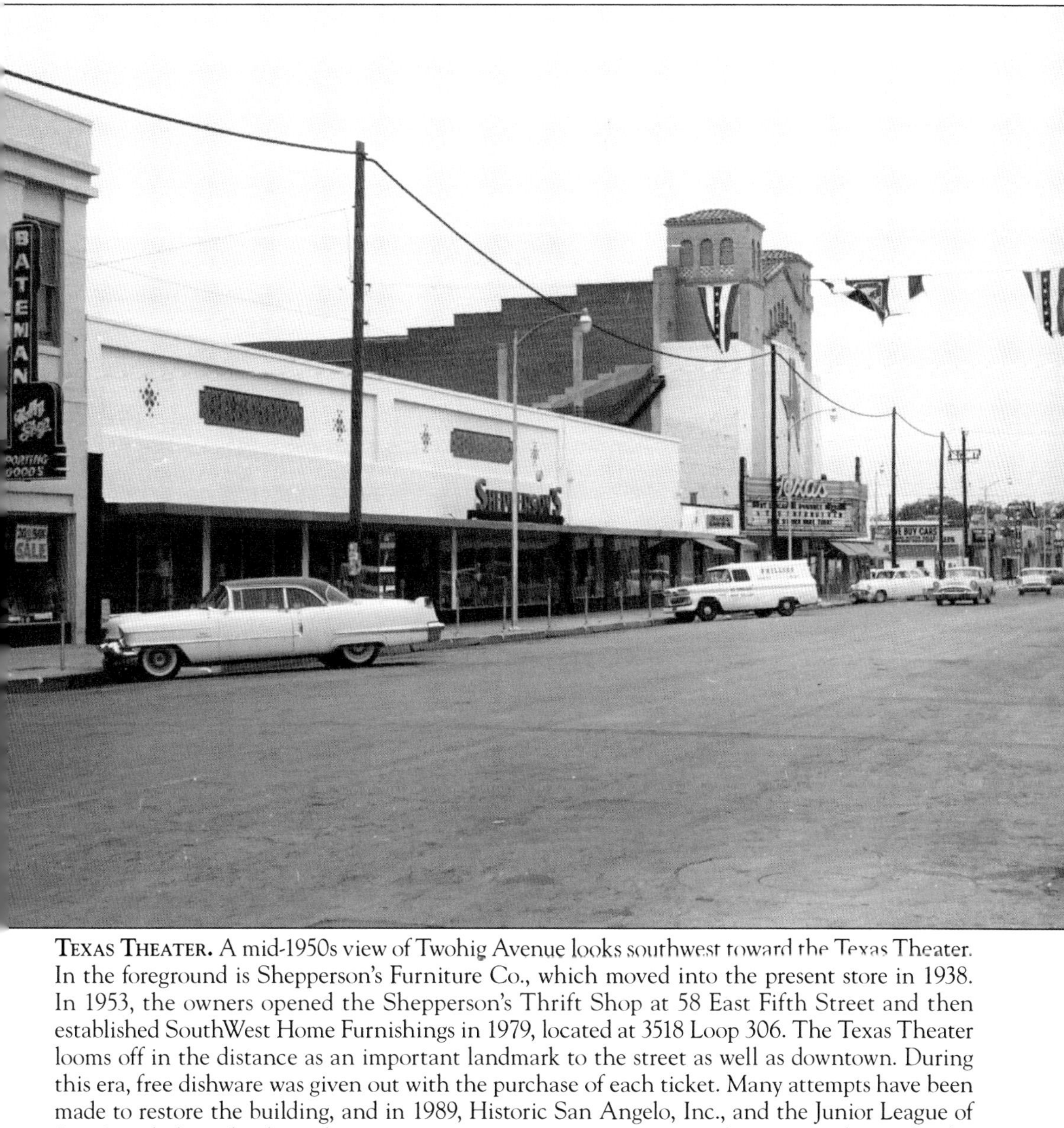

Texas Theater. A mid-1950s view of Twohig Avenue looks southwest toward the Texas Theater. In the foreground is Shepperson's Furniture Co., which moved into the present store in 1938. In 1953, the owners opened the Shepperson's Thrift Shop at 58 East Fifth Street and then established SouthWest Home Furnishings in 1979, located at 3518 Loop 306. The Texas Theater looms off in the distance as an important landmark to the street as well as downtown. During this era, free dishware was given out with the purchase of each ticket. Many attempts have been made to restore the building, and in 1989, Historic San Angelo, Inc., and the Junior League of San Angelo brought three theater restoration experts to town to explore uses and costs for the building. The structure still sits empty but is being preserved for rehabilitation and/or restoration. Farther down the street, the Star Lanes Building is visible. An interior photograph of its snack bar is on page 65. (WTC.)

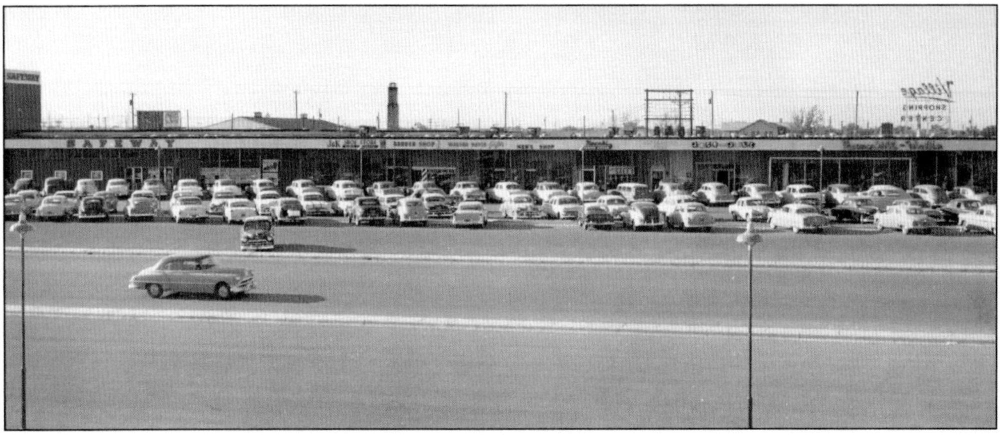

Village Shopping Center. In May 1952, developer Ted B. Brown broke ground in a pasture in the Ted Brown addition, located in the 2200 and 2300 blocks of West Beauregard Avenue, a wide residential thoroughfare. The new shopping center was constructed in one of the fastest growing areas of town, with 4,000 families within a one-mile radius. It was the first major shopping center constructed outside of downtown. Brown spent six years researching shopping center designs and traveling to sites before constructing the Village. William A. White designed this center as well as other projects for Brown. Storefronts were built in widths of 16.5 feet, 33 feet, and 50 feet, and in any depth up to 108 feet. The owner would provide the floor covering, light fixtures, heating and cooling equipment, as well as the storefront. The center provided basement storage for each store. The tenant would furnish the store's outside sign. Note the neon sign on the right-hand side of the photograph; it can still be seen from Sherwood Way. (WTC.)

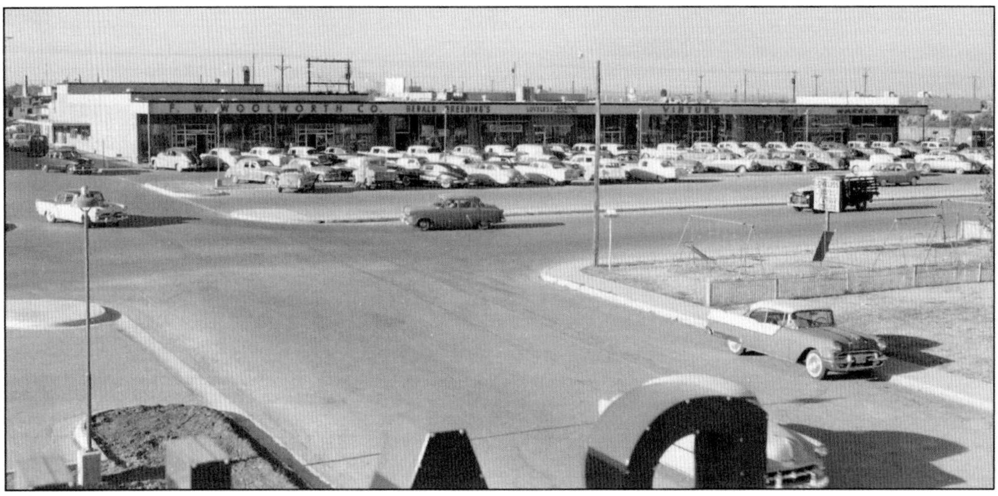

Village Shopping Center. The first three stores to open in May 1952 included Safeway Food Store, Jackson's Necchi Sewing Circle, and Shorty Harwood's Village Barber Shop. In August 1952, Cottage Maternity Shop, Jack & Jill Shop, Walter Davis Gifts, and Bauer-McCann Ladies Wear opened. Later, in 1952–1953, Syl's Bakery, J&K Shoe Shop, the Camera Shop, Elda Dougherty's School of Dancing, Herring Station Post Office, Village Beauty Salon, Loveless Juvenile Furniture Co., Warren Drug, F.W. Woolworth, and W.W. Virtue's department store were added. By June 1955, the center was fully occupied. In August 1955, Hemphill-Wells Co. opened a suburban branch where Bauer-McCann was originally located. In July 1979, Hemphill-Wells moved to Sunset Mall, and M.L. Leddy's later moved from its downtown location to a site in the Village Center. (WTC.)

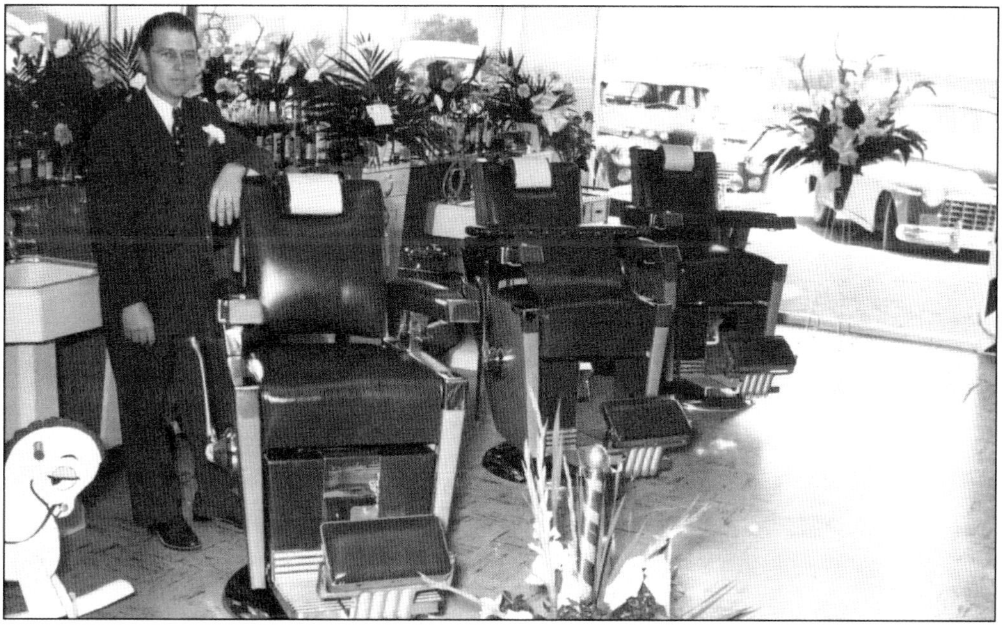

Shorty Harwood's Barber Shop. Shorty Harwood's Village Barber Shop was one of the first three stores to open at the new Village Shopping Center in May 1952. This photograph appears to record the grand opening of Clifton V. "Shorty" Harwood's Barber Shop. Shorty previously worked at the St. Angelus Barber Shop. (Courtesy of Barney's Studio.)

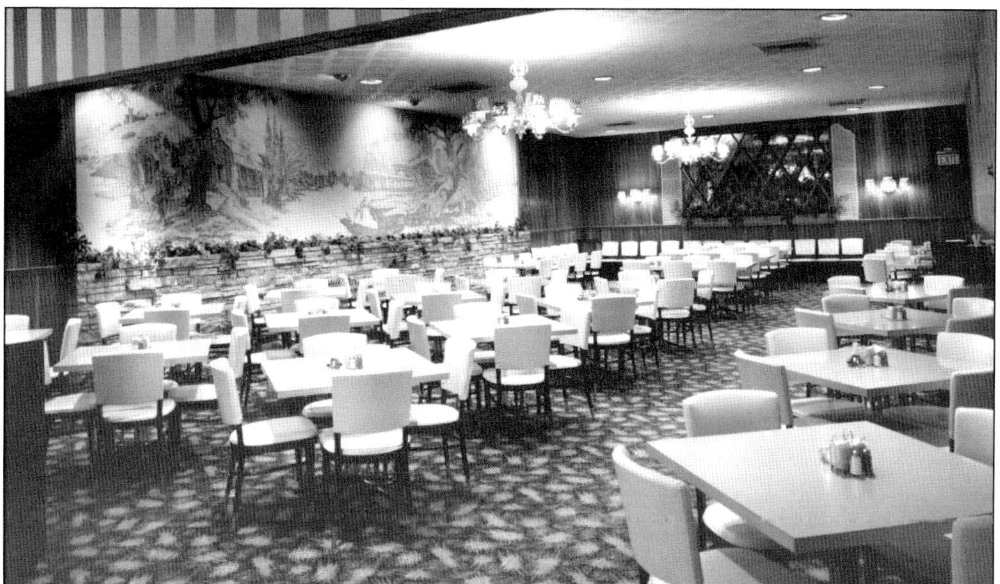

Luby's Cafeteria. Harry Luby started the New England Dairy Lunch cafeterias in 1911 in Springfield, Missouri. The business expanded, but Luby, wanting to avoid having to run a large company, retired after bringing his ideas to Waco, Texas. His son Robert M. Luby established his first Luby's Cafeteria in Dallas in 1934, and a second cafeteria opened in Alamo Heights in 1948. San Angelo had two of the company's cafeterias: Luby's Downtown at 114 South Irving Street and Luby's Village Cafeteria, pictured, at 2215 West Beauregard Avenue. (WTC.)

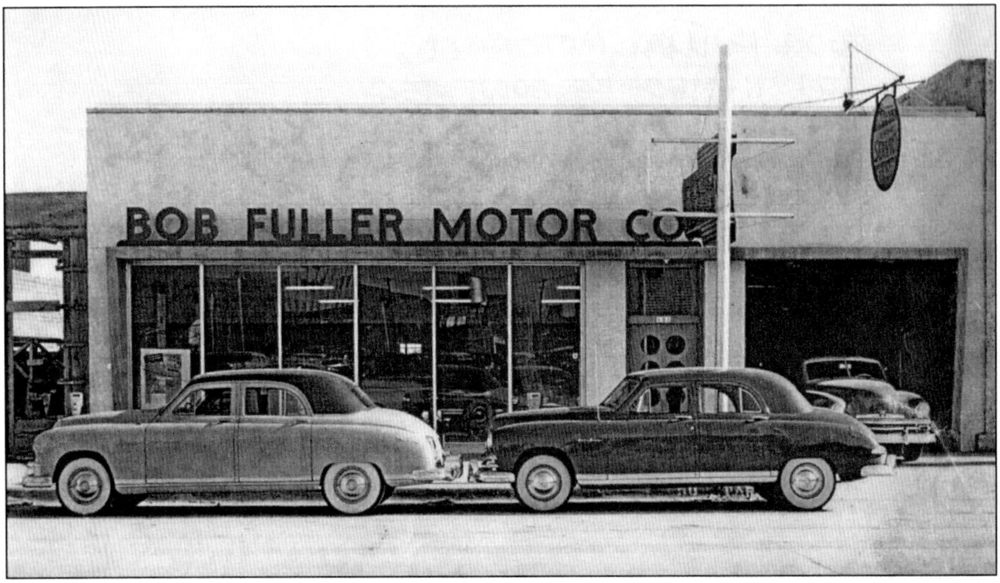

BOB FULLER MOTOR CO. The Bob Fuller Motor Co., the sales and service branch of Kaiser-Frazer Automobiles, was located at 121 West Twohig Avenue. Many car dealerships were located in the downtown area during this period. In the case of Fuller, its used car lot was located at 1816 West Beauregard Avenue. The facade is restrained in design, with a zigzag-shaped showroom window, projected eyebrow trim, and a variation of bold Gill Sans lettering used as the main ornamental feature of the facade. The front door utilized an Art Deco motif. Two hanging signs were added to identify the business and its service entrance. The car with the two-tone paint is a 1949 Frazer Manhattan four-door sedan, and the other one at the curb is a 1949 Kaiser Deluxe four-door sedan. In 1952, "Frazer" was dropped from the name of the corporation, which ceased production of passenger cars in 1955. Some construction activity next door can be seen on the left-hand side of the photograph. The building was removed at an unknown time and is now a vacant lot. (FC.)

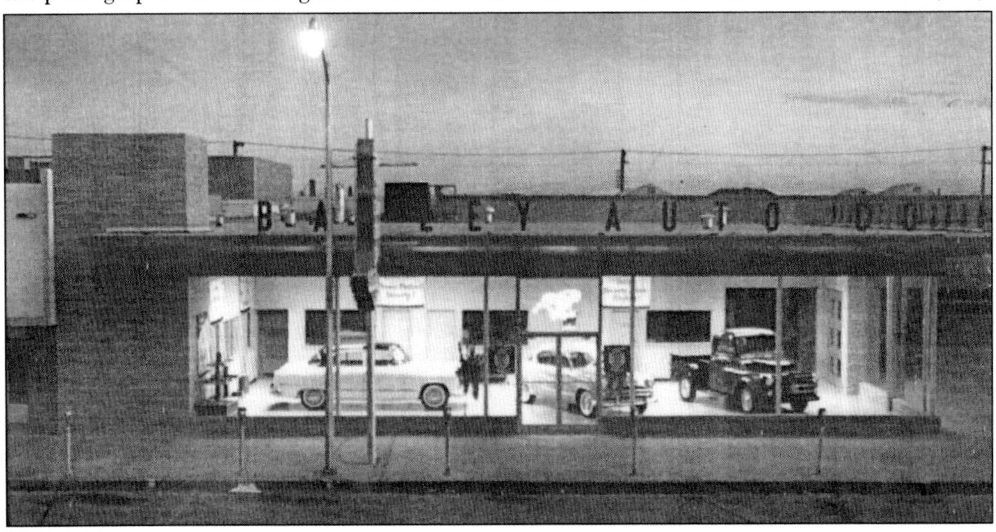

BAILEY MOTORS. A showroom-and-service facility was built in 1952 at 15 West Concho Avenue to sell Dodge cars and trucks. The architect responsible for the design is not known. A flat roof with overhangs was incorporated into the design of the building, and the use of glass was maximized to display the vehicles. (FC.)

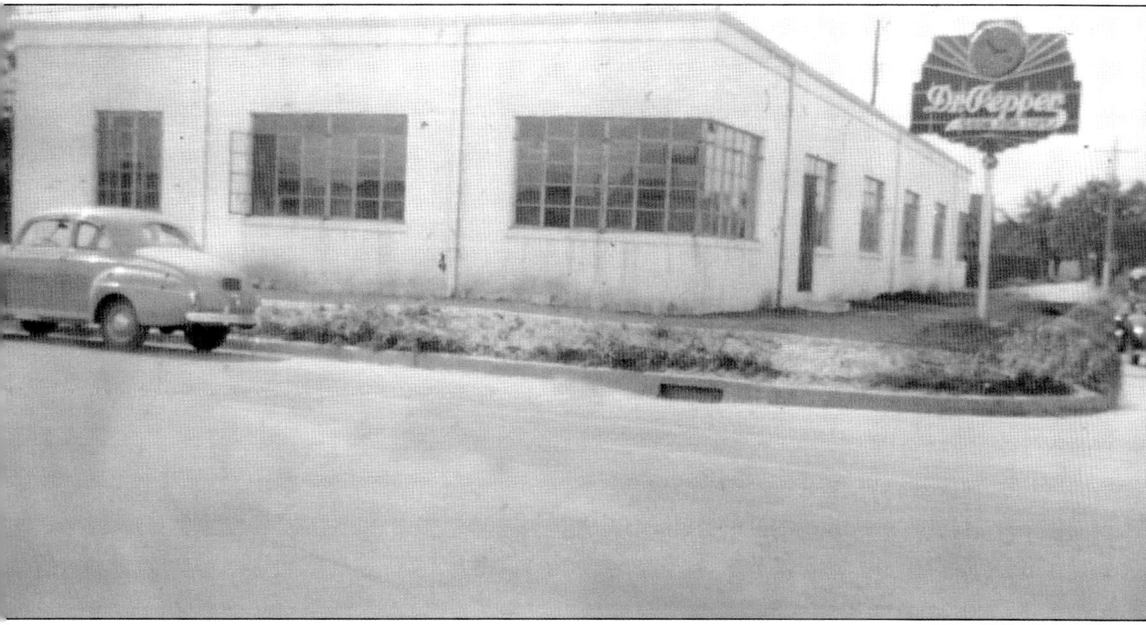

Dr. Pepper Bottling Plant. The Dr. Pepper bottling plant was located at 505 North Oakes Street, one of eight bottling plants located in San Angelo. The building survives, with its concrete block walls, metal sash windows, and barreled roof. The other bottling plants in the early 1950s included Coca-Cola Bottling Company at 69 North Chadbourne Street; Barq's Bottling Company at 79 East Avenue K; Grapette Bottling Company at 306 North Chadbourne Street; Pepsi-Cola Bottling Company at 315 North Chadbourne Street; 7 Up Bottling Company at 61 East Washington Drive; Nehi-Crown Bottling Company at 31 East First Street; Nesbit Orange Bottling Company at 51 East Washington Drive; and Nu-Grape Bottling Company at 1825 West Avenue N. While this seems like a lot of bottling plants for a city the size of San Angelo, according to the Texas State Bottlers Association in 1955, the average per capita consumption of 187 bottles of soda pop nationally was in sharp contrast to the 400 bottles per capita consumed locally. (Courtesy of Dr. Pepper Museum & Free Enterprise Institute.)

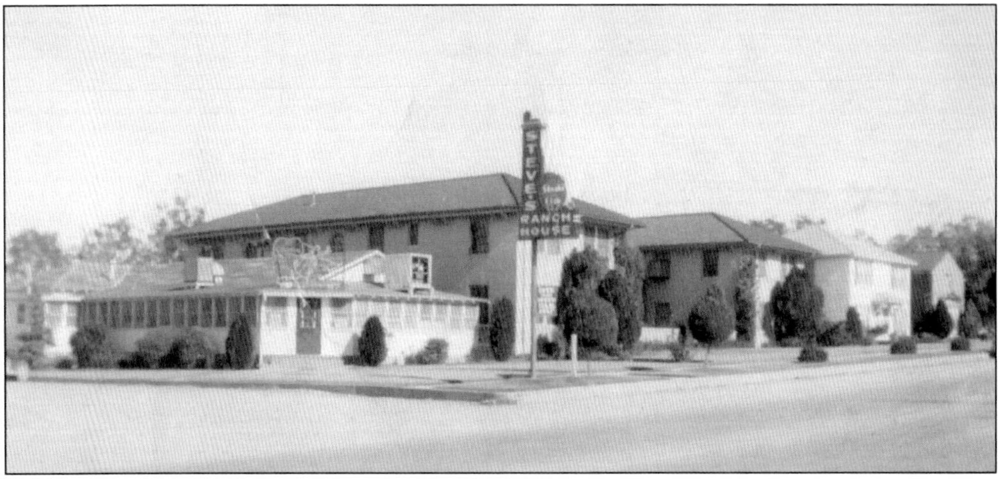

Steve's Ranch House. Steve's Ranch House was typical of the many "eating" houses located east of the Santa Fe Park and municipal golf course. The interior was of Western ranch style. The restaurant opened in August 1941, remodeled in 1952, and closed in 1957. Remodeling included an additional dining room, air-conditioning, and a huge fireplace. Unfortunately, the "Oh Uncle" neon sign was removed during remodeling. (WTC.)

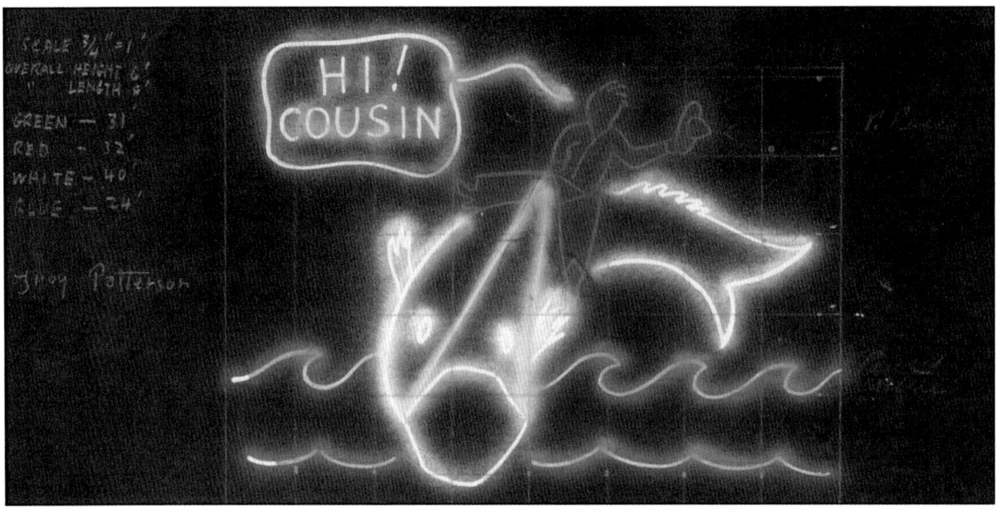

Neon Sign. The "Hi! Cousin" neon sign graced Steve's Ranch House for 11 years until the restaurant was remodeled in 1952. Neon signs were commonly used for exterior advertisement purposes from 1920 to 1960. The sign, consisting of a cowboy riding a huge fish while waving his 10-gallon hat and greeting everyone with the words, "Hi! Cousin," became a trademark for the restaurant. This rare shop drawing has survived and is signed by Troy Patterson, owner of Troy Patterson Outdoor Advertising & Neon Co. Patterson produced many other neon signs used by businesses in the region. The drawing indicates that 32 feet of red tubing was used for the cowboy, 40 feet of white tubing for the fish, 24 feet of blue tubing for the water, and 40 feet of green tubing for the balloon and lasso. A transformer fed about 15,000 volts, causing the gas to ionize, resulting in the glow. Noble gases (neon, argon, helium, xenon, and krypton) are mixed with a small amount of mercury to create a particular color. Each gas has a distinctive color. Neon gives a red color; argon enhanced with mercury creates a bright blue; krypton is a yellow-white light. Coating the inside of the glass tube with phosphors combined with different gases produces over 150 different colors. (WTC.)

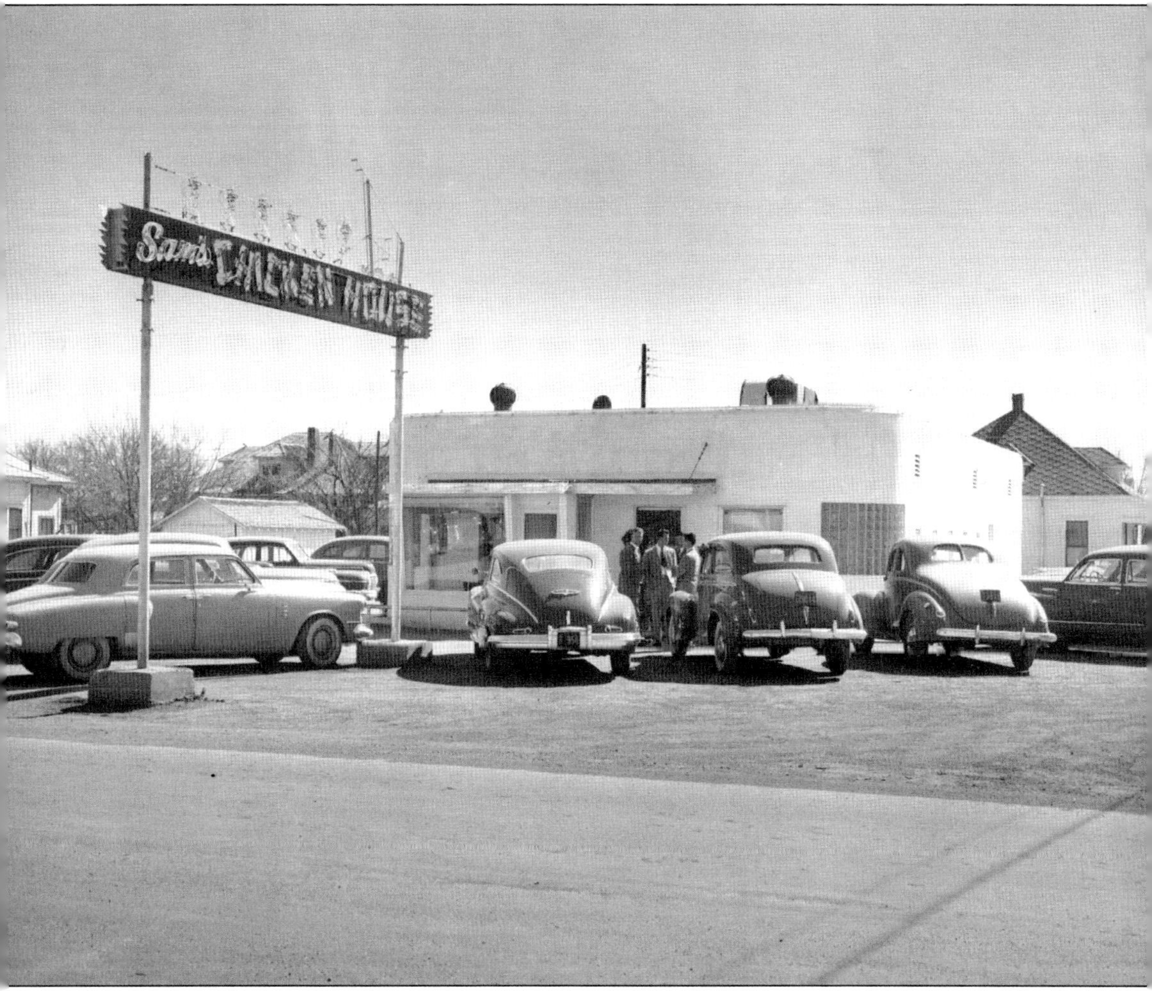

SAM'S CHICKEN HOUSE. Operated by Sam DeChearo, Sam's Chicken House at 1717 West Beauregard Avenue opened in the mid-1940s and closed in the late 1960s. With the restaurant's name spelled out in rustic lettering, the exterior sign also featured animated neon chickens walking toward Sam's Chicken House. The restaurant served whole or half chickens, fried chicken, steak fingers, and fried shrimp. It featured Armour's corn-fed steaks and was open from 6:00 a.m. to 2:00 a.m. (WTC.)

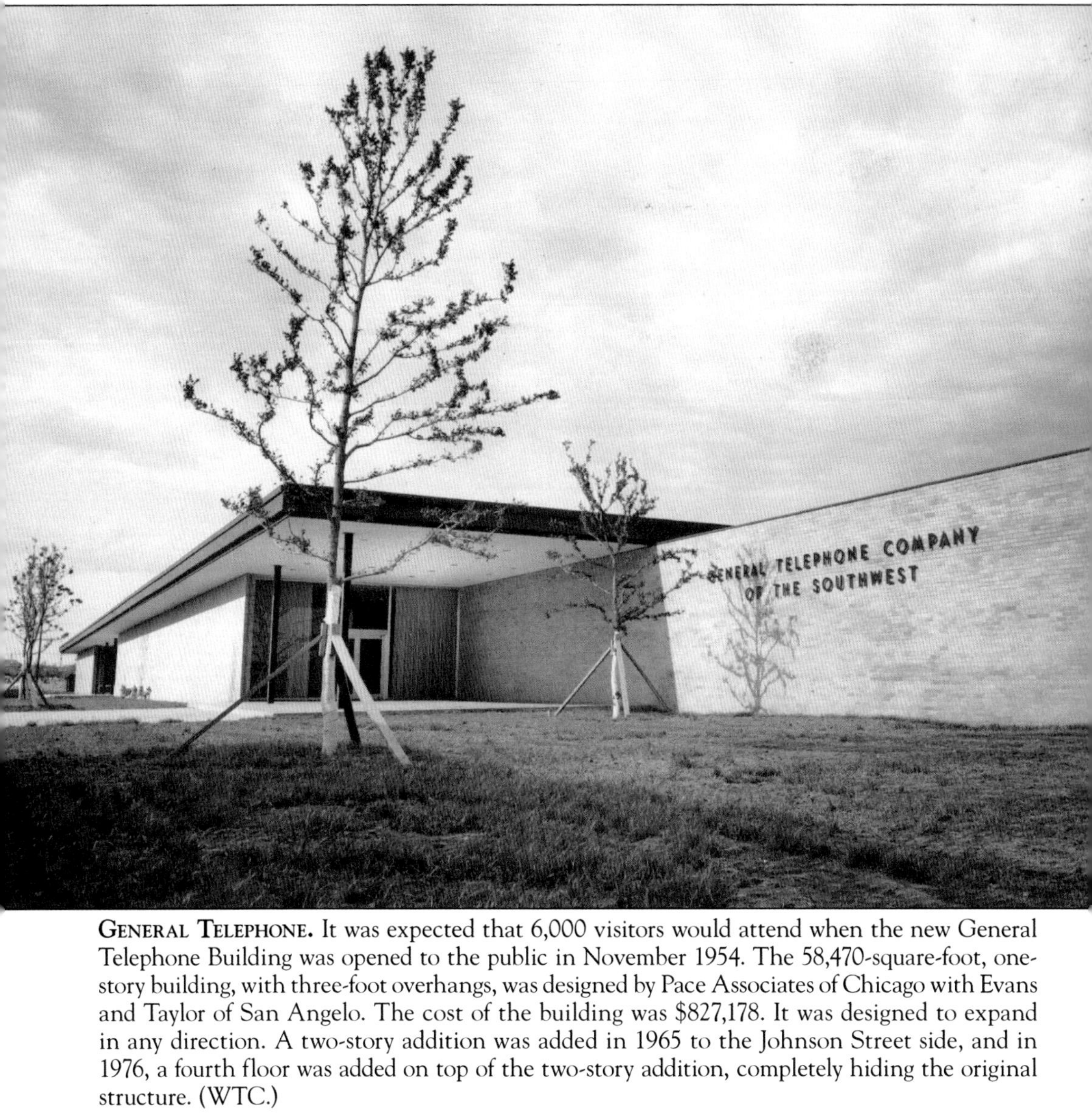

General Telephone. It was expected that 6,000 visitors would attend when the new General Telephone Building was opened to the public in November 1954. The 58,470-square-foot, one-story building, with three-foot overhangs, was designed by Pace Associates of Chicago with Evans and Taylor of San Angelo. The cost of the building was $827,178. It was designed to expand in any direction. A two-story addition was added in 1965 to the Johnson Street side, and in 1976, a fourth floor was added on top of the two-story addition, completely hiding the original structure. (WTC.)

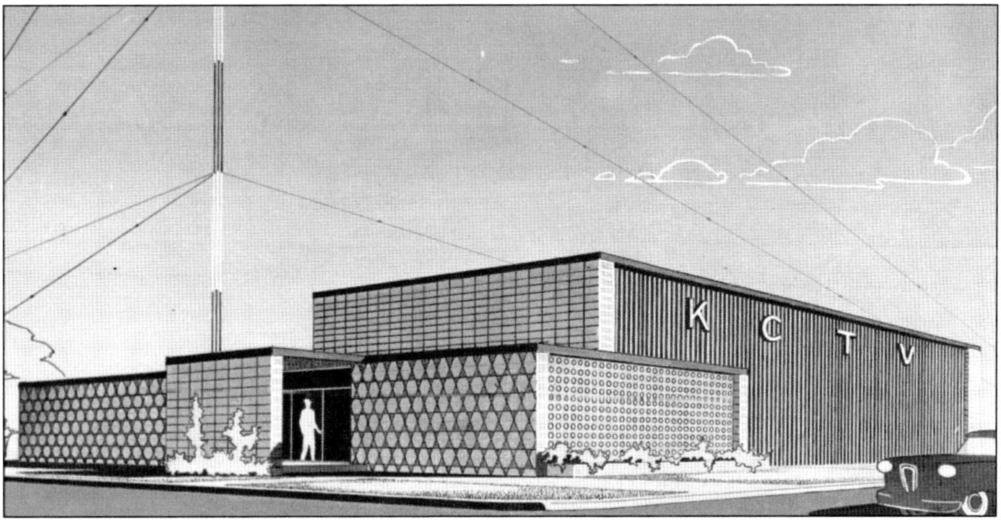

KCTV. The first television station in San Angelo started tests in June 1953 and began commercial programming on July 5 as KTXL (now KLST-TV) Channel 8. Since the beginning, the station has had three sets of call letters: KTXL, KCTV, and KLST. One early advertisement suggested patrons drive out to see the new TV tower and then drop by to select their television sets. At the time, a new 21-inch, black-and-white GE Ultra-Vision console with blond veneer and swivel casters sold for $414.95. (WTC.)

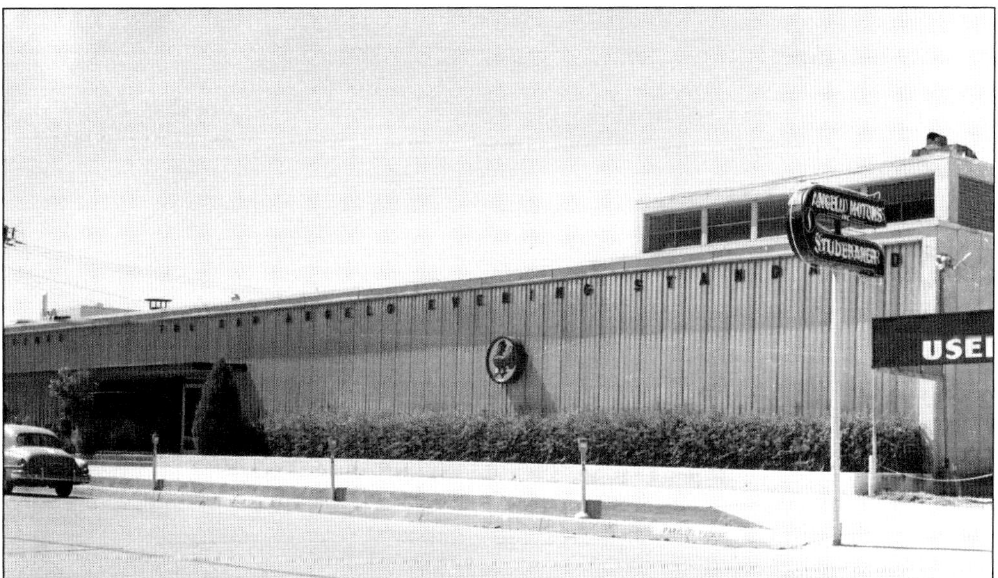

STANDARD-TIMES. The local daily newspaper has been published since 1884. In the 1920s, Houston H. Harte joined with Bernard Hanks to form the newspaper chain, Harte-Hanks, Inc., which soon included the San Angelo *Standard-Times*. In 1951, the newspaper constructed a new plant at Harris Avenue and Irving Street. Designed by Donald Goss and erected by contractor Bill Warner of Warner Construction, it provided a total of 38,000 square feet divided equally between the basement and first floor. Goss designed the foundation so it could be expanded upward to as much as 10 stories. In 1984, a major rehabilitation project resulted in 10,000 additional square feet, the relocation of mechanical and electrical equipment, and a remodeling of the facade. (WTC.)

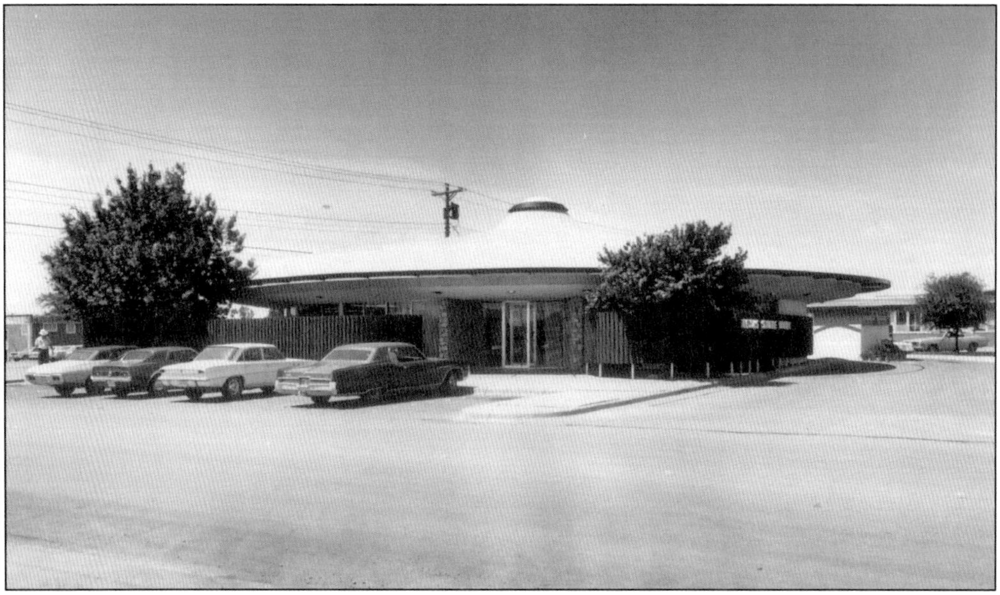

Texas State Bank. Now hidden behind a four-story office building, the "Bank of Tomorrow" was designed by Donald Goss, architect, with William A. White. Goss and Mark McLaughlin, bank director, traveled to Phoenix to look at round bank buildings. Walter Bimson, chairman of the Board of Valley National Bank in Phoenix, felt that "sculpture" bank buildings would help growth, so his city had lots of banks to visit. Goss and McLaughlin returned from their visit, and Goss designed a round, inverted-saucer-shaped roof that provided natural lighting over the circular lobby. The bank opened its doors on February 16, 1963. Increase in business necessitated the construction in 1977 of a four-story tower facing Sherwood Way. The distinctive reflective-glass facade was designed by Goss, Drake & Donaldson, architects. (Courtesy of Texas State Bank.)

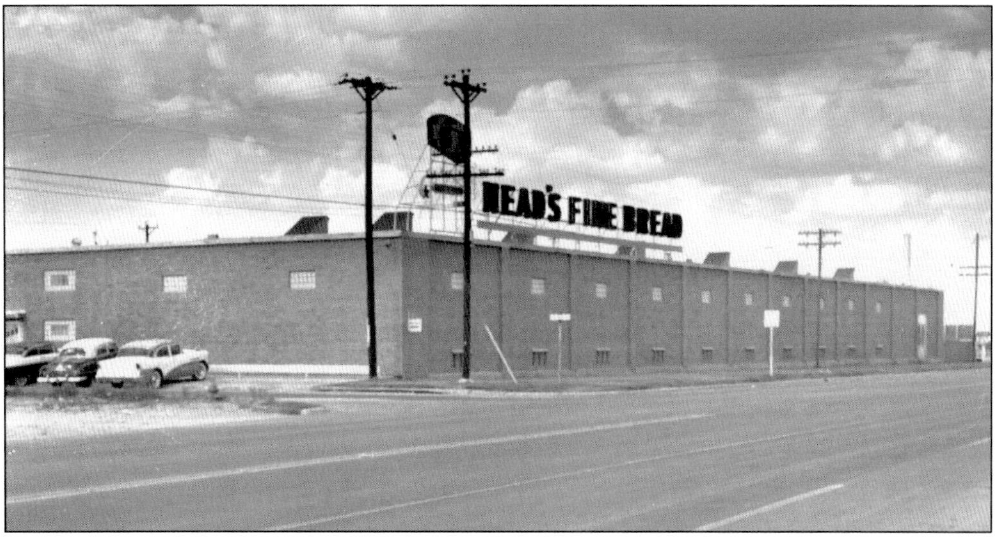

Mean's Bread. Mean's Bread at 3130 Sherwood Way was a major producer of bread products until the late 1960s. Mean's moved from 18 North Main Street in the mid-1950s. At that time, other bakeries included Boehm's Bakery, Green's Bakery, Spiegle and Hughes, Gustine Pie Factory, Eddie's Pie Shop, M System Stores, McClure's Bakery, Barnett's Quality Products, and Henson's Bakery. (WTC.)

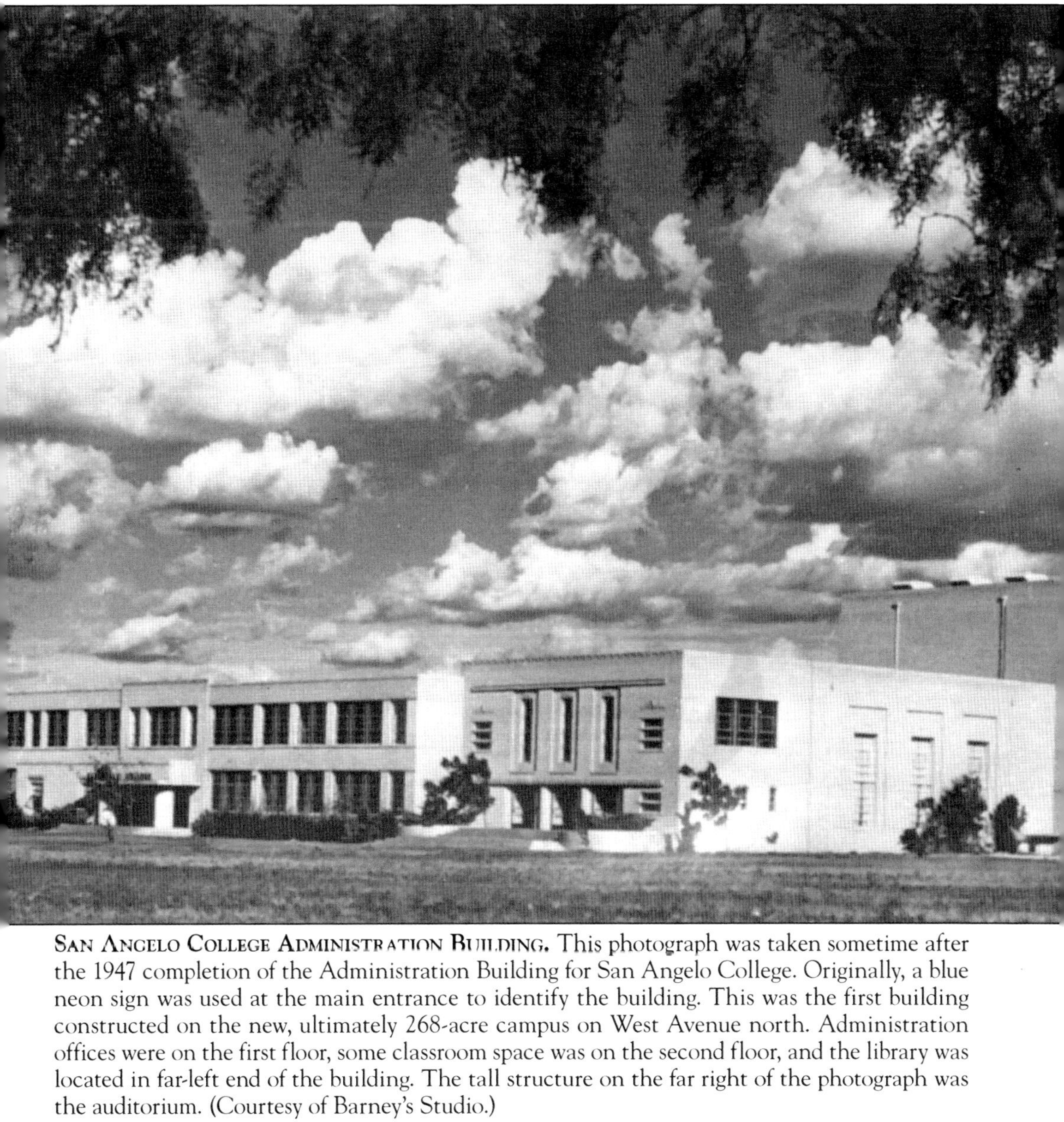

SAN ANGELO COLLEGE ADMINISTRATION BUILDING. This photograph was taken sometime after the 1947 completion of the Administration Building for San Angelo College. Originally, a blue neon sign was used at the main entrance to identify the building. This was the first building constructed on the new, ultimately 268-acre campus on West Avenue north. Administration offices were on the first floor, some classroom space was on the second floor, and the library was located in far-left end of the building. The tall structure on the far right of the photograph was the auditorium. (Courtesy of Barney's Studio.)

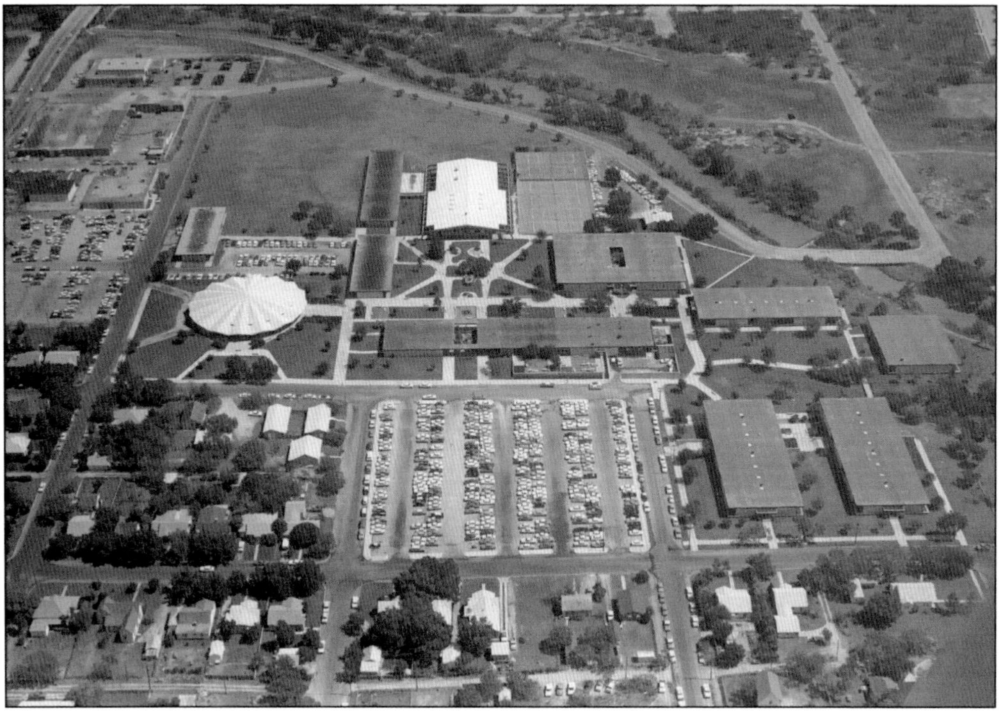

Aerial View of Central High School. The Central High School was designed by Caudill, Rowlett & Scott (CRS) of Houston and associate architect Max D. Lovett of San Angelo. CRS had an extensive background in designing schools. The architects received an AIA Award of Merit for designing America's first campus-type high school. Visitors from around the United States and from other countries toured the facility. (CRS Center, College Station, Texas.)

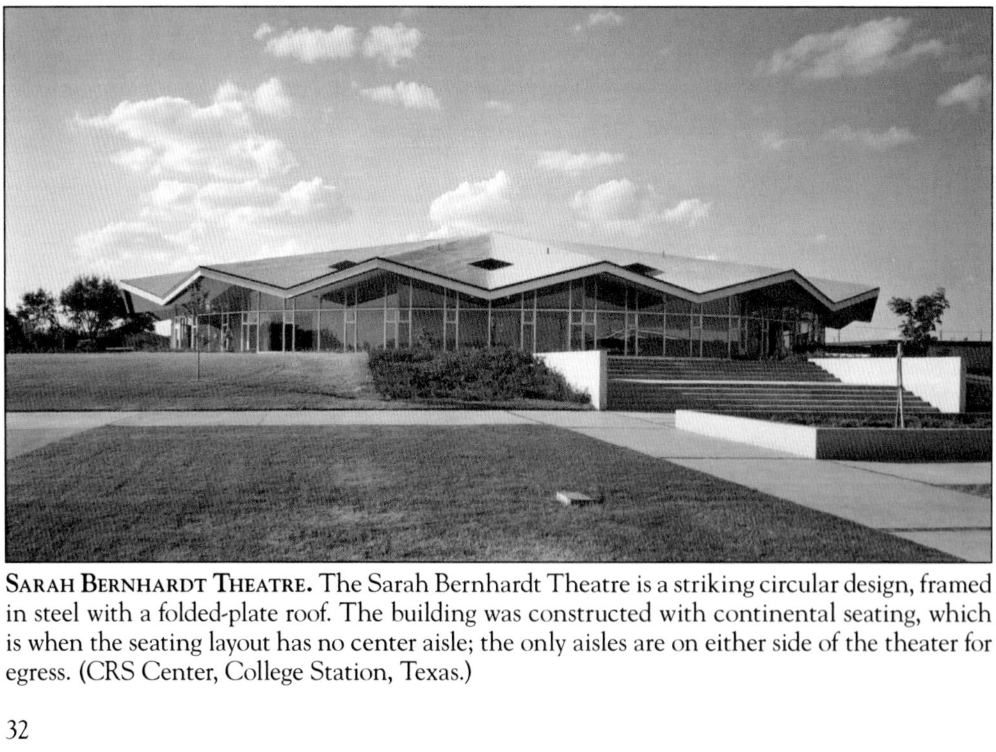

Sarah Bernhardt Theatre. The Sarah Bernhardt Theatre is a striking circular design, framed in steel with a folded-plate roof. The building was constructed with continental seating, which is when the seating layout has no center aisle; the only aisles are on either side of the theater for egress. (CRS Center, College Station, Texas.)

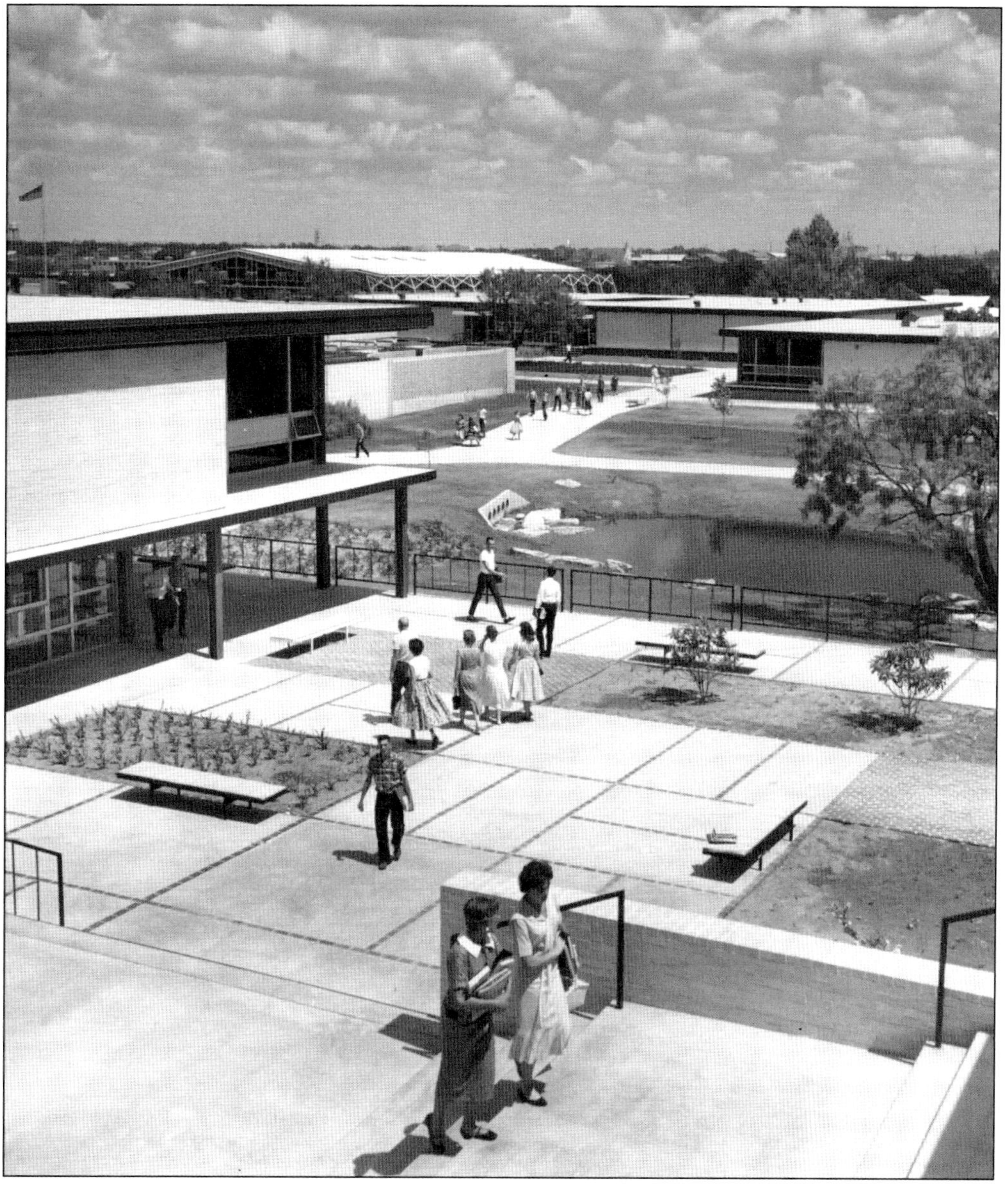

CENTRAL HIGH SCHOOL COURTYARD. The price tag in 1958 for the school was $3.5 million, which included purchasing the land. It was built for 2,150 students but could actually accommodate 2,500; today, there are close to 3,000 students. It contains 11 separate buildings in 208,086 gross square feet. All but three of the buildings have year-round air-conditioning. The design consisted of separate academic buildings for sophomores, juniors, and seniors and structures for the library, elective subjects, administration, fine arts, and a gymnasium with enclosed swimming pool, space for physical education, and shops. (CRS Center, College Station, Texas.)

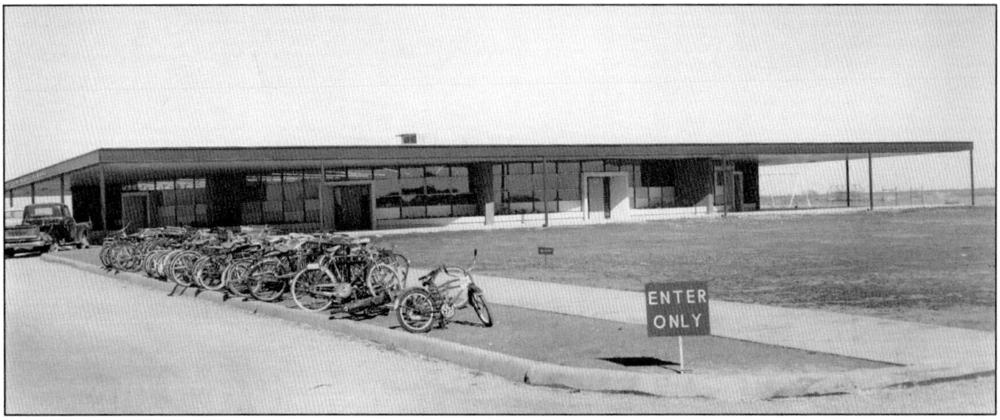

BELAIRE ELEMENTARY SCHOOL. This photograph shows an overall view of Belaire Elementary School, which was built in 1955 as part of an expansion program by San Angelo Independent School District. The school is located in the Belaire addition at 700 Stephens Street. The design of the school was unique for its use of air-conditioning and its overall circular footprint capped by a flat square roof. The design of the overhanging roof allowed classes to be held outside during good weather and protected the windows from the sun, thus reducing the cost to run the air-conditioning. The school was designed by W.W. Caudill of Caudill, Rowlett & Scott, architects, of Houston, with Donald Goss of San Angelo as associate architect. The 20,022 square feet of floor space was built for $8.96 per foot by Burk Construction Company. Because of Burk's low bid, one of the alternate options, air-conditioning, was added to the contract. (CRS Center, College Station, Texas.)

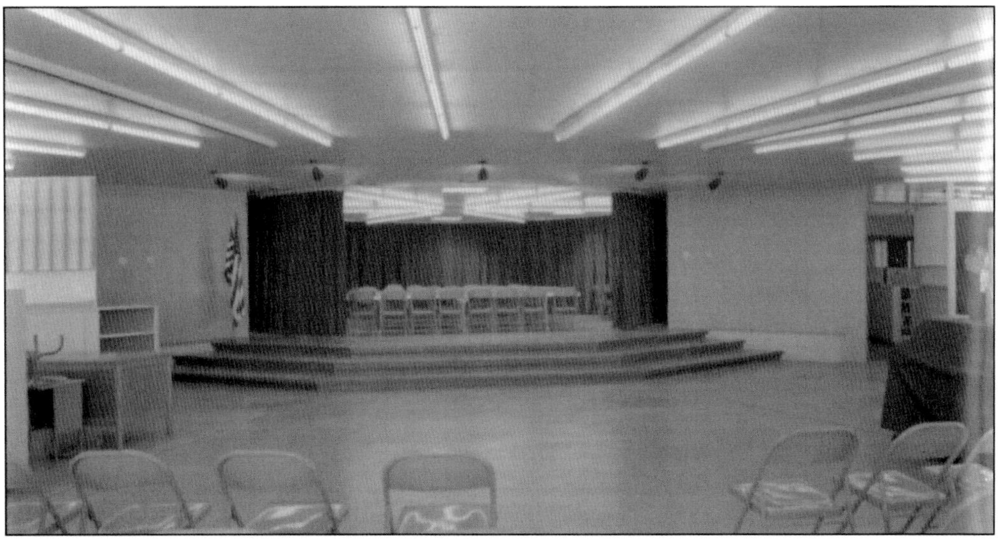

BELAIRE ELEMENTARY SCHOOL. In the mid-20th century, air-conditioning of schools was considered to be prohibitively expensive. But Belaire's wedge-shaped classrooms reduced the ductwork by 50 percent, and window shading reduced operation costs. Part of the reason to use air-conditioning was to keep out plane noise from Goodfellow Air Force Base. The school design included eight classrooms, a kitchen, and administration offices built around a circular, all-purpose room used as a dining room and stage. Partitions between three rooms could be folded, creating an auditorium with the stage. In 1965, a separate building for the library was constructed, followed by six additional classrooms in 1983. A fire in 1994 destroyed much of the original building, but the district rebuilt the school, and it is still in use. (CRS Center, College Station, Texas.)

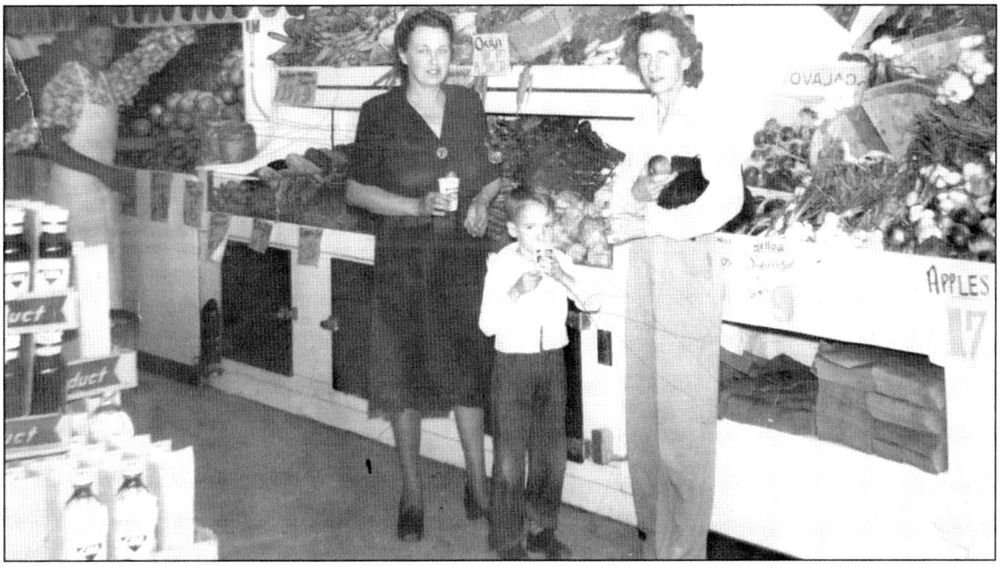

Abbott's Supermarket. This interior view of Abbott's Supermarket, located at 1505 South Chadbourne Street, shows a scene typical of many neighborhood stores in the 1950s. The 1952 *Polk City Directory* listed over 130 retail grocery stores in San Angelo. The people in the photograph are unidentified, but clearly visible is the price of apples, which was 17¢. This store, like others, carried different items besides groceries, such as shoes and clothing. Many of these stores would deliver groceries to homes. Unfortunately, most have closed, and Abbott's was added to the list in October 2011. The pressure of the mega–grocery stores and the trend toward one-stop shopping are among the reasons that most of these neighborhood stores have disappeared. (Courtesy of Bobby Abbott.)

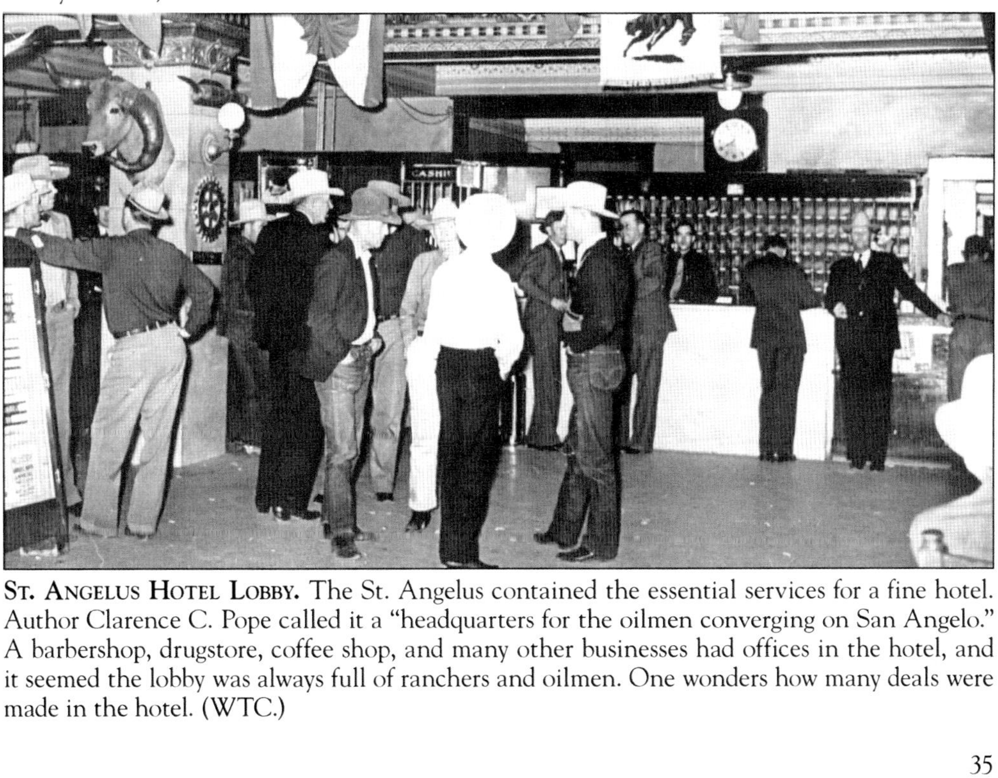

St. Angelus Hotel Lobby. The St. Angelus contained the essential services for a fine hotel. Author Clarence C. Pope called it a "headquarters for the oilmen converging on San Angelo." A barbershop, drugstore, coffee shop, and many other businesses had offices in the hotel, and it seemed the lobby was always full of ranchers and oilmen. One wonders how many deals were made in the hotel. (WTC.)

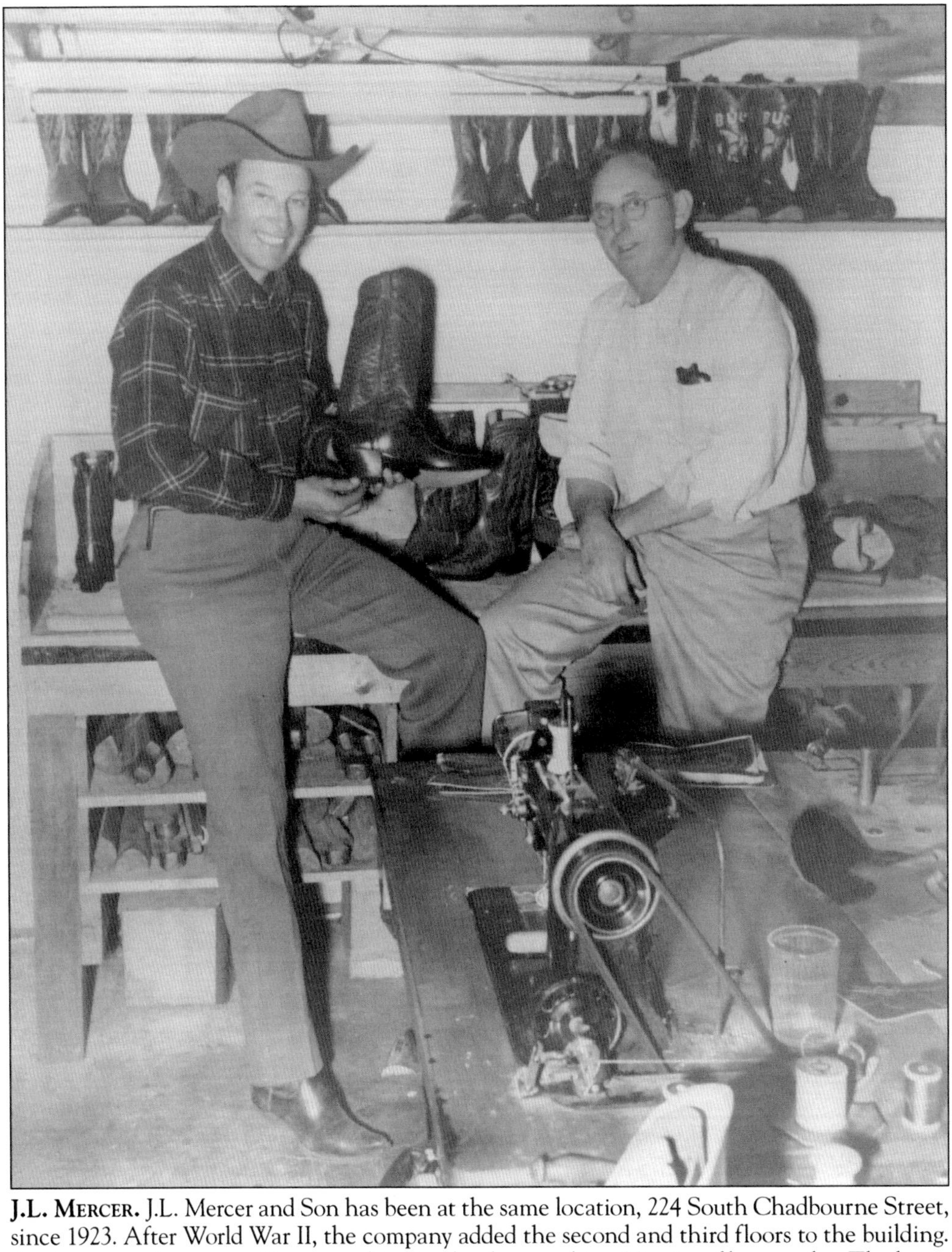

J.L. Mercer. J.L. Mercer and Son has been at the same location, 224 South Chadbourne Street, since 1923. After World War II, the company added the second and third floors to the building. At that time, there were 15 men working in the shop, making 20 pairs of boots a day. The boots sold from $35 a pair. This photograph is believed to have been taken in the early 1950s, with J.L. Mercer on the right and "Wild" Bill Elliot on the left. Wild Bill was a Hollywood film actor specializing in playing the rugged heroes in Westerns, best known in the *Red Ryder* series of 16 movies. He was in the area to pick up a horse in Sterling City and stopped by to purchase a pair of boots. Mercer managed to have a professional photograph made to record the event. Other well-known people who owned Mercer boots included Lyndon B. Johnson, John Wayne, and Charlie Daniels. (Photograph courtesy of J.L. Mercer and Son.)

LANE BROS. TRUCKING CO. Many service and transportation businesses, based in San Angelo, like the Lane Bros. Trucking Co., provided important support to oilfield operations west of the city. (WTC.)

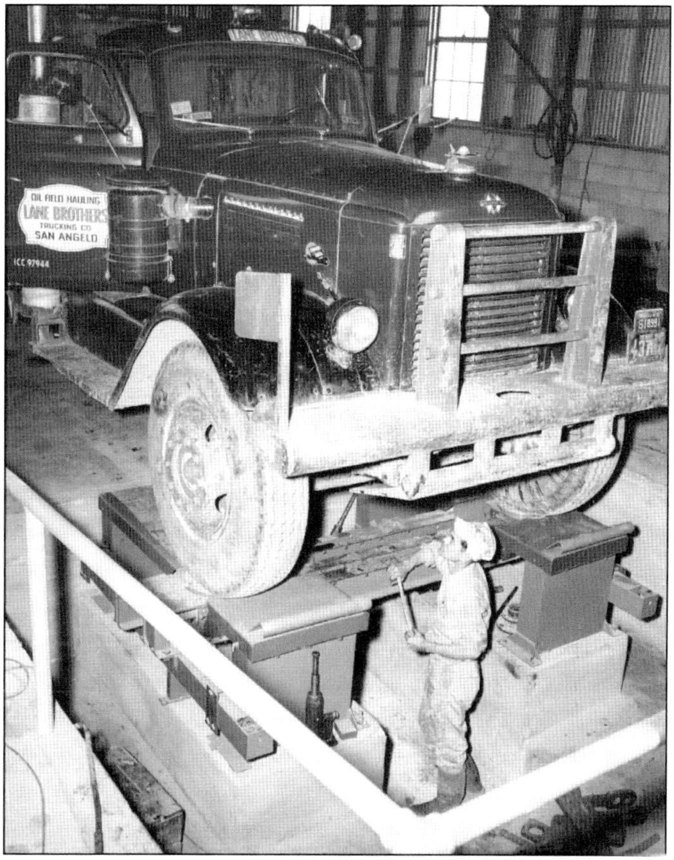

GMC SERVICE AREA. As the industry developed after World War II, the service area became an important part of the business. Besides providing parts for the service department, the service area also sold wholesale parts and displayed accessories to entice potential customers. This photograph was taken at the Concho Motor Truck Co. at 5 West Concho Avenue. (WTC.)

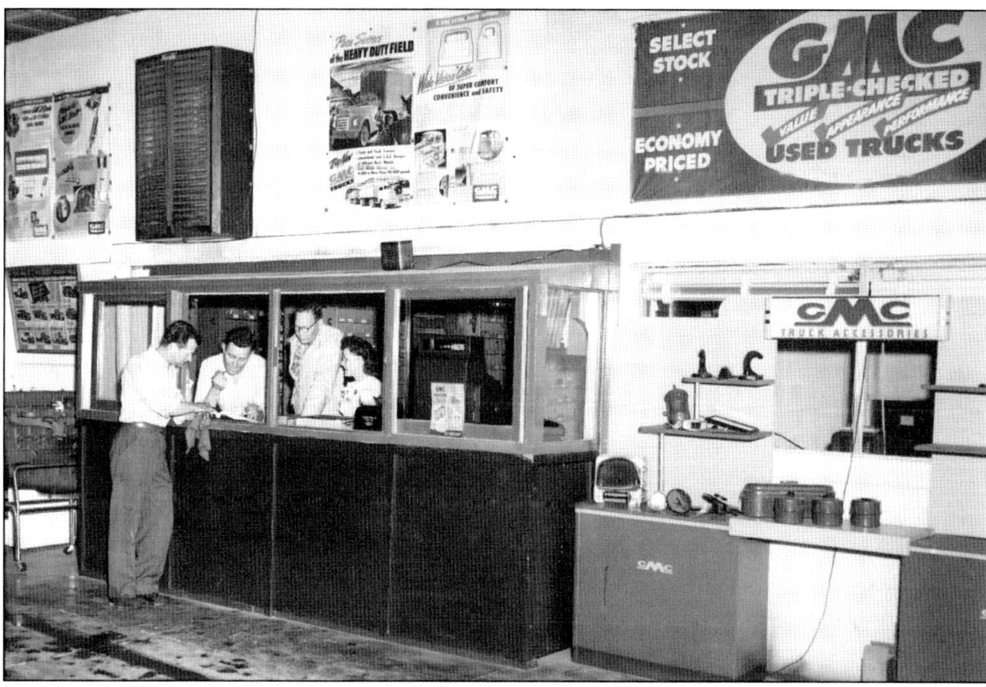

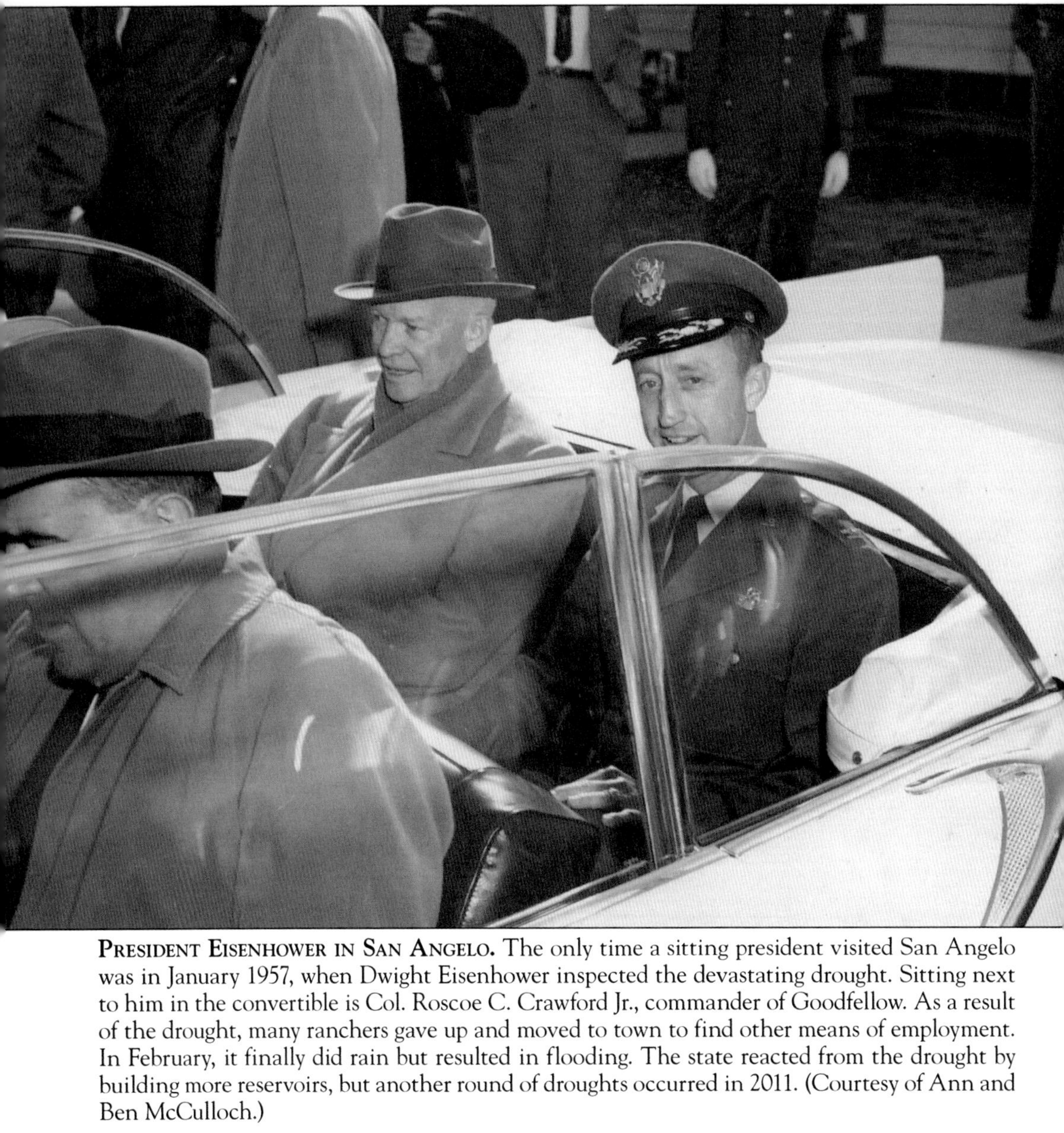

President Eisenhower in San Angelo. The only time a sitting president visited San Angelo was in January 1957, when Dwight Eisenhower inspected the devastating drought. Sitting next to him in the convertible is Col. Roscoe C. Crawford Jr., commander of Goodfellow. As a result of the drought, many ranchers gave up and moved to town to find other means of employment. In February, it finally did rain but resulted in flooding. The state reacted from the drought by building more reservoirs, but another round of droughts occurred in 2011. (Courtesy of Ann and Ben McCulloch.)

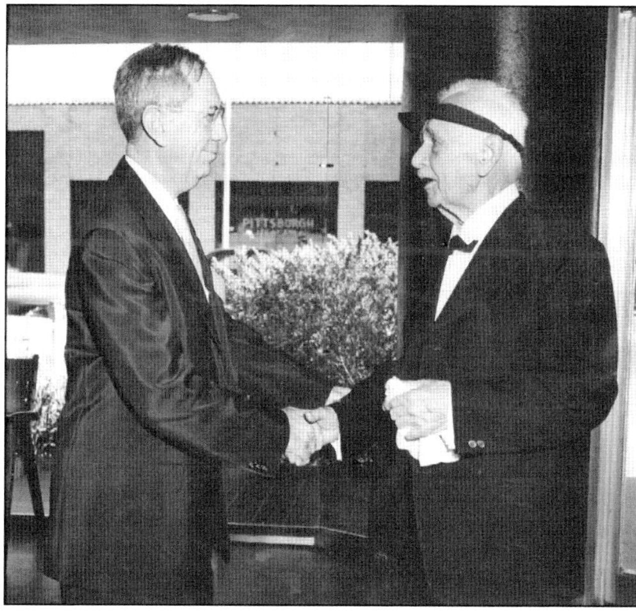

Harte and Ruffini. Shown before a meeting in 1958 are newspaper magnate Houston Harte, (left), and architect Oscar Ruffini, who designed over 35 buildings in a four-block area in downtown San Angelo as well as many other buildings in different communities. Harte considered Ruffini's weathered board-and-batten frame studio and house a blight on Chadbourne Street and wanted it to be moved or razed. Eventually, Ruffini moved out of his house and into the St. Angelus Hotel. See page 50 for pictures of Ruffini's studio and house. (WTC.)

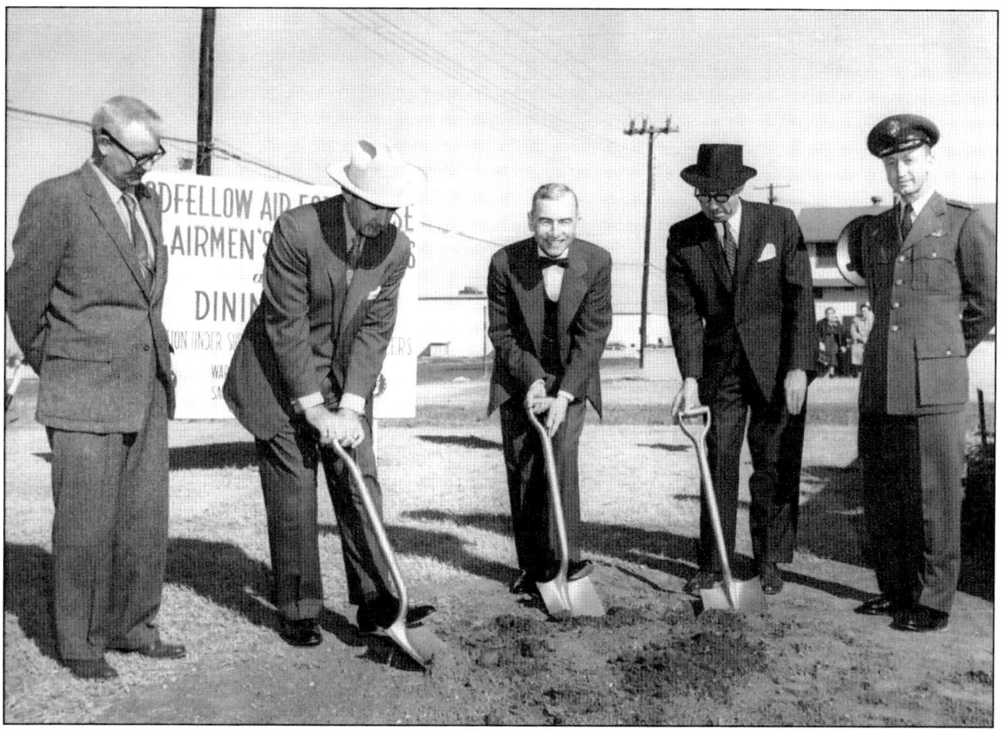

Expanding Goodfellow. This photograph records the ground breaking for the construction of a dining hall and two dormitories in February 1956. Pictured are, from left to right, M.D. Bryant, mayor of San Angelo; Gov. Allan Shivers; Secretary of the Air Force Donald Quaries; Congressman O.C. Fisher; and Col. Roscoe C. Crawford Jr., commander of the 3545th Pilot Training Wing at Goodfellow Air Force Base. Secretary Quaries was here to announce that Goodfellow Air Force Base had become a permanent installation. The base was originally constructed in 1940 as a temporary facility and had continued to be regarded as such until Quaries's announcement. (WTC.)

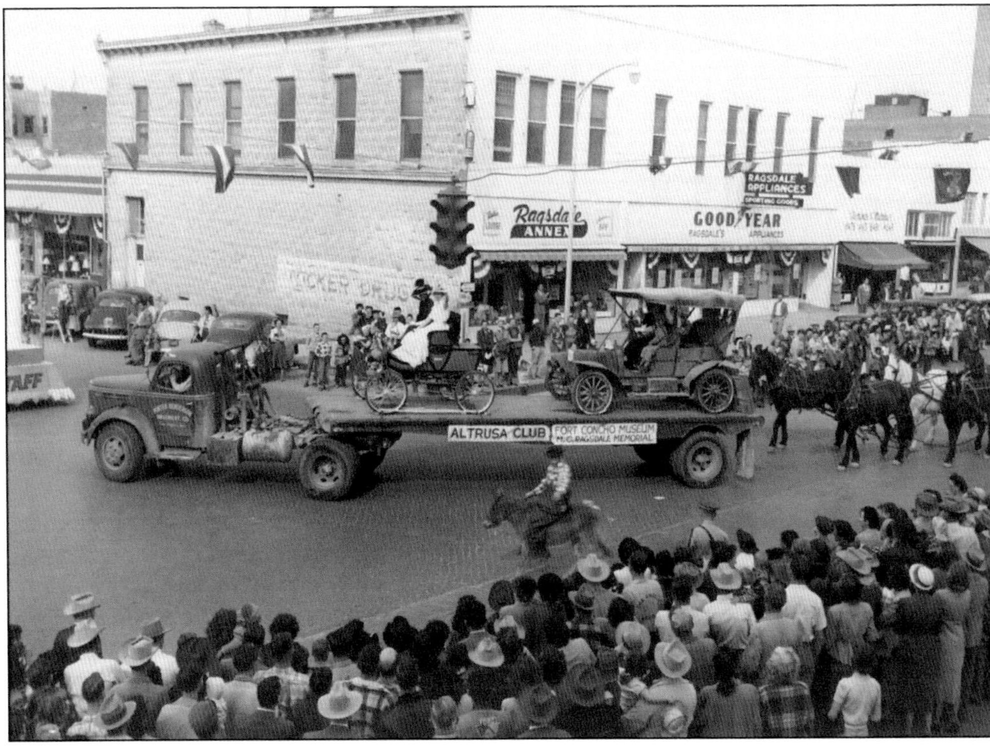

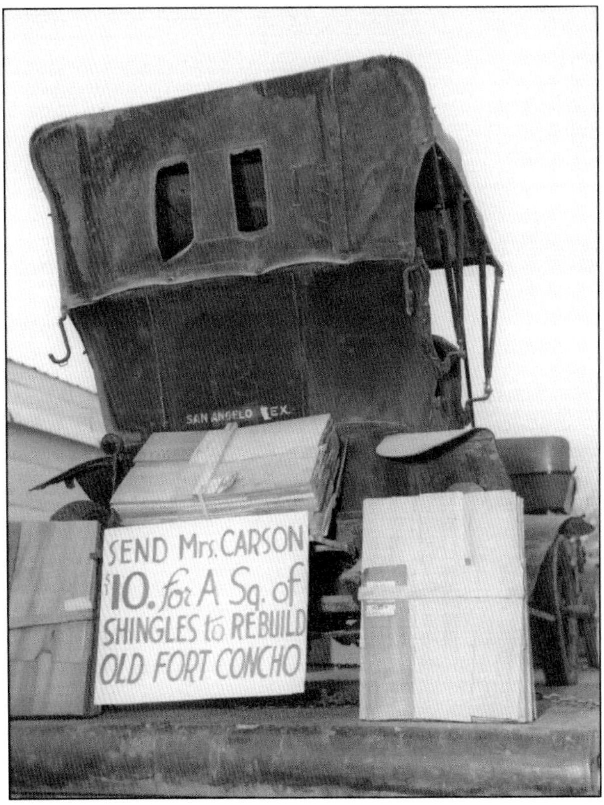

Antique Cars on Trailer. A 1894 Stanley Steamer and a 1908 Franklin are transported on a trailer during a parade through downtown. (FC.)

Gineva Wood Carson, Fort Concho. Gineva Wood Carson worked tirelessly for three decades to collect money for charity. As shown here, she raised money to purchase wood shingles to restore one of the historic buildings at Fort Concho. The City of San Angelo began to acquire many of the buildings, and the fort and museum were made a unit of city government by 1955. Later, in the 1960s, the fort hired its first professionally trained museum director. (FC.)

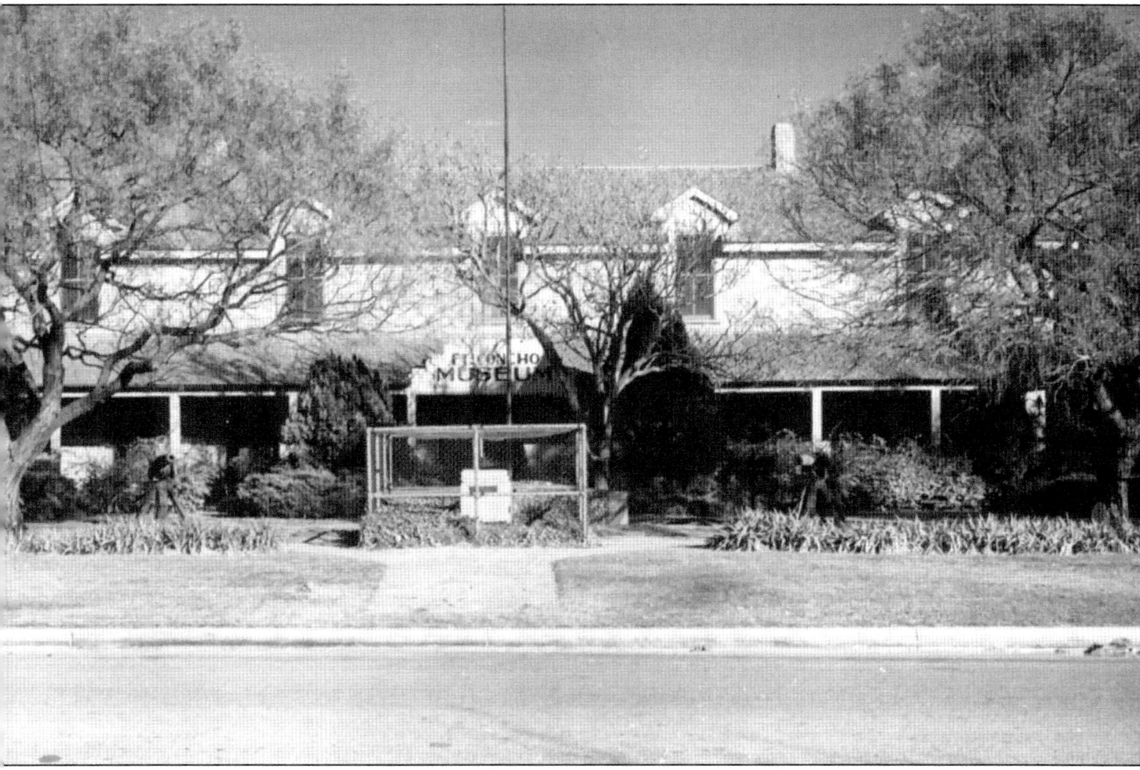

Fort Concho Museum. In 1923, the local chapter of the Daughters of the American Revolution launched a project to save the fort, but funds fell short, and so, a marker was erected at the site. During the 1920s, Gineva Wood Carson created the West Texas Museum. In 1930, she moved the museum to the fort. This photograph dates from the early 1950s. (FC.)

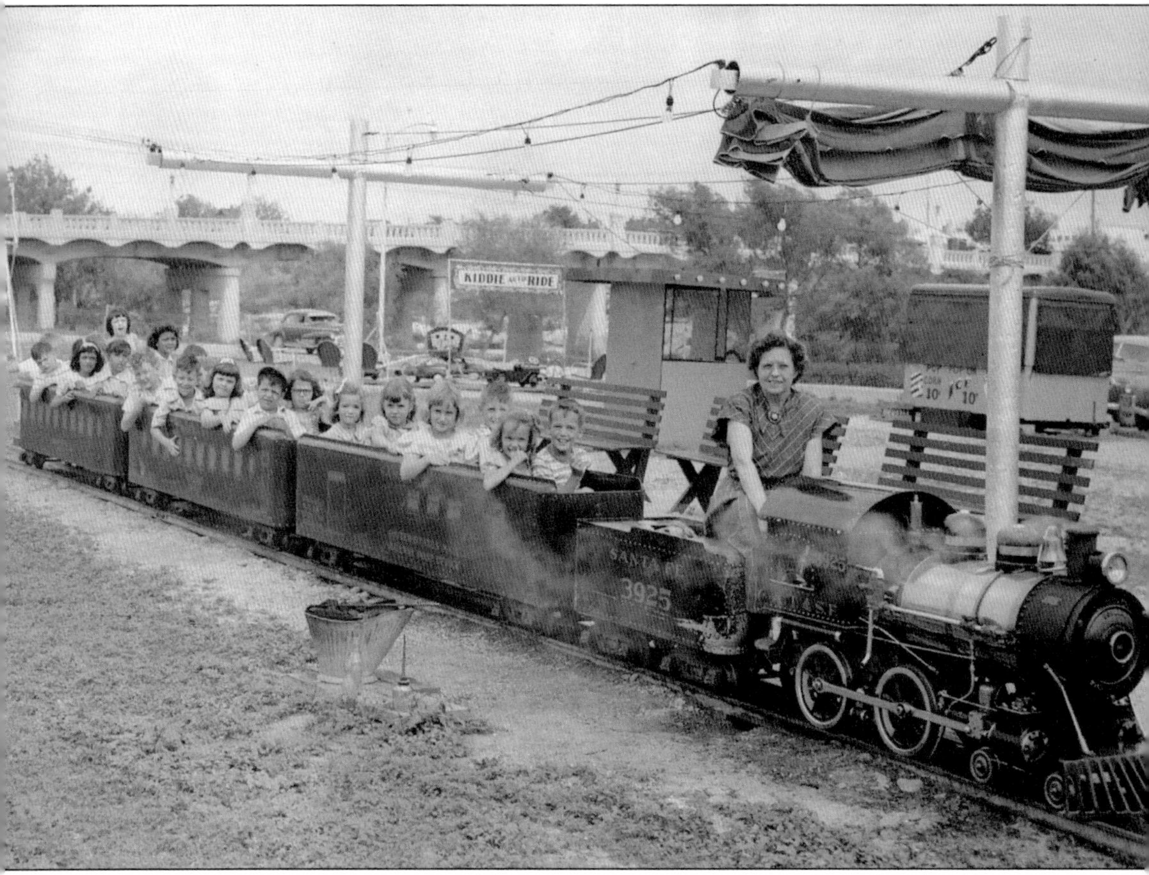

Neff's Amusement Park. Pictured here is Hazel Neff operating the red-and-gold miniature Santa Fe steam locomotive at Neff's Amusement Park. Neff's, as it was called, was a popular place for family entertainment for 50 years. Roy and Hazel Neff initially started the park in 1948 near the Lone Wolf Bridge. The next year, it was moved to the Concho River across from the present-day RiverStage and stayed there until it closed in 1998. The park equipment was then sold off in pieces. In 2001, Funland Amusement Park, run by Ernie Baker, opened at the same site and quickly closed after a year of operations. Hazel ran and repaired all the rides and made popcorn and cotton candy when Roy was at his day job. Roy worked at the park in the evenings and on weekends. Their daughter Kay Reed started selling tickets at the age of seven, and several generations of teenagers were hired to help run the park. (Courtesy of Carolyn Kersten.)

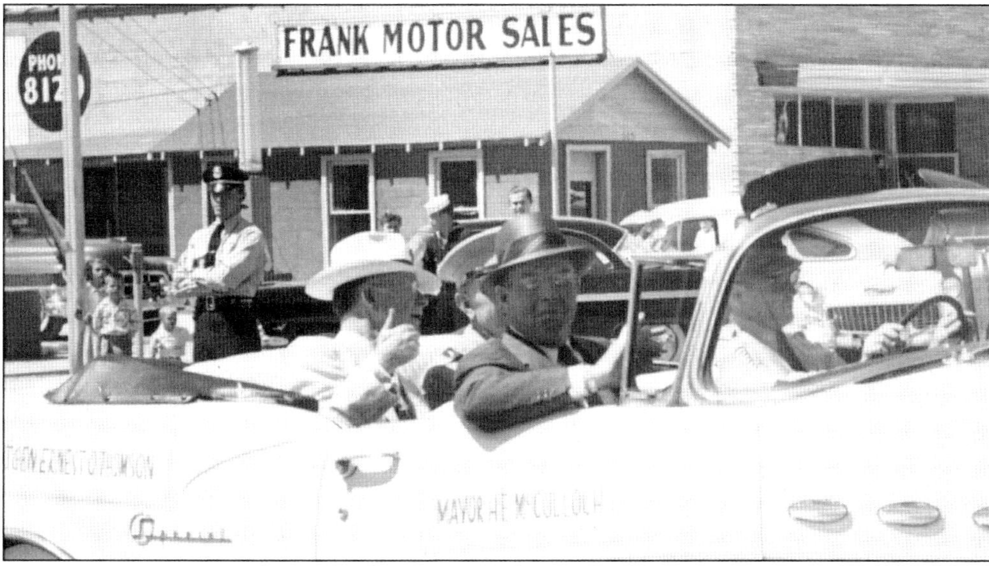

MAYOR H.E. MCCULLOCH IN PARADE. Mayor H.E. McCulloch is seen in the Armed Forces Parade, held on May 19, 1956. The parade was described as being a mile in length and comprising many Army Reserve and National Guard units and floats. Riding in the Buick Special convertible with the driver, from left to right, were Lt. Gen. Ernest O. Thompson, Texas Railroad commissioner; Brig. Gen. Clayton P. Kerr, center; and Mayor H.E. McCulloch sitting in the front passenger seat. (Courtesy of Ann and Ben McCulloch.)

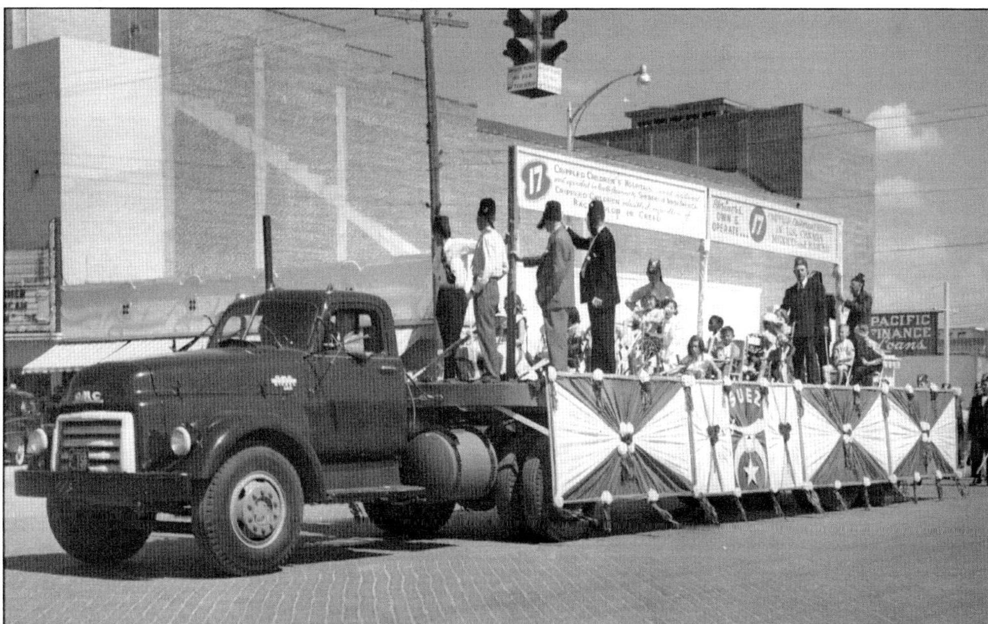

SHRINERS PARADE FLOAT. A dispensation was granted to the Suez Temple, Ancient Arabic Order Nobles of the Mystic Shrine, on June 22, 1950. With a membership of 834, the club started sponsoring circuses in San Angelo in 1948. The Shriners can be seen in many local parades, such as the one pictured here, and are involved in community events. They provide invaluable support for the Shriners Hospital for Children. (WTC.)

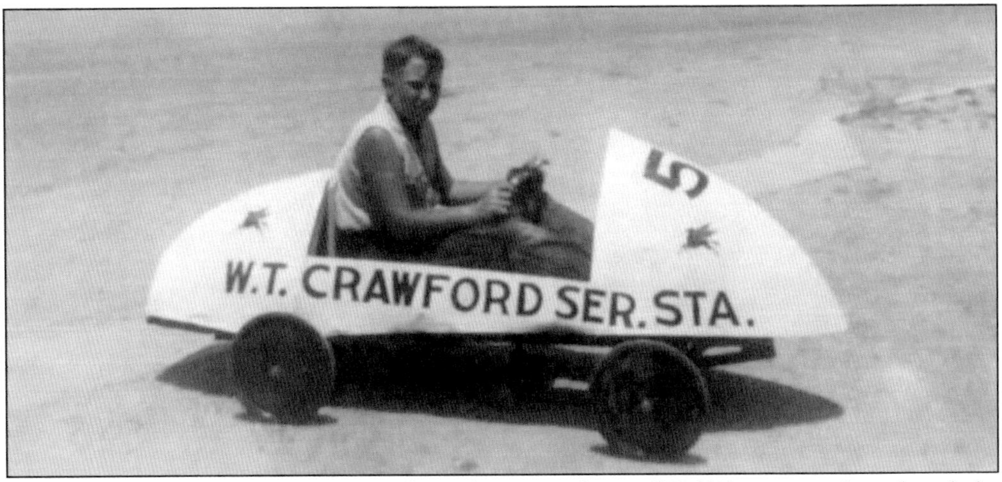

SOAPBOX DERBY. Washington Drive Hill was the scene of several YMCA-sponsored soapbox derby races between the late 1940s and mid-1950s. This photograph, taken about 1945, shows Hubert "Whit" Whittley sitting in car No. 5. Whittley's dad went to Angelo Iron and Metal and found half of a gas tank, originally belonging to an airplane, to serve as the body. Whittley's racing career was short, as he lost both of his heats and was out of the race. The July 1955 race, as described by the San Angelo *Standard-Times*, had "a crowd of about 124 [who] braved the treeless wastes of Washington Drive for the two-hour event." (Courtesy of Sandy and Whit Whittley.)

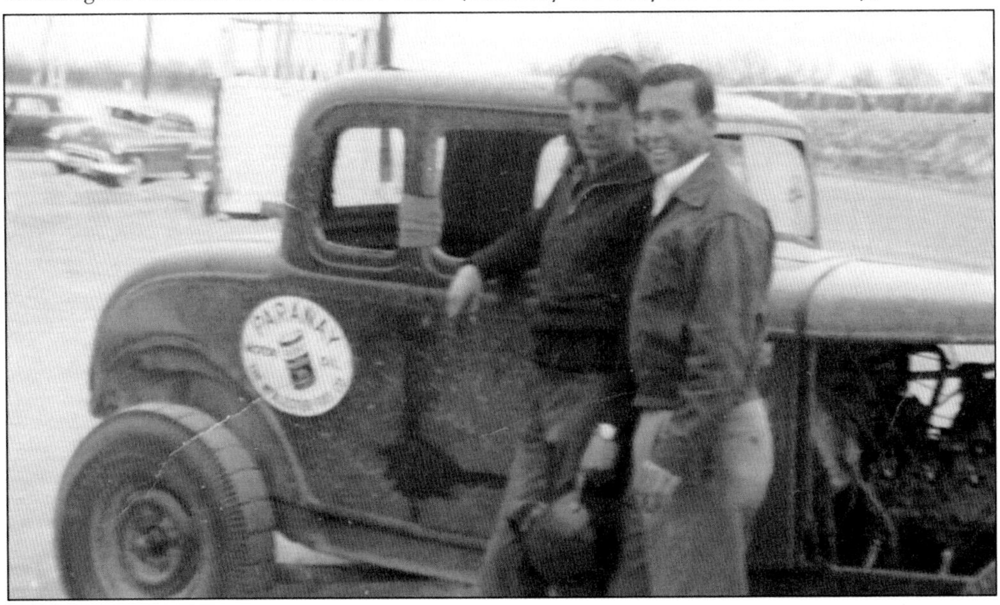

AUTO RACING. Automobile racing was a popular sport and pastime. At one point in the 1950s, two tracks competed for cars and drivers, as well as spectators. During a bargain-day event in 1954, Ben Toile, the director of Speedbowl, charged $1 per carload, resulting in an attendance of over 2,000. This photograph was taken in 1952 at the Speedbowl, a dirt track located on Christoval Road. On the right is sponsor Erwin Otto Goetz; the racer with him is unidentified. In 1953, a second track was constructed out on Arden Road. It was called Raceway Park. Later, a banked, paved racetrack was constructed, called Lakeside Speedway, located at Kickerbocker and Mathis Field. Mathis Field was the scene of drag racing, sponsored by the YMCA and San Angelo Police Department. (Courtesy of Gary Goetz.)

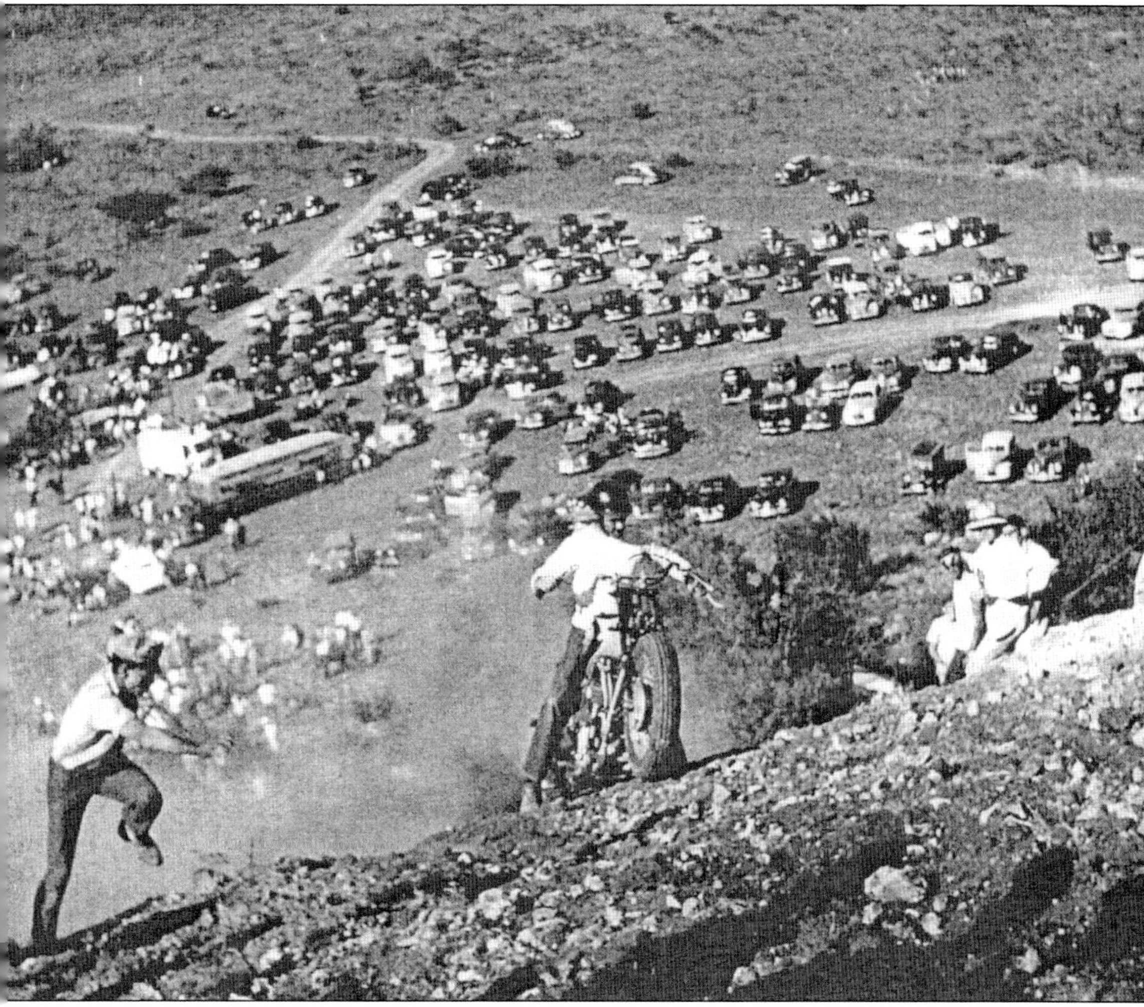

HILL-CLIMB. Motorcycle enthusiasts in Europe believed mechanical steeplechasing, also called scrambles or hill-climbs, would be the answer to the popular horse steeplechasing. The sport found its way to San Angelo in 1949. The event was repeated in March 1954 at the Claude Linthicum ranch, seven miles west on Arden Road. The half-mile course up a 280-foot rocky hill challenged all climbers, and the event drew a good crowd. San Angelo entries included Bobby Cook, Charles Blumentritt, Cliff Peiser, Harrell Mathis, Thomas Sparks, Richard Bachus, Tody Cobalt, and Wayne Kiser. An unidentified driver in this photograph masters the hill. (FC.)

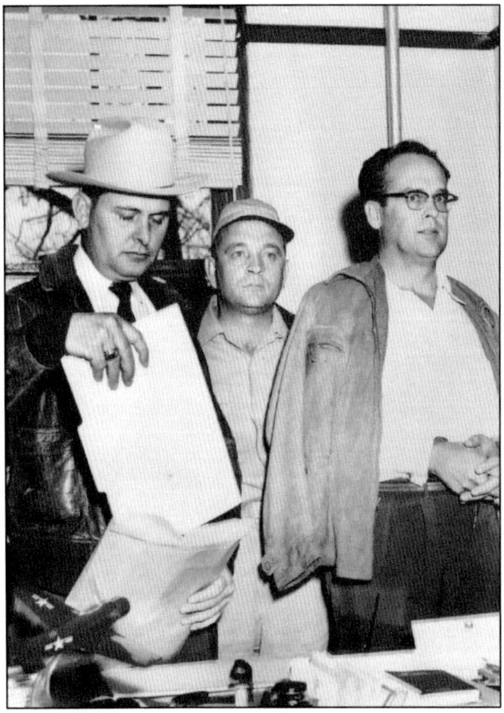

WEAVER BOMBING. On the quiet morning of January 19, 1955, a car bomb exploded at 303 West Beauregard Avenue, shattering the calm of a peaceful residential neighborhood. Killed in the incident was 52-year-old Helen Harris Weaver, wife of architect Harry Weaver. Harry Washburn, Mrs. Weaver's former son-in-law, on the right, was convicted of murder and sentenced to life in prison. Texas Ranger Ralph Rohatsch (left) charged Carl Henninger (center) as Washburn's accomplice. Testimony showed that the assassination attempt actually targeted architect Weaver, who had protested against his wife giving money to Washburn. (Private collection.)

MAYOR M.D. BRYANT (1954–1956), ENTERTAINING FOREIGN OFFICERS. Mayor Bryant entertained many visitors to San Angelo at his ranch, including these Chinese air force officers. (Courtesy of US Air Force, Goodfellow Air Force Base, Texas.)

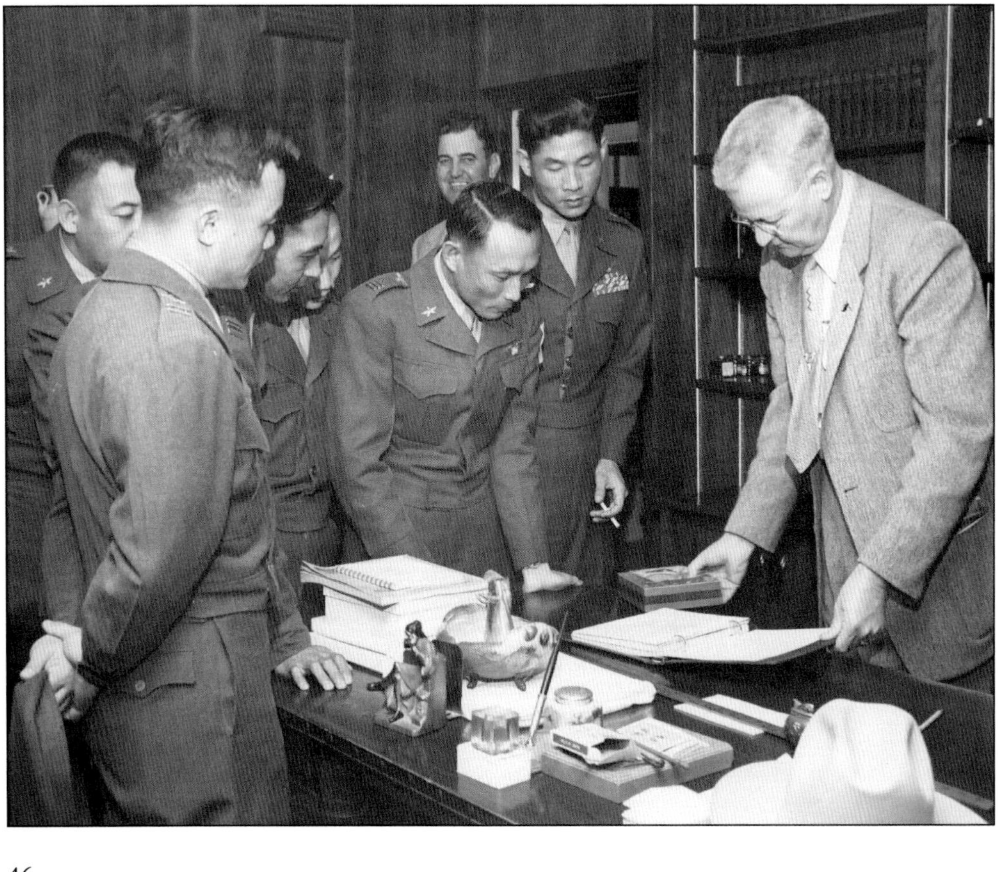

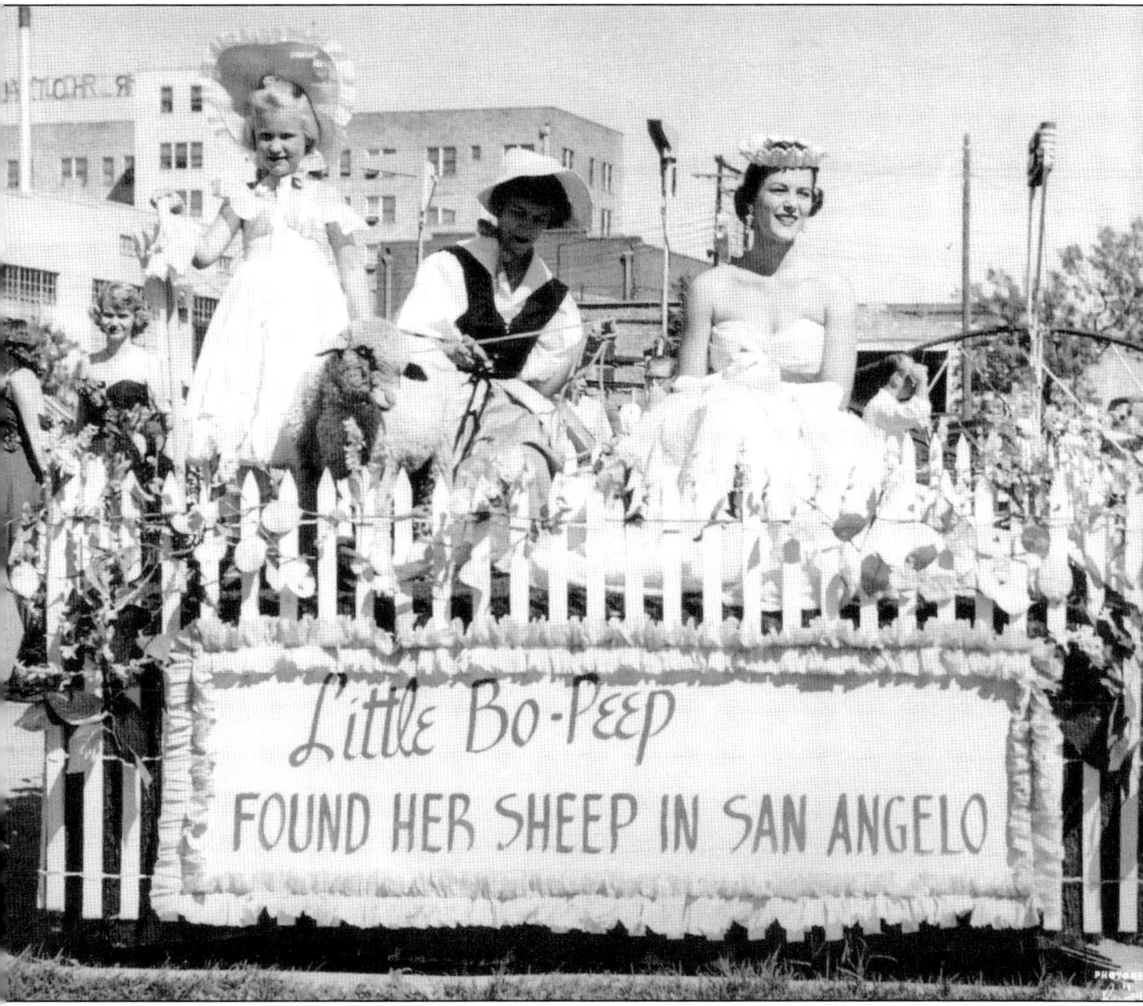

KATHRYN GROMATSKI, FIRST MISS WOOL, 1952. The Miss Wool of Texas pageant was originally held in 1952 in San Angelo and continued annually until 1972. In 1958, the pageant became national, with contestants representing wool-producing regions around the United States. The pageant was sponsored by the National Wool Growers Association, the American Sheep Producers Council, and the Wool Bureau, Inc., and was always held in the San Angelo Coliseum. (Courtesy of Barney's Studio.)

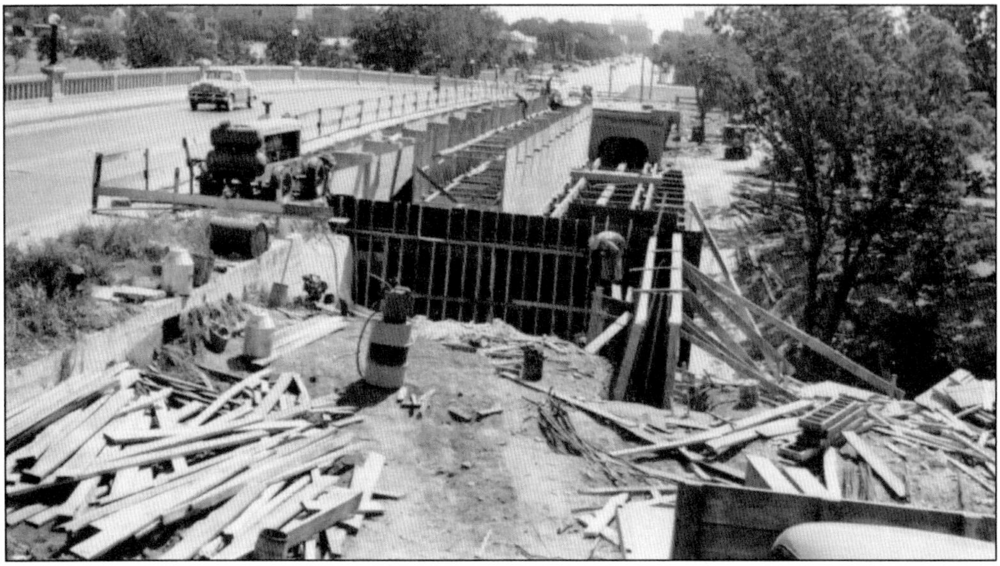

Beauregard Avenue Bridge. A scrapbook of detailed photographs of the construction from January 1951 until its completion on October 11, 1951, chronicles the work. Unfortunately, the name of the person who took these photographs is not known, other than that he was the bookkeeper for the project contractor. Gerald Lackey wrote a narrative summary of the work in February 2005. This photograph, dated June 11, 1951, shows the bridge looking east. (WTC.)

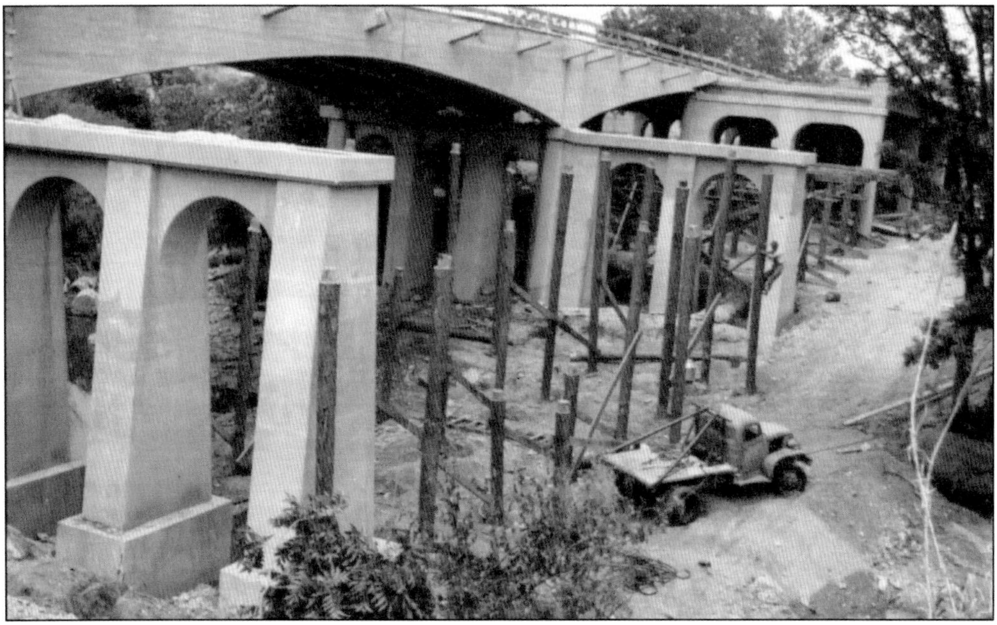

Beauregard Avenue Bridge. Nearly all of the work was done by hand. The most interesting part of the construction project was the 200-foot-long cantilever span over the river. The ends of the spans are free to move horizontally and vertically to adapt to loads and changing weather conditions. The work required a considerable amount of pine poles to support the form work. On August 12, a flood came down the Concho River, and the workers stayed at the job to save the supports. If they had not been successful, it would have meant the loss of several months' work and financial disaster to the contractor. This photograph was taken on June 27, 1951, looking east. (WTC.)

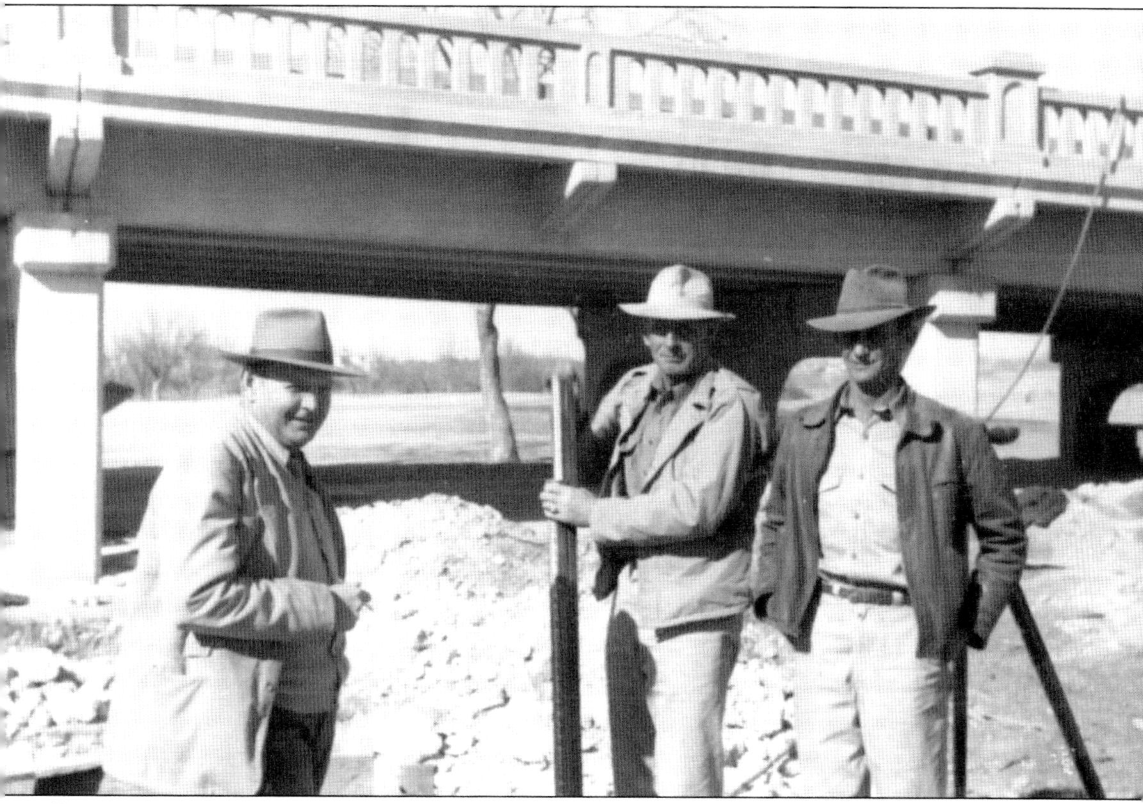

Beauregard Avenue Bridge. In 1929, the Beauregard Avenue Bridge was constructed over the Concho River. By the late 1940s, the western part of the city was experiencing rapid growth, and Beauregard Avenue was becoming congested. In 1950, Beauregard Avenue, also US Highway 67, was widened to four lanes from Sherwood Way to the Concho River. The Beauregard Avenue Bridge was only two lanes at the time and therefore needed to be widened to complete the project. The two-lane bridge was in sound condition and so did not need to be replaced. Officials decided that the bridge added to the aesthetics of the river park area below, and so, it decided to widen the structure, even though it was not the most economical solution. Shown here at the construction site are A.J. Jennings, senior resident engineer (left); W.B. Hoppe, project engineer (center); and Bob Baker of Bob Baker Construction. The firm Thomas & Ratliff received the contract and sublet the work to Baker Construction. (WTC.)

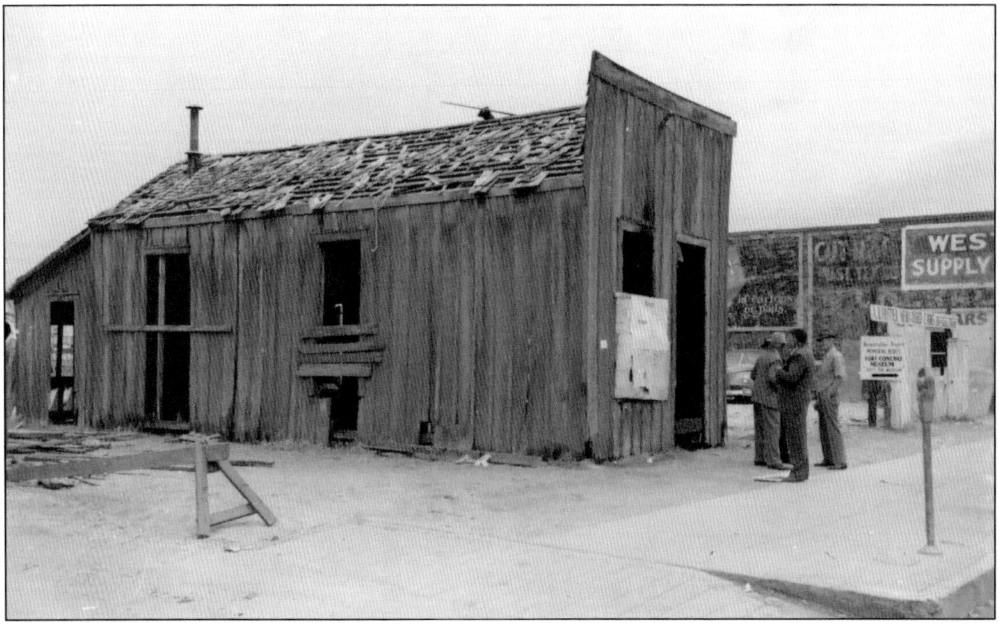

Ruffini's Studio and House. Oscar Ruffini was an early architect in San Angelo, and the many buildings he designed certainly had an impact on the development of the city. His studio and house were located at 11 South Chadbourne Street in a "toolshed"—a board-and-batten frame building with a false front and lean-to addition. Very few architect offices from this period have survived, and nor have original drawings, specifications, and tools. (FC.)

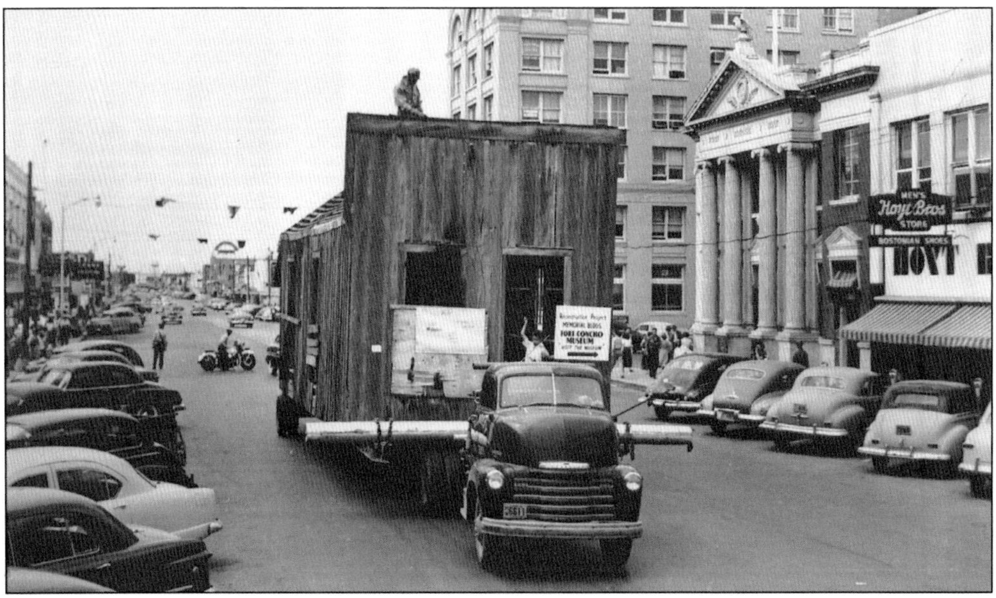

Moving Ruffini's Studio and House. The city commission eventually ordered Oscar Ruffini's weather-beaten house demolished because it was a "public hazard and nuisance." The local newspaper reported that no repairs had been allowed for years because the zoning ordinance prohibited it. The importance of the building was finally recognized, and Henry Ragsdale and Billy Hanks, cochairmen for the Fort Concho Moving Group, made arrangements with Briley Bros. to relocate the structure in May 1951 to Fort Concho. (FC.)

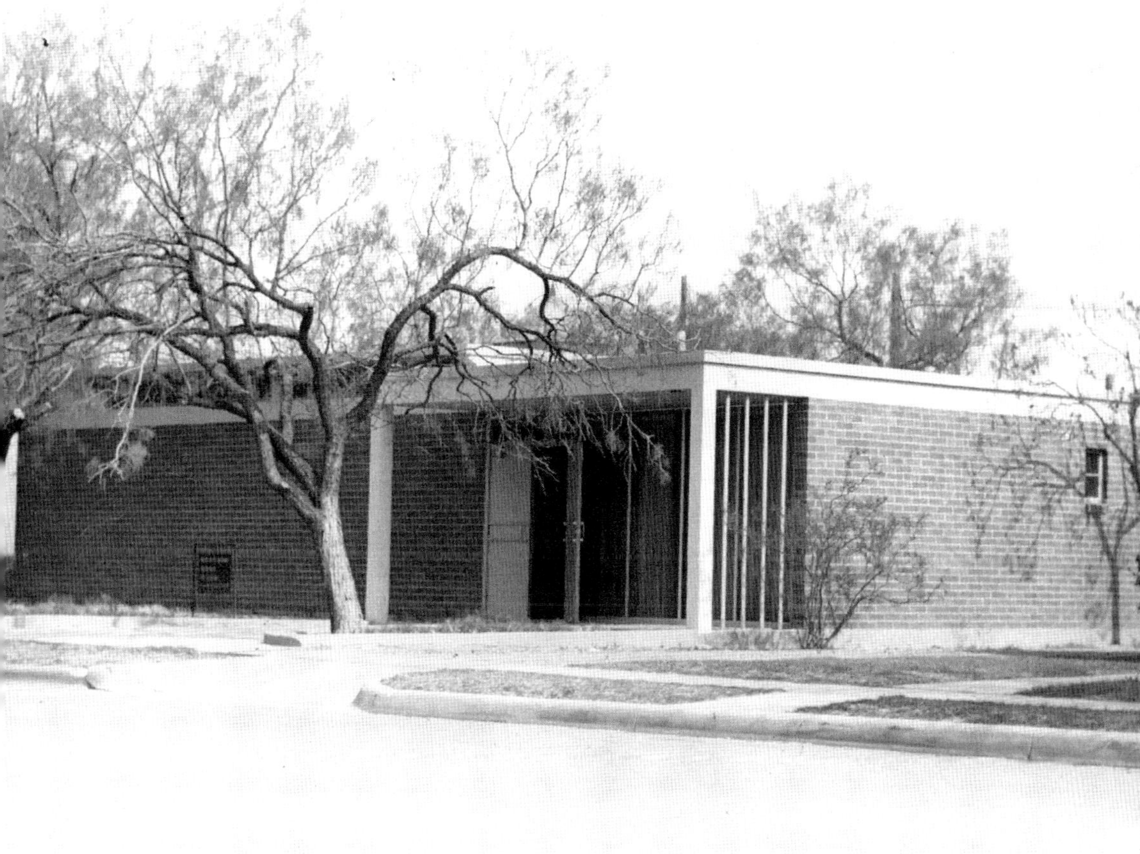

KENDALL ART GALLERY. In 1948–1949, architect Donald Goss designed the original portion of the Helen King Kendall Memorial Art Gallery at 119 West First Street. Construction of the second wing, known as the "In Our Image" wing, occurred in 1950–1951, with the studio wing at the back completed the following year. The art gallery is home to the San Angelo Art Club, the second-oldest continuous art organization in Texas. The club organizes many exhibits of local artists and conducts classes throughout the year. (Courtesy of Barney's Studio.)

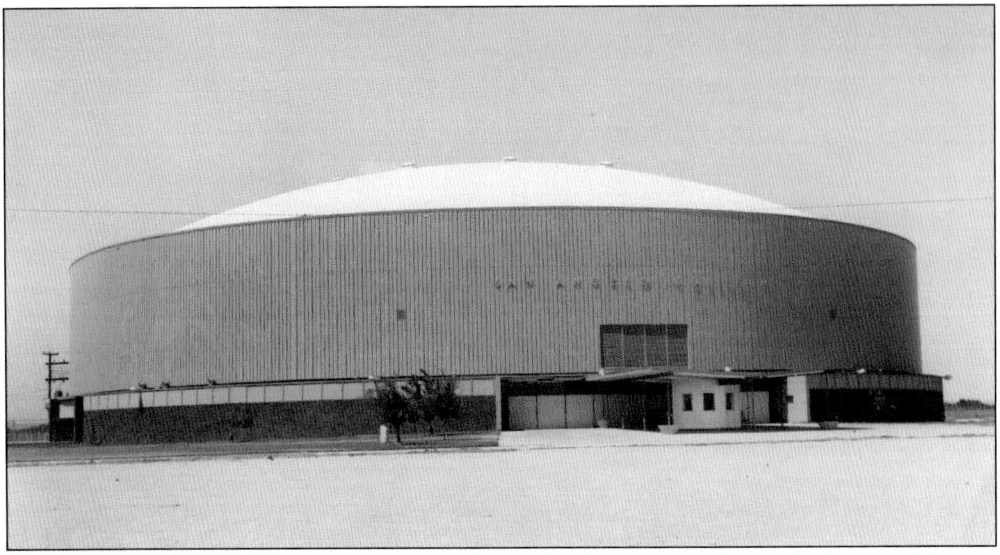

San Angelo Coliseum. Built in 1959 as the home for the San Angelo Stock Show and Rodeo, the San Angelo Coliseum has a seating capacity of 5,260. The original one was destroyed in a tornado in 1953. Beside the stock show, it is used for concerts, trade shows, and exhibits. Having the rodeo indoors helps to eliminate the negative effects of unexpected weather situations. In 2011, the structure was renamed the Foster Communication Coliseum. (WTC.)

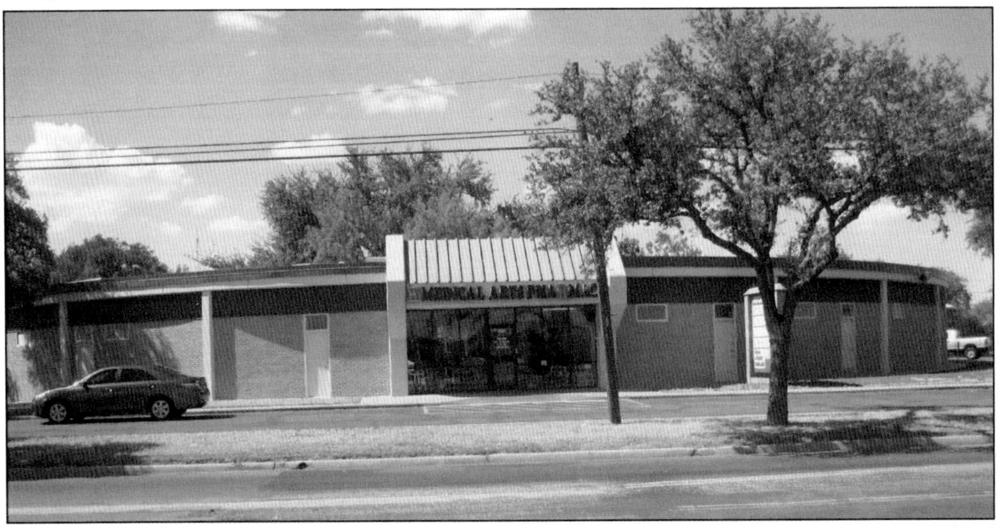

Medical Arts Building. In the 20th century, the first specialized buildings for private medical practitioners began to appear. After World War II, the shift from the center of town to areas with more space for new construction and adequate parking is illustrated by the Medical Arts Building, located at Pecos and Howard Streets. This circular building with an arcade in the courtyard was designed in 1956 by Mauldin, Ballard and Associates of San Angelo and cost $250,000 to build. One of the key points of the design is flexibility. The number of suites or offices could be shifted around, and the design called for a second floor, which was not built. Dr. Perry J.C. Byars Jr. was corporate president; Dr. Sam H. Gainer, vice president; Dr. Gordon A. Pilmer, secretary-treasurer; and Dr. J.J. Reese and Dr. Lloyd R. Hershberger, directors. In this case, the Medical Arts Building was occupied by independent doctors with no business affiliations other than joint ownership of the building. (Photograph by author.)

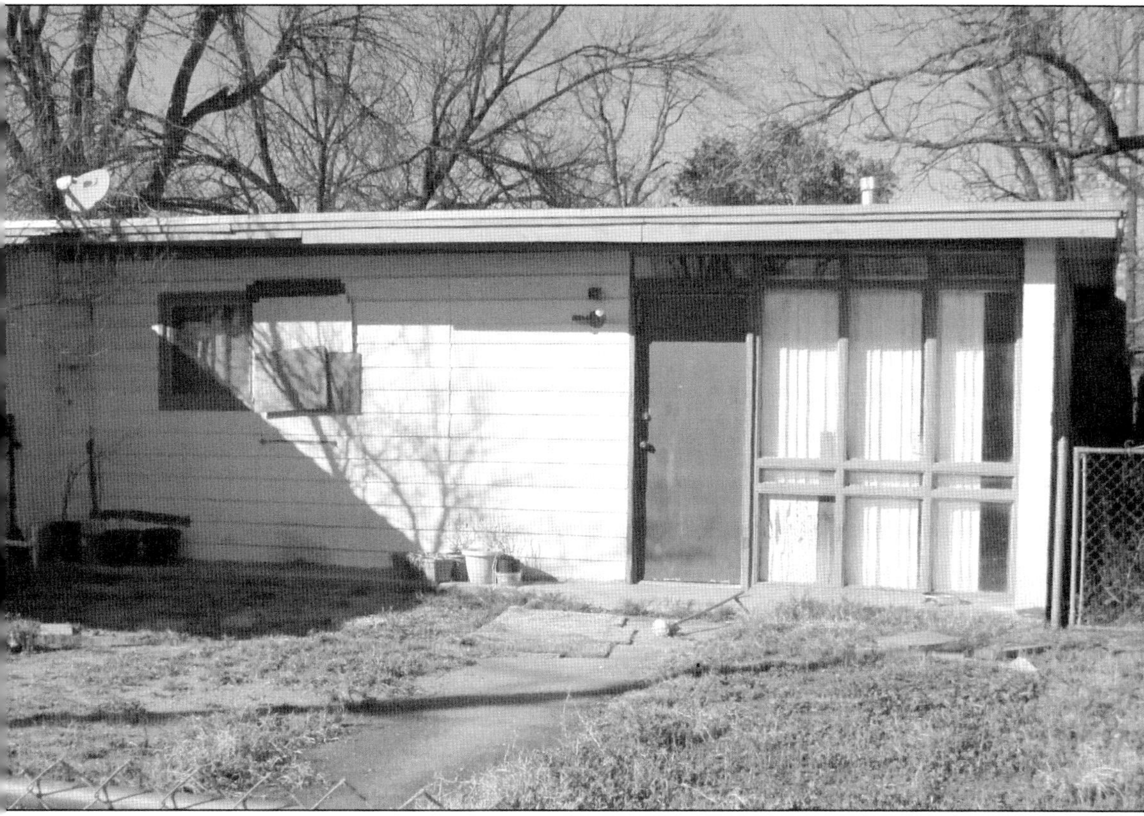

San Angelo Plan. In 1951, John Moss designed a 550-square-foot house costing $3,000, called the "San Angelo Plan." The total construction cost generated quite a lot of excitement. It was a two-bedroom, one-bath house, constructed on a concrete slab, with sidewalls of solid masonry and wood siding on the front and rear walls. Marilu Flores and Mrs. Hugh Norton planned the color scheme for the first house in earth tones to blend with the brick masonry. It was built by T&M Development Co. of San Angelo, headed by Moss, A.L. Turner, and John Armstrong. Lee Jones of San Angelo Federal Savings and Loan Association helped with financing. Many of these houses were constructed in San Angelo, at least 39 different cities in Texas, and states such as Shreveport, Louisiana; Morristown, Tennessee; Charlotte, North Carolina; and Artesia, New Mexico. Stories and photographs appeared in *Southern Building Supplies*, the *Gulf Coast Lumberman*, and *Architectural Forum*. In December 1951, Sen. Lyndon Johnson and a group of individuals flew in on a DC-4 from Johnson City to inspect the first house constructed in the Ben Ficklin addition. He came away very impressed and stated, "This is the beginning of what should be a revolution in housing development. I am amazed and thrilled." (Photograph by author.)

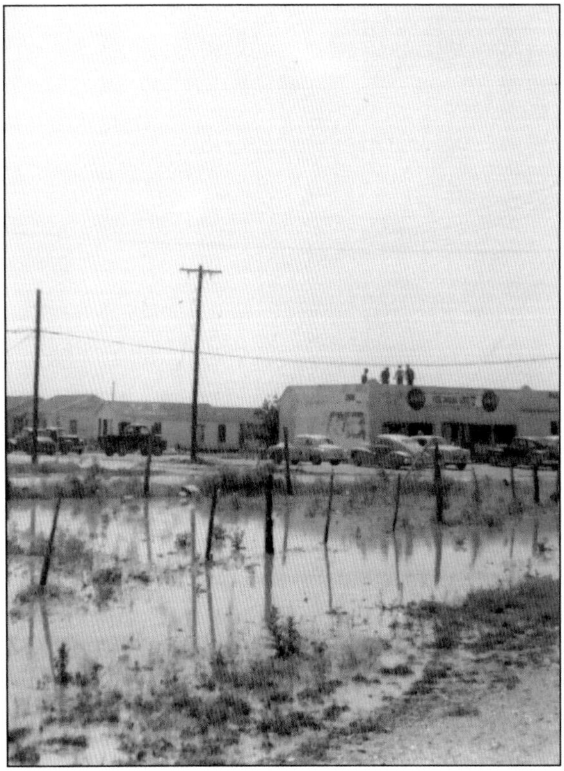

Tornado, Holman Grocery. Holman Grocery No. 2 at 3820 North Chadbourne Street survived the 1953 tornado and became a viewing platform to observe the destruction. Heavy rain and hail immediately followed the tornado, eliminating the possibility of fires from broken gas mains and downed electric lines. James DeLong, who took this photograph, pulled off the road at the Y on Chadbourne Street during the tornado, and fallen overhead wires got entangled in the hood ornament of his Frazer automobile. Not knowing if they were live, he kept backing up and turning to eventually free the car from the wires. While in the process of maneuvering the car, a large house roof flew over his car. By that time, his knees were knocking. James was on his way to have a first date with local girl Artie McDowell, whom he would eventually marry, but the storm delayed the meeting for a few weeks. (Courtesy of James DeLong.)

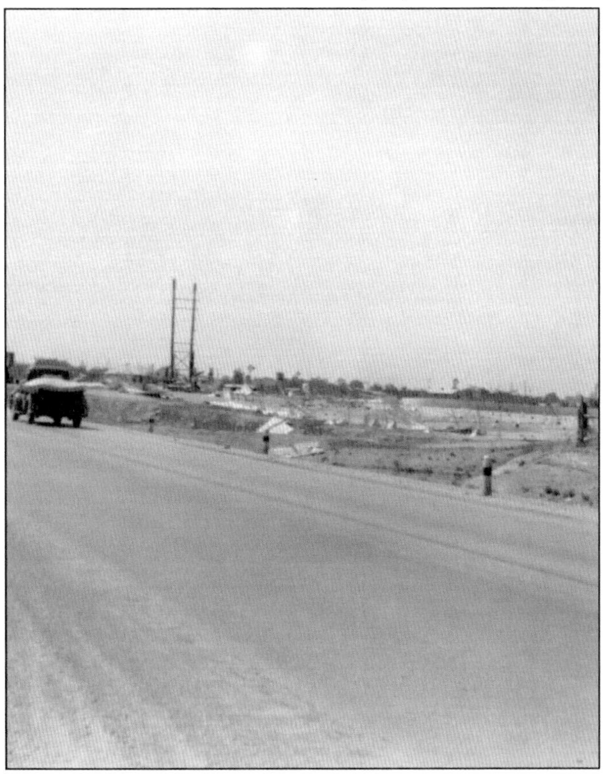

Rocket Drive-In. James DeLong witnessed the destruction of the Rocket Drive-In screen as the May 11, 1953, tornado created a half-mile-wide path of destruction through Lake View on its way to Waco. DeLong returned home to collect his camera to record the damage. The Rocket Drive-In, located at 4001 North Chadbourne Street, was rebuilt and continued to operate for another 17 years. San Angelo followed the national trend during the peak of drive-in popularity in the 1950s and 1960s with six other drive-ins in town: the Atomic, located at 2505 North Main Street; Belvue, at 654 North Bell Street; Jet, 3506 Sherwood Way; Stardust, 2501 North Randolph Street; Starlite, Mertzon Highway and Arden Road; and the Twilight at South Chadbourne Street and the Old Christoval Road. (Courtesy of James DeLong.)

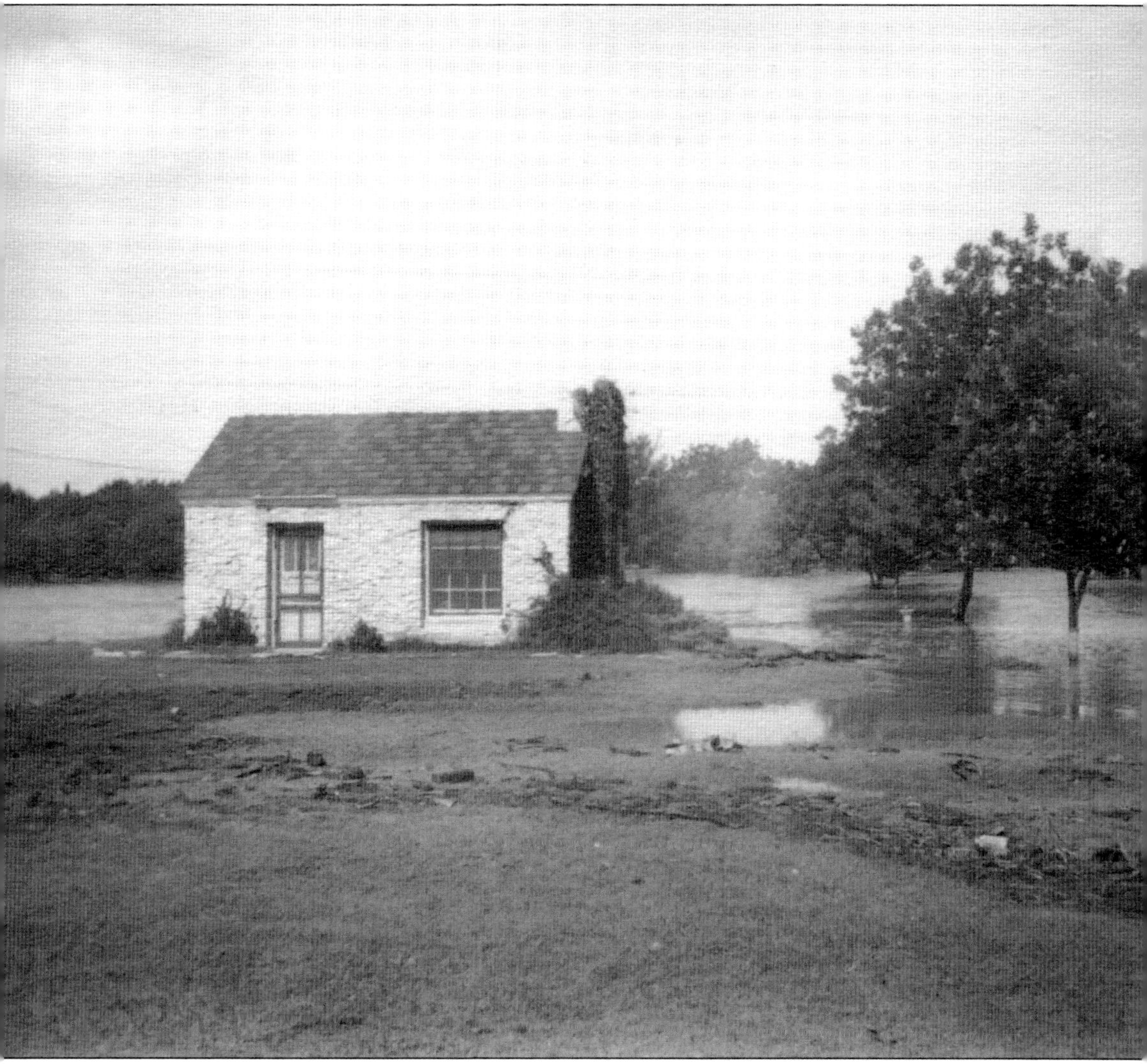

Flood at Clubhouse. The flood of 1936 was certainly one of the worst in the 20th century, but flooding also occurred at other times in San Angelo, as witnessed in the early 1950s. Here, the Concho River left its bank and inundated areas around the Santa Fe golf course clubhouse near West Beauregard Avenue. (Courtesy of Barney's Studio.)

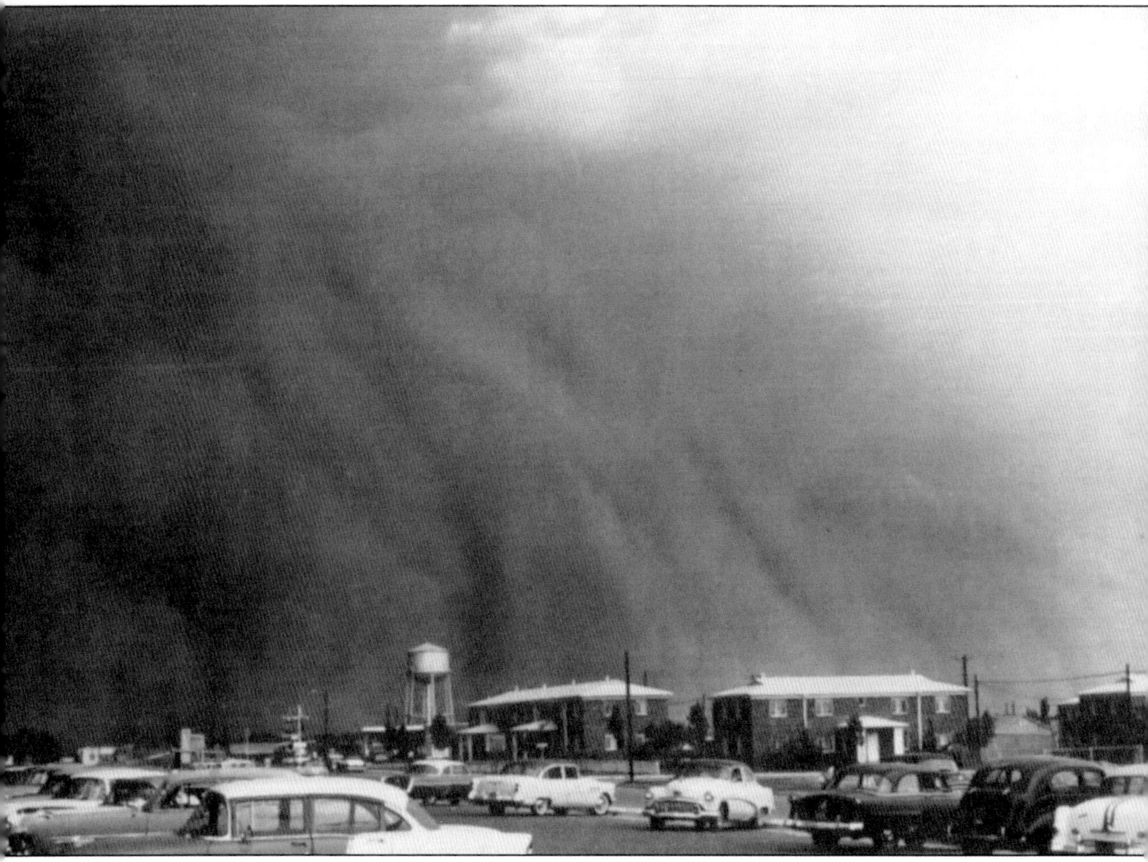

Dust Storm. A monster dust storm was recorded in this 1950s photograph, looking from the Village Shopping Center on Beauregard Avenue toward the public housing complex. (WTC.)

Two

1960s

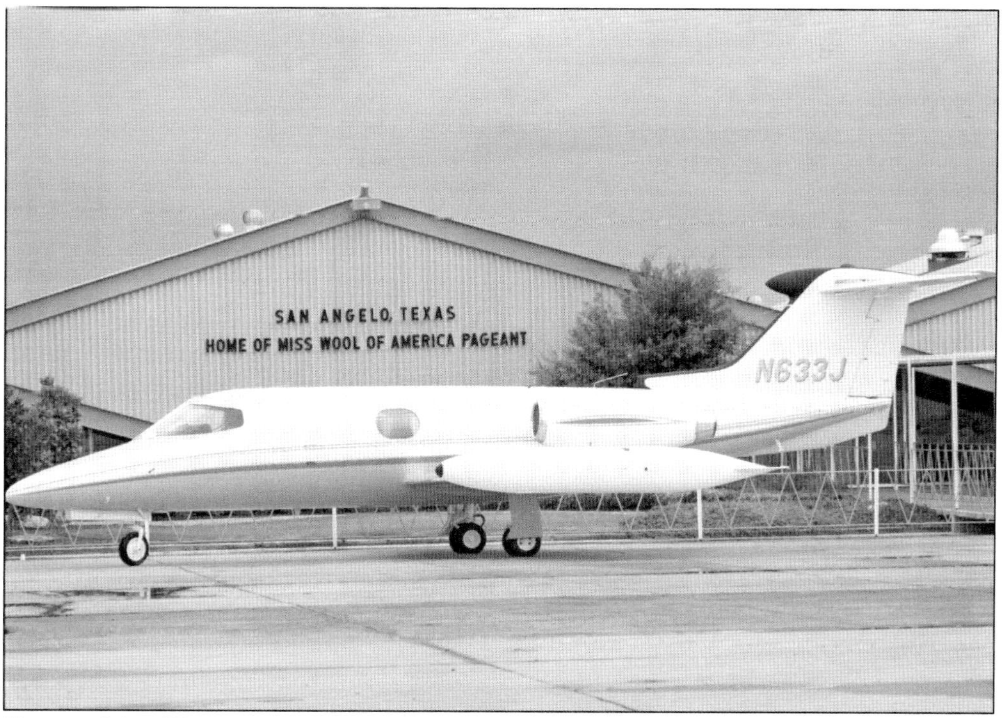

Home of Miss Wool of America Pageant. This is a photograph of the San Angelo Municipal Airport, located at Mathis Field. In 1970, it served West Texas with 11 scheduled fights daily. San Angelo is the home of the Miss Wool of America pageant. The wool and mohair industry has been an important part of the San Angelo business world since the first sheep were brought into the county in the 1870s. In the 1950s, a pageant was created to help promote the industry centered in West Texas. It continued into the national scene with help from television until the 1970s. (WTC.)

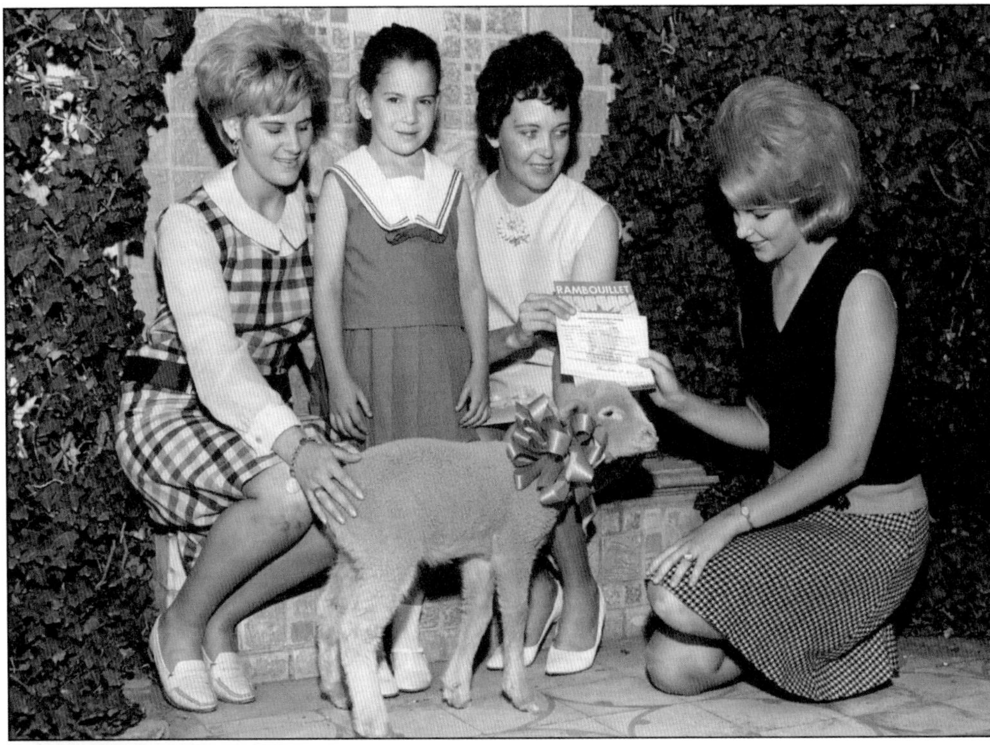

MISS WOOL AT TS&GRA HEADQUARTERS. Janice Archer, Miss Wool of Texas for 1965, is in the courtyard of the Texas Sheep & Goat Raisers Association Headquarters. Six-year-old Becy Hodges, daughter of Clinton and Joyce Hodges of Sterling City, presented Janice Archer a registered Rambouillet ewe lamb. (Courtesy of the Texas Sheep & Goat Raisers Association.)

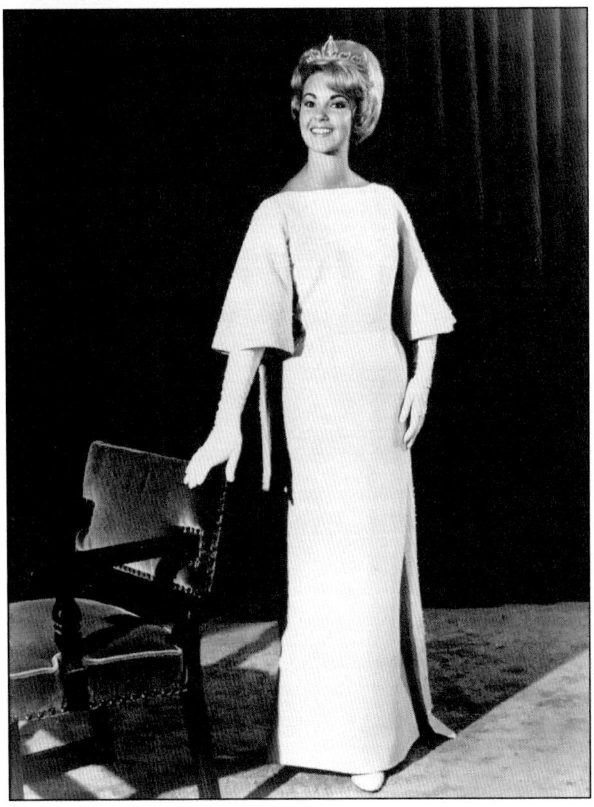

MISS WOOL MODELING A GOWN. Miss Wool of Texas for 1965, Janice Archer is modeling a coronation gown. The dress and sweep train are of sheer white wool and the butterfly sleeves, bodice, and train are trimmed with sunburst crystals. (Courtesy of the Texas Sheep & Goat Raisers Association.)

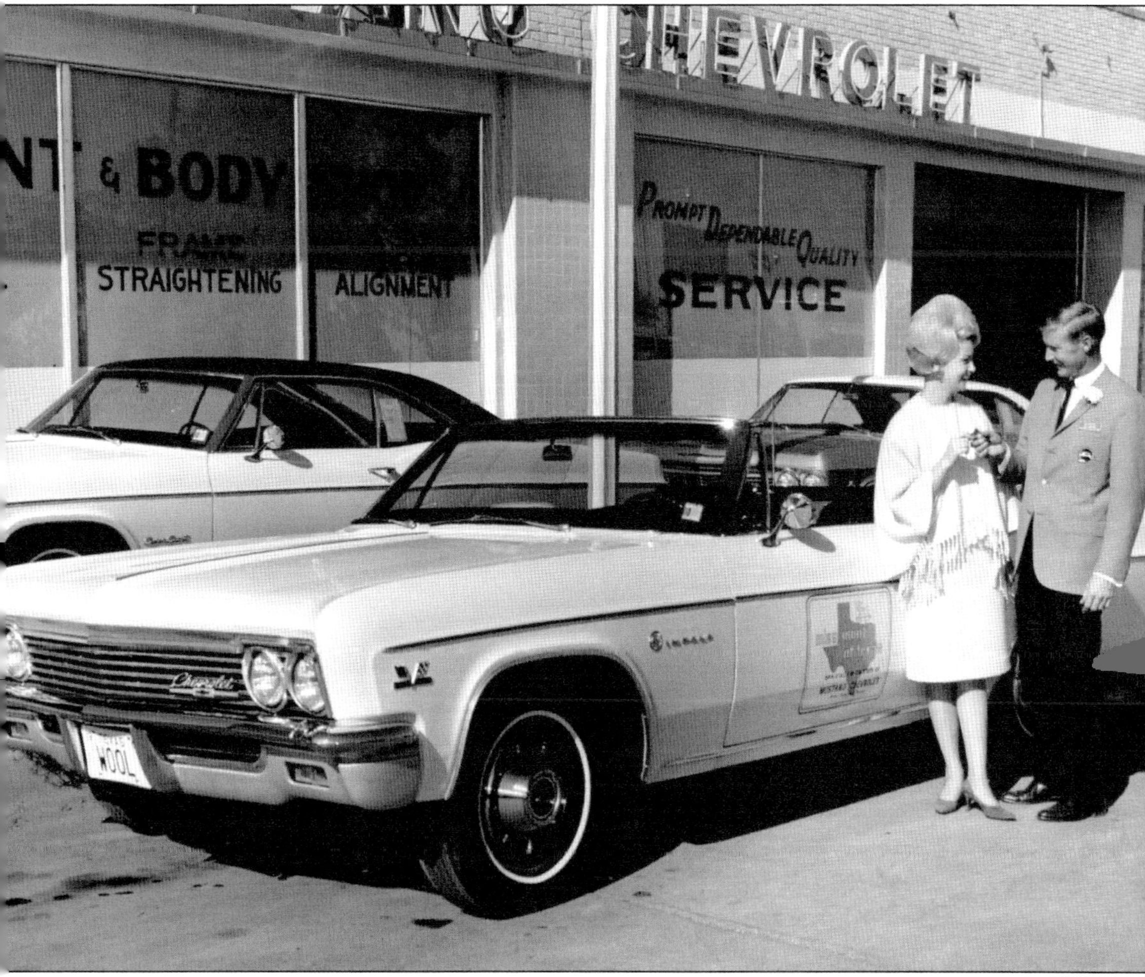

MISS WOOL OF TEXAS. Janice Archer was provided an Impala convertible by Mustang Chevrolet to drive and attend events around Texas. Note the special license plates bearing "WOOL." Miss Wool received the keys from Ben Bessent, Mustang Chevrolet sales manager. (Courtesy of the Texas Sheep & Goat Raisers Association.)

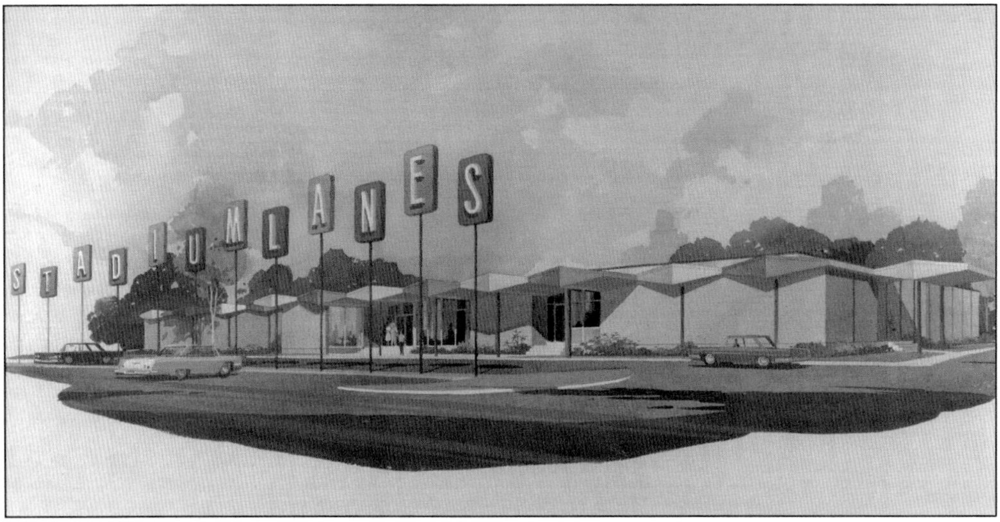

STADIUM LANES. The architectural presentation drawing of the Stadium Lanes, located on Knickerbocker Road, reflects the design work of Zentner & Marcum, architects. The facility opened for business in 1963. George Alexander had just returned from the Air Force Reserves, and his first job with the family business was to construct the bowling alley using tilt-up wall construction. Workers poured 39 panels on the ground at the site, with pink-and-white marble aggregate exterior finish, and lifted them into place with a crane. The exterior of the building reflects the design vocabulary of the period, with Harlequin-shaped decorative fascia and the Stadium Lanes sign's individually suspended up-and-down letters. The building continues to be used as it was originally designed. (Courtesy of Alexander Construction Company, George Alexander.)

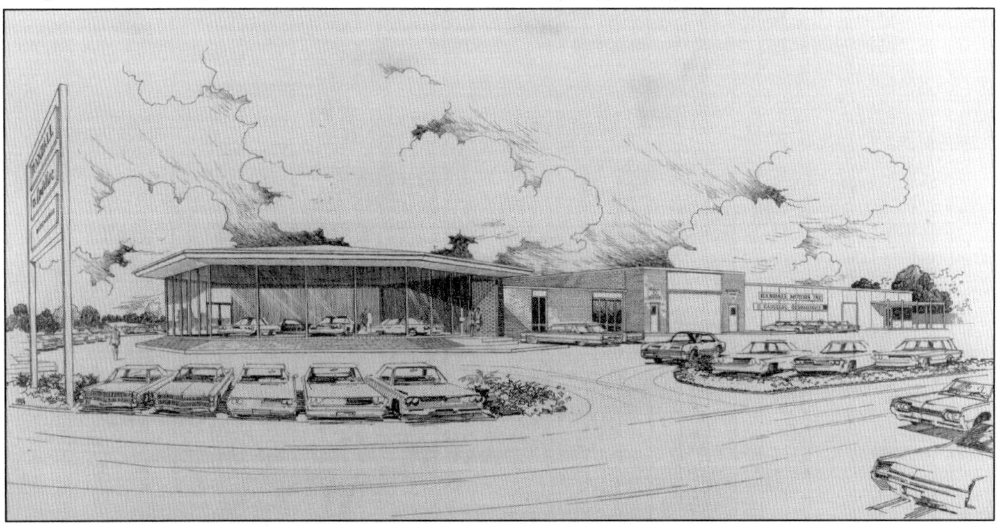

RANDALL DEALERSHIP. Randall Motors, located at 801 West Avenue North, was designed by Zentner & Marcum, architects. Until the 1970s, the appearance of the new car models were kept hidden from the public until the last moment by covering them while in transit and covering the display windows with brown paper. On a Saturday in January 1952, it was estimated that 3,500 to 4,000 people viewed the introduction of the new models of Cadillacs and Oldsmobiles at the old location on South Oakes Street. The debut included coffee and donuts, as well as organ music by Mary Carter and her daughter Sabre. A special door prize was a new Norge refrigerator. (Courtesy of Randall Motors, Inc., George K. Randall.)

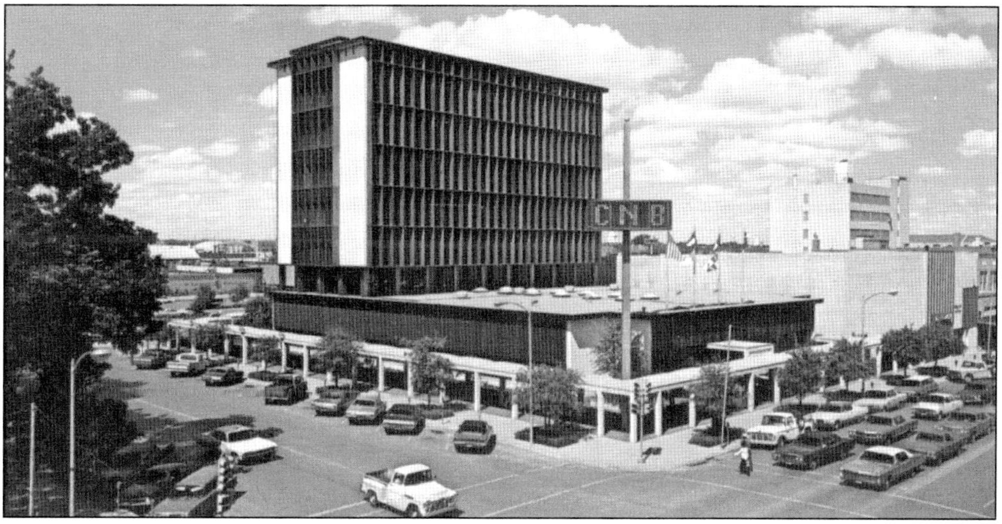

Central National Bank. The Central National Bank was constructed in 1967 after the St. Angelus and five other buildings at the corner of Beauregard Avenue and Irving Street were demolished. It was designed by O'Neil Ford's architectural firm, Ford, Powell & Carson. The firm is noted for using regional materials and technology. Mexican artisans created the covered concrete and brick roofs that surround the building. (FC.)

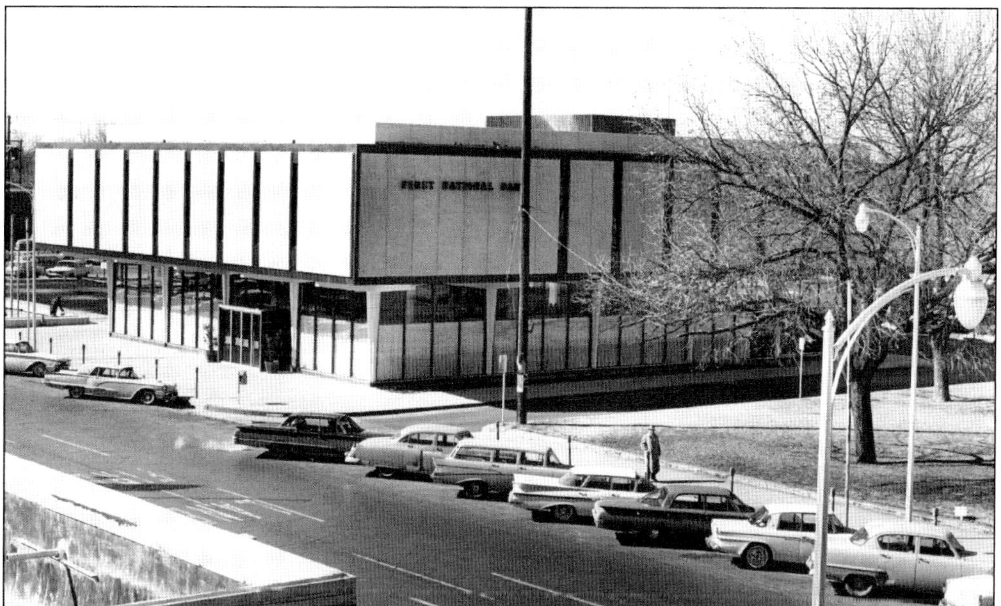

First National Bank. On October 29, 1960, ground breaking ceremonies took place at the site of the new First National Bank Building, located at 124 West Beauregard Avenue. The design of the building followed the New Formalism style, in which the building is freestanding with strictly symmetrical elevations, smooth wall surfaces, and a flat projecting roof. The building was designed by Pierce and Pierce, architects, of Houston, in partnership with the local architectural firm of Lovett and Sellers. It was built by contractors Templeton & Cannon. George F. Pierce and Abel B. Pierce received an award of commendation from the Houston chapter of the AIA for the bank building. (WTC.)

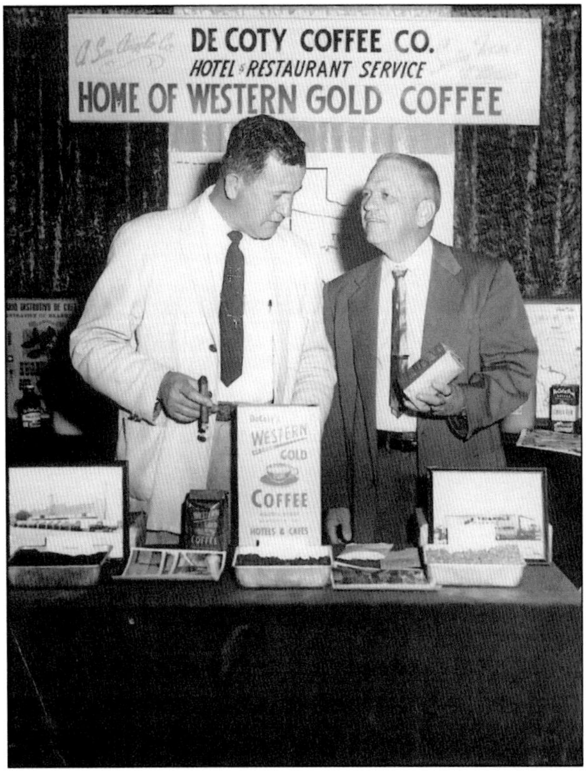

Nickel and Ducote. Two local businessmen, Homer Nickel (left) and Curry Ducote, discuss coffee at a local merchandise show. Nickel ran a successful fencing business called Twin Mountain Fence Company, established in 1947, and also owned the Log Cabin Steak House on Arden Road. Ducote and C.T. Sr., his father, owned the DeCoty Coffee Company, established in 1929 and housed in a number of locations before it was moved to 618 South Chadbourne Street in 1937. In 1964, the owners constructed a new, larger plant at 1920 Austin Street. On display are pictures of the various business locations, as well as samples of green and roasted coffee beans. Their brand name Western Gold Coffee refers to the gold rim one observes around the top of the coffee line in a white coffee cup—the sign of good coffee made from quality beans. (Courtesy of Laura Ducote.)

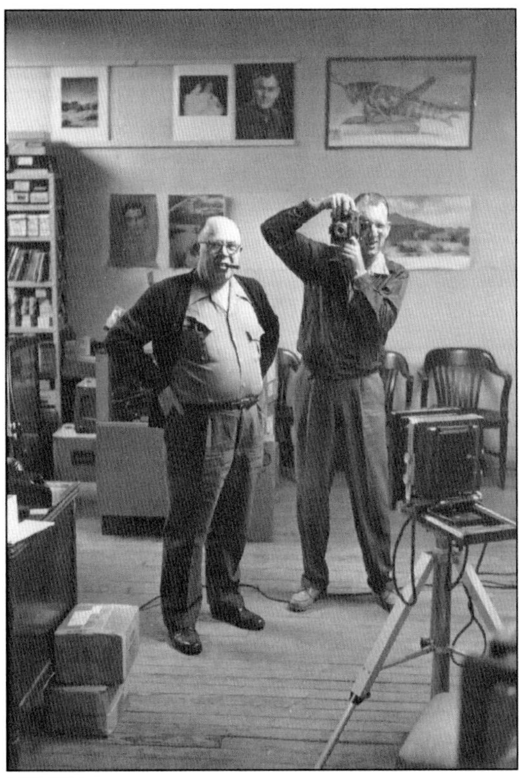

Barnhart and Witter. Local photographers Barney Barnhart (right) and Lloyd Witter pose for the camera in Witter's studio. Barnhart moved to San Angelo in 1947 and set up Barney's Studio as a photographic business at 521 West Beauregard Avenue. In 1951, he moved to 1107 Beauregard Avenue after a fire destroyed the studio. In April 1963, he moved it to 3111 Beauregard Avenue, where his daughters have run it since their father's death in 1991. Barnhart concentrated on portraits and commercial and aerial photographs for clients and was very active in many community affairs, such as the Jaycees. Witter moved to San Angelo in 1935 and operated a photofinishing and portrait studio until he retired in 1978. In the 1960s, his studio was located at 26 1/2 West Concho Avenue. He was involved in the Rotary Club and was asked to judge the most photogenic girl at San Angelo College for 1962–1963. Witter wrote that it was a rare privilege, but fraught with a certain amount of danger. (Courtesy of Barney's Studio.)

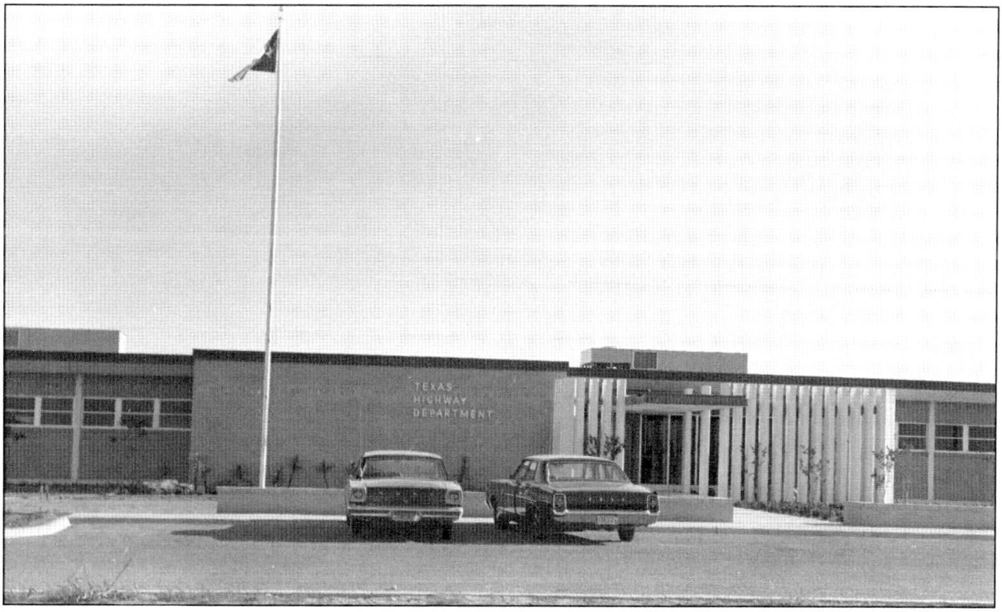

Texas Department of Transportation District Office. Design for the new San Angelo District offices for the Texas Department of Transportation, then known as the Texas Highway Department, located at 4502 Knickerbocker Road, commenced in 1963, and the complex was completed in 1968. The district offices were previously located on Avenue L. Leonard Mauldin, an architect in association with Louis A. Drake, designed the 44,000-square-foot complex of warehouses, shops, and offices. (Courtesy of *Texas Highways*.)

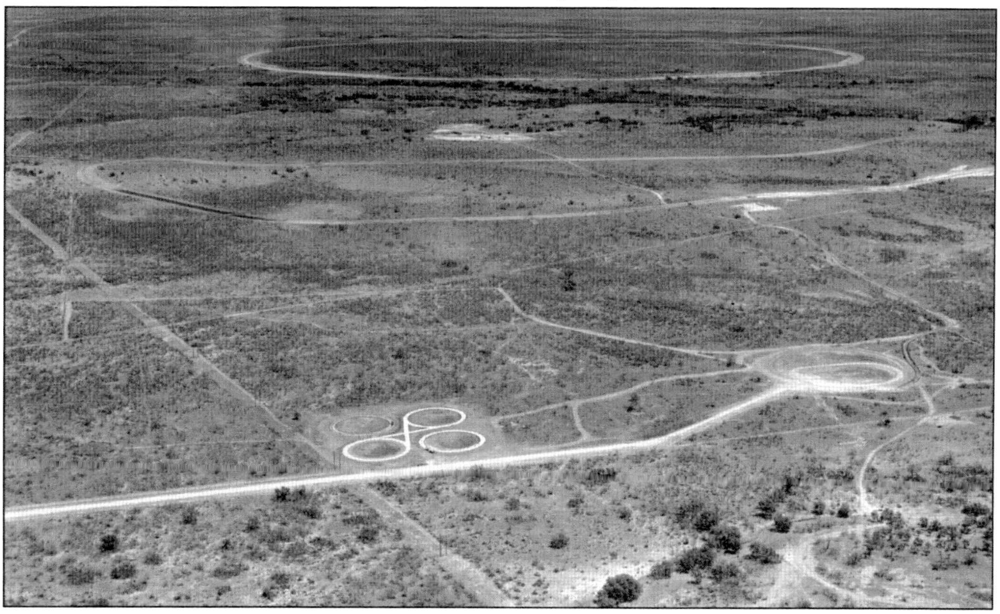

Goodyear Proving Grounds. The vast proving grounds facility on Highway 277 North began operations in 1944. Major improvements date from 1957 and include a five-mile-high speed circle, a meandering 20-mile paved, figure-eight turnpike road, a 2.5-mile tractor tire straightaway, a five-mile wandering gravel road, and a headquarters building. The test site now covers 7,300 acres of rolling landscape on the former Crownest Ranch. (WTC.)

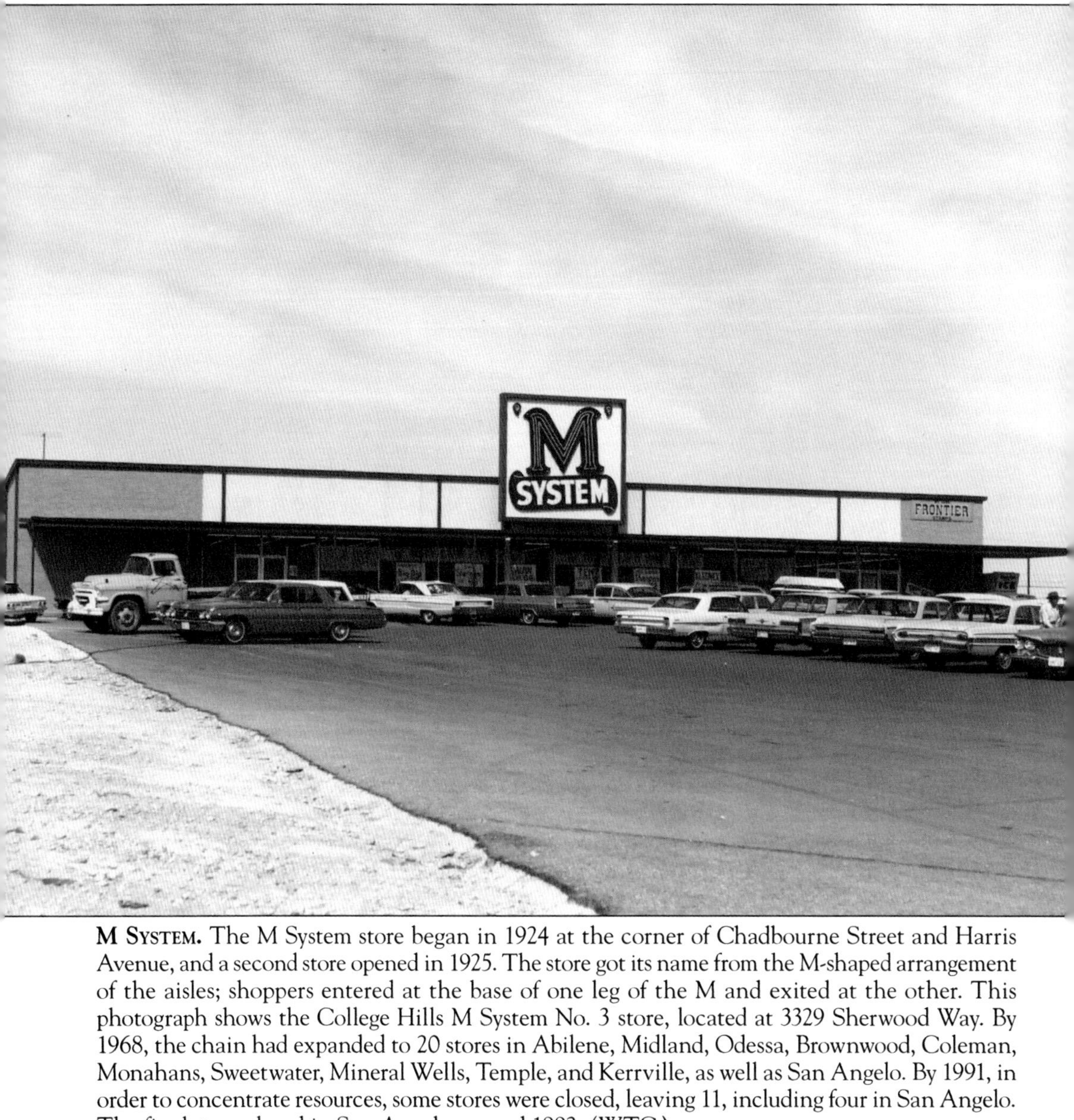

M System. The M System store began in 1924 at the corner of Chadbourne Street and Harris Avenue, and a second store opened in 1925. The store got its name from the M-shaped arrangement of the aisles; shoppers entered at the base of one leg of the M and exited at the other. This photograph shows the College Hills M System No. 3 store, located at 3329 Sherwood Way. By 1968, the chain had expanded to 20 stores in Abilene, Midland, Odessa, Brownwood, Coleman, Monahans, Sweetwater, Mineral Wells, Temple, and Kerrville, as well as San Angelo. By 1991, in order to concentrate resources, some stores were closed, leaving 11, including four in San Angelo. The final store closed in San Angelo around 1992. (WTC.)

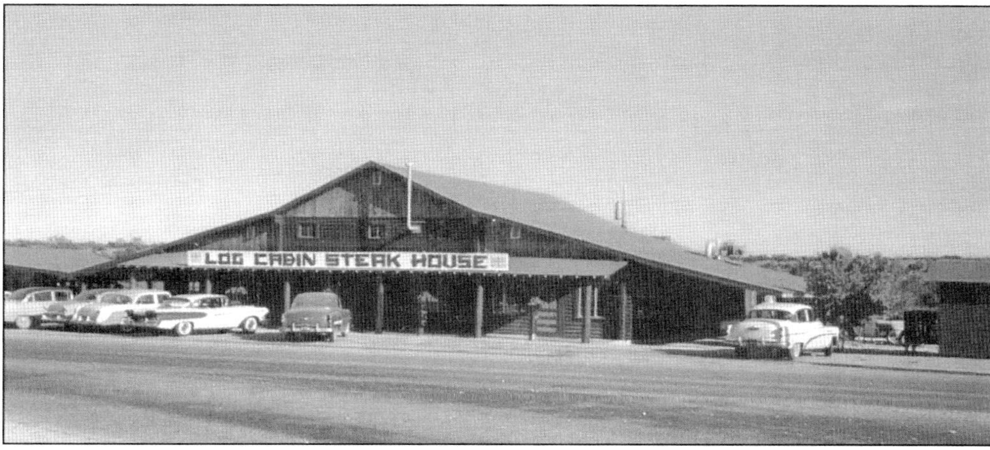

Log Cabin Steak House. Homer Nickels built the Log Cabin Steak House on Arden Road around 1959. The logs came from Gunnison, Colorado. It only took three days to assemble the walls, but a month to complete the roof structure, according to Robert Nickels, Homer Nickels's son. It was a very popular restaurant, serving steaks, chicken, and seafood. Set afire in 1974 during a robbery, it burned to the ground, never to be rebuilt. (WTC.)

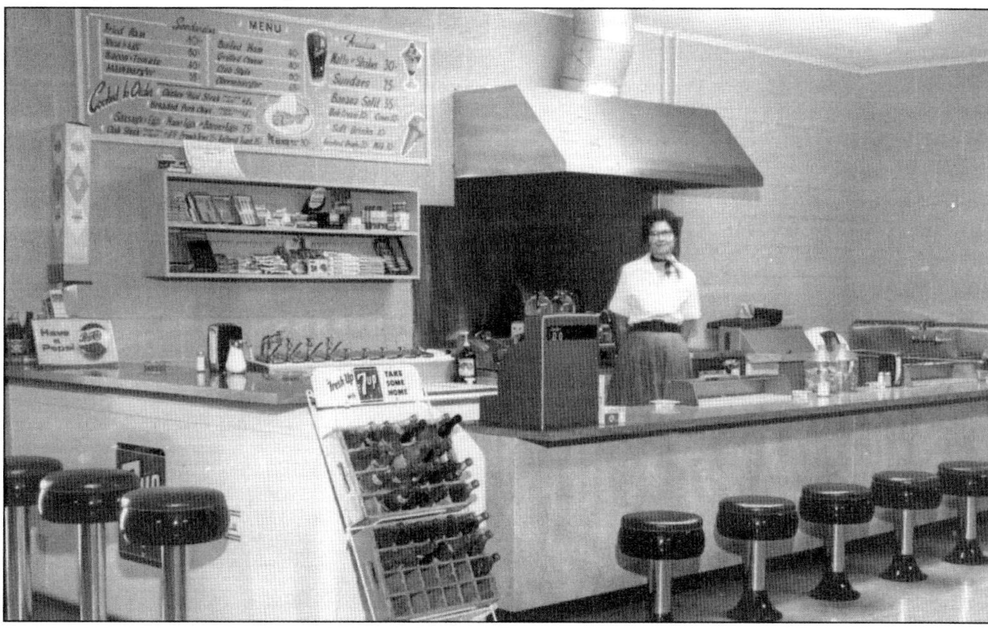

Star Lanes. A popular hangout while bowling was the snack bar in the Star Lanes, located at 125 West Twohig Avenue. Note the hamburger and the banana split on the menu, each costing 35¢. In 1955, the San Angelo Bowl was opened after being destroyed by lighting in 1952. In 1966, the name was changed to Star Lanes. It finally closed its doors in 1981. It sported state-of-the-art equipment, with 12-lanes and automatic pin-setting machinery. Down the street in the basement at 17 East Twohig Avenue was the DeLuxe bowling alley with six lanes. It was operating before World War II and closed around 1964. The Stadium Lanes opened in 1963, and the Sherwood Lanes, located at 2725 Sherwood Way, opened in 1954. Sherwood Lanes originally had 16 lanes with an elaborate interior but expanded with an additional eight lanes and modern pin-setting equipment by 1960. It closed in 2001 and was briefly a hobby center. Part of the building was removed and remodeled by the owner, who owns the Sherwood Way retail strip center. (WTC.)

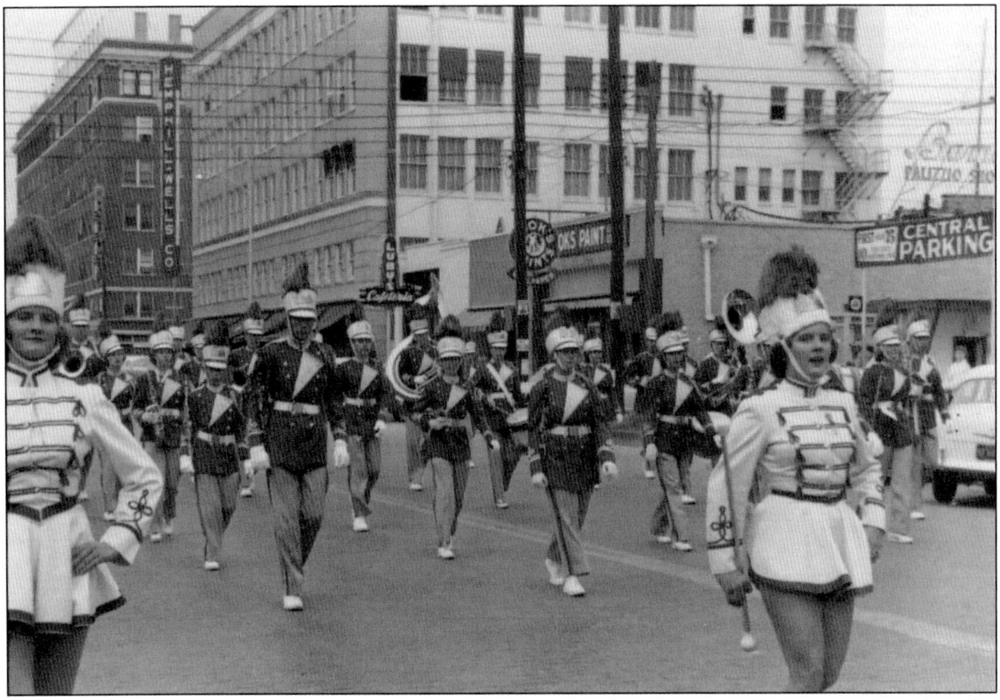

LAKE VIEW HIGH SCHOOL BAND. The homecoming parade is an annual event in San Angelo. This photograph, taken November 3, 1956, by Lloyd Witter, shows the Lake View High School marching band in the San Angelo College Homecoming Parade on Irving Street. See page 62 for a photograph of Witter. Note the Hemphill-Wells Building and the entrance sign for Luby's Cafeteria. (WTC.)

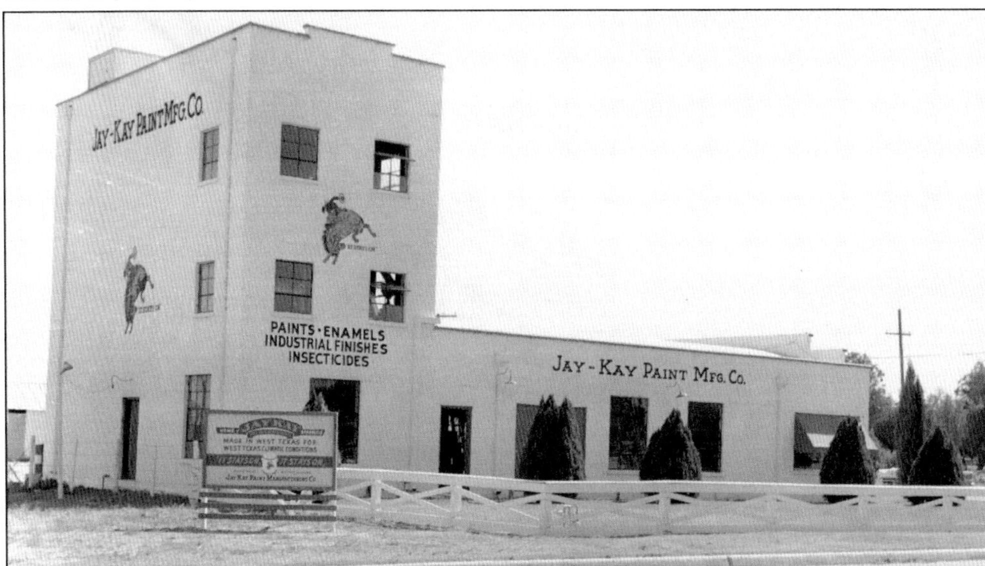

JAY-KAY PAINT MANUFACTURING CO. The Jay-Kay Paint Manufacturing Co. was located on Avenue N in a three-story industrial building with steel sash windows. Products associated with the company included paints, enamels, industrial finishes, and insecticides. The logo was a bucking horse with the tag line "It stays on." (WTC.)

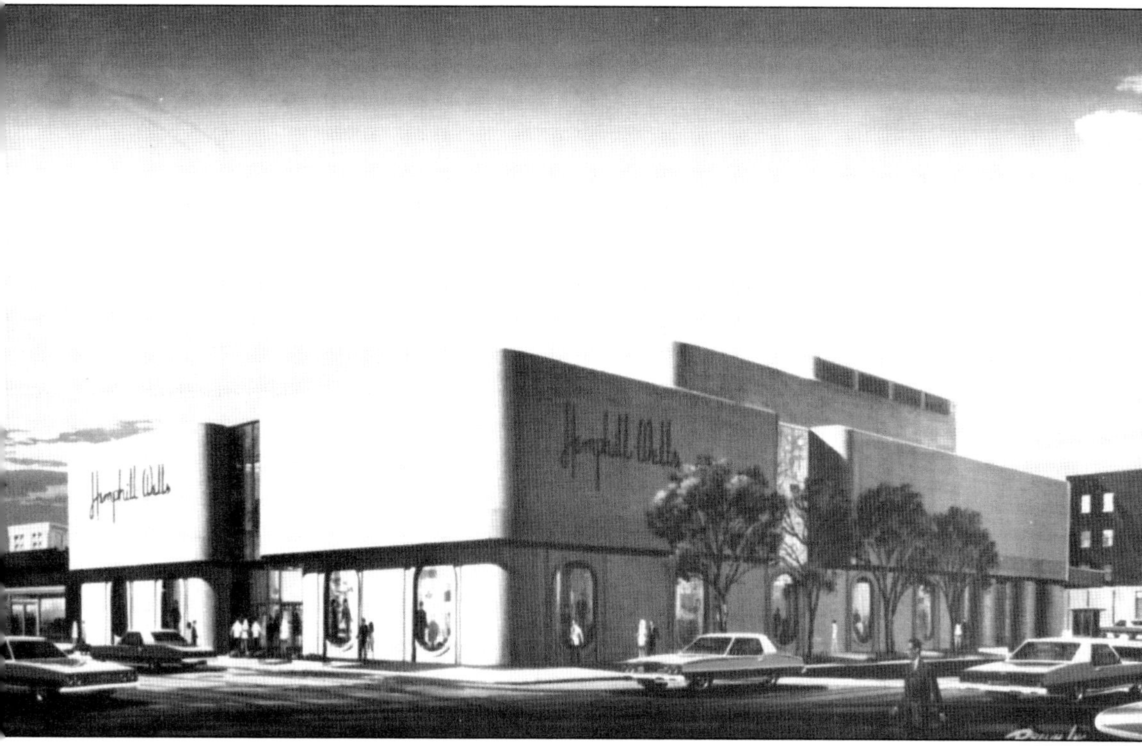

HEMPHILL-WELLS REOPENING. On February 12, 1973, Hemphill-Wells reopened in its brand new store at the southeast corner of Beauregard Avenue and Irving Street. The company closed this location on May 10, 1971, and moved to temporary facilities until the new building was completed. Local architects Chakos, Zentner & Marcum designed the building, and Brockstein and Son of Houston designed the interior. The ribbon-cutting event at 8:40 a.m. included local dignitaries and company officials; the Rev. Michael Waco of the First Christian Church gave the invocation. The exterior of the building was strikingly different from most commercial buildings in town, with its curved brick corners, giant display windows, and large wall relief by Remo Scardigli depicting West Texas life. The 85,000-square-foot interior was also striking, with its vivid contemporary colors on all three floors, escalators (as well as a self-service elevator), Furr's cafeteria on two levels, and even a post office substation on the lower level. The ground-floor shops included men's clothing, shoes, cosmetics, and a smoke shop. The lower level included "domestics," luggage, a bookshop, and boys' clothing. The upper floor contained women's wear, a bridal salon, beauty salon, and house-decorating items. The store closed in January 1986. (WTC.)

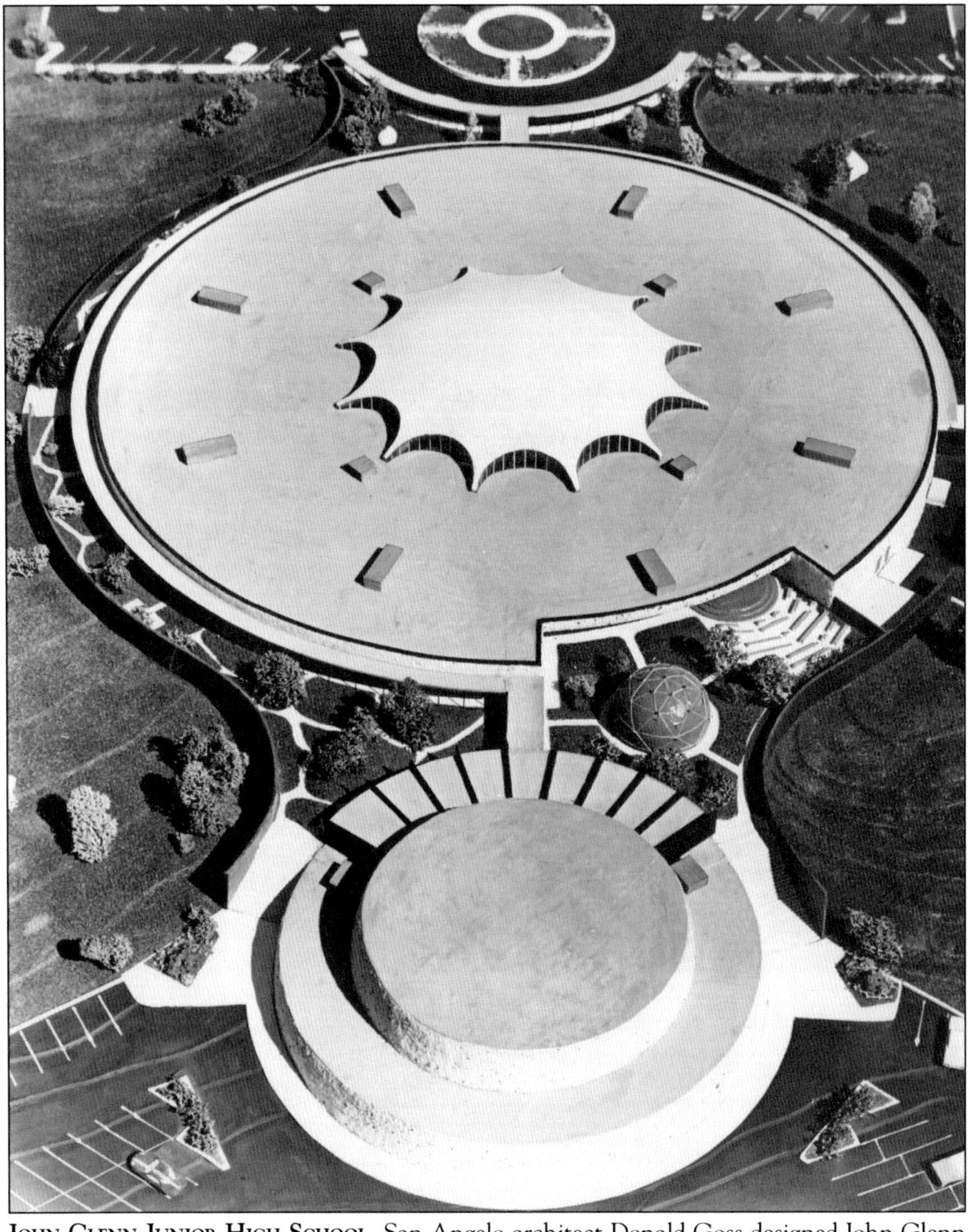

John Glenn Junior High School. San Angelo architect Donald Goss designed John Glenn Junior High School (now Glenn Middle School), which was formally dedicated on October 14, 1967. The unique design of the school, sometimes called Space Age architecture, is only part of the story. In 1967, John L. Givens, principal at Lee Junior High, was named project director to develop a new nongraded program of teaching-learning to accommodate the city's highest and lowest socioeconomic groups. The school district officials named it for NASA astronaut John Glenn, a well-known national hero whose flights in space symbolized advancements in the knowledge of science and technology. John Glenn and his wife, Annie, attended the formal dedication. The intent was that the innovative design and education approach would propel San Angelo into the future. (WTC.)

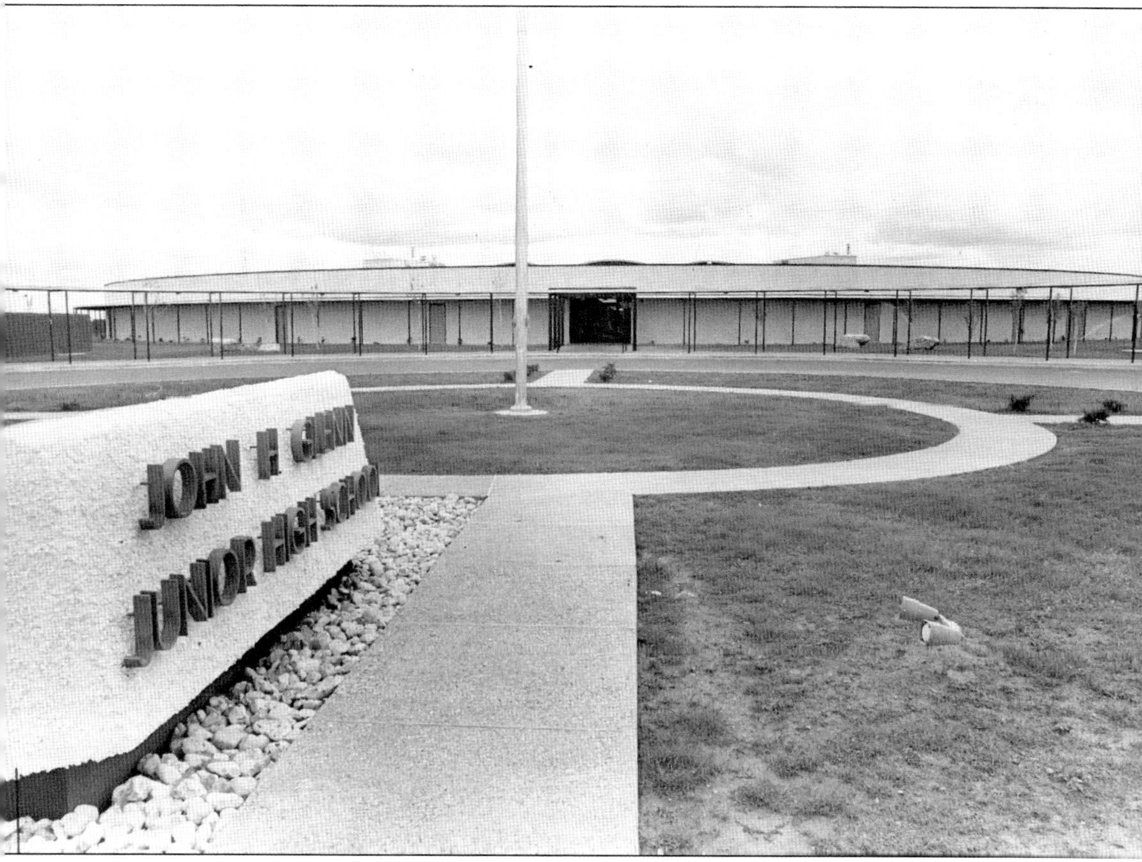

John Glenn Junior High School. Donald Goss designed the school utilizing a circular footprint, with a separate but connected circular building to house the gymnasium, choral program, and arts and crafts. The main building was designed with everything built around the core, called the learning mall, where the library was located. The next ring of rooms surrounding the learning mall included the math testing center and student center, as well as classrooms for natural science, social science, language arts, and typing. There were aids in subject research fields in the learning mall to help students carry out their independent study projects. The outer ring contained science laboratories, speech and homemaking classrooms, offices, and support facilities. (WTC.)

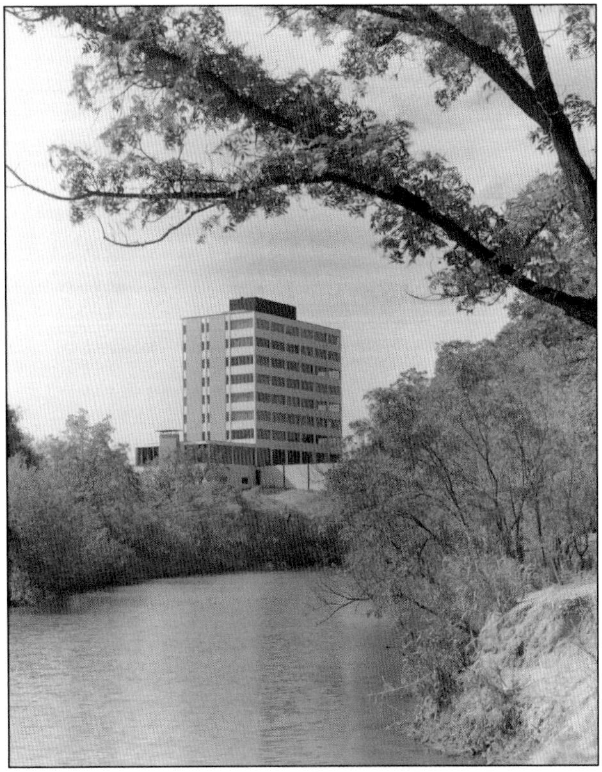

River Terrace Apartments. Donald Goss designed the River Terrace Apartments on the south side of the Concho River on Avenue D in the International style in 1962. It is believed to be one of the first condo apartments in Texas. The initial owners were John I. and Cele Moore, E.S. and Minnie Mayer, Dulcie Baumgart, H.E. and Eva Lee McCulloch, Houston and Isabel Harte, and Gilliean Blackstone. John I. Moore lived on the top floor and displayed his animal trophies in the lower level of the building, which he called the "Boar's Nest." (WTC.)

Trade Show in the Coliseum. The San Angelo Coliseum was designed for more than the stock show and rodeo. Shown here is an unidentified trade show on the floor of the coliseum. (Courtesy of Barney's Studio.)

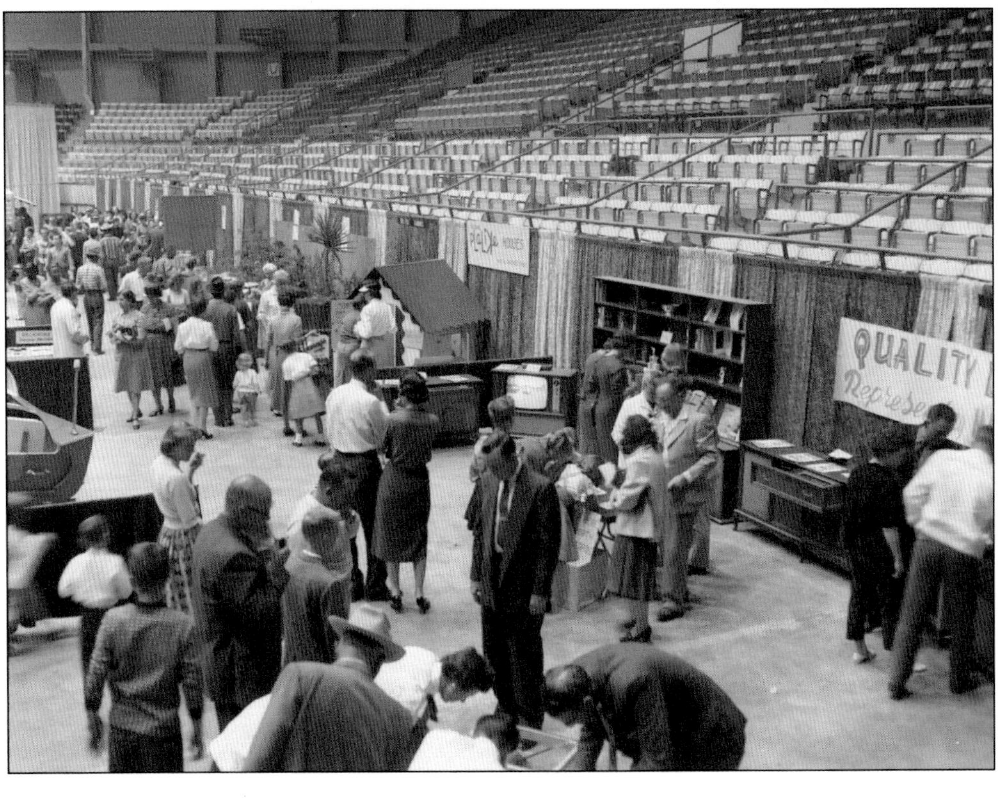

Three
1970s

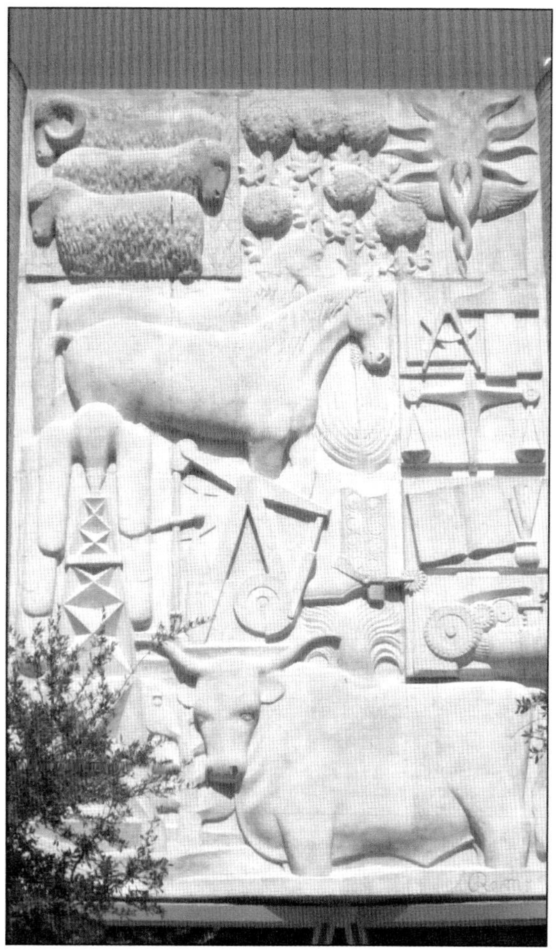

REMO SCARDIGLI SCULPTURE. On October 10, 1972, workers installed a 15-by-24-foot decorative relief cast concrete sculpture by artist Remo Scardigli on the Irving Street facade of the new Hemphill-Wells store, which opened in February. Designed using "stylized naturalism," the piece reflected the West Texas economy. Scardigli was born in Ponte Bugianese, Italy, in 1910 and immigrated to Portland, Oregon, in 1920. He worked in California and Mexico before moving to San Angelo. In addition to his sculpture, he also made jewelry. With help from local artists and students, he created this sculpture on the floor of his studio, located at 145 North Oakes Street in an old brick two-story building across the street from Edison Junior High. He constructed an armature of wood to reduce the amount of relief clay, which varied in thickness from one-fourth of an inch to three inches. After Scardigli modeled the clay, he poured plaster over the whole piece, then mixed cement and sand by hand and poured it into the plaster mold to create the final appearance. Welding plates were added to the back of the sculpture for attachment to the new building. (Photograph by author.)

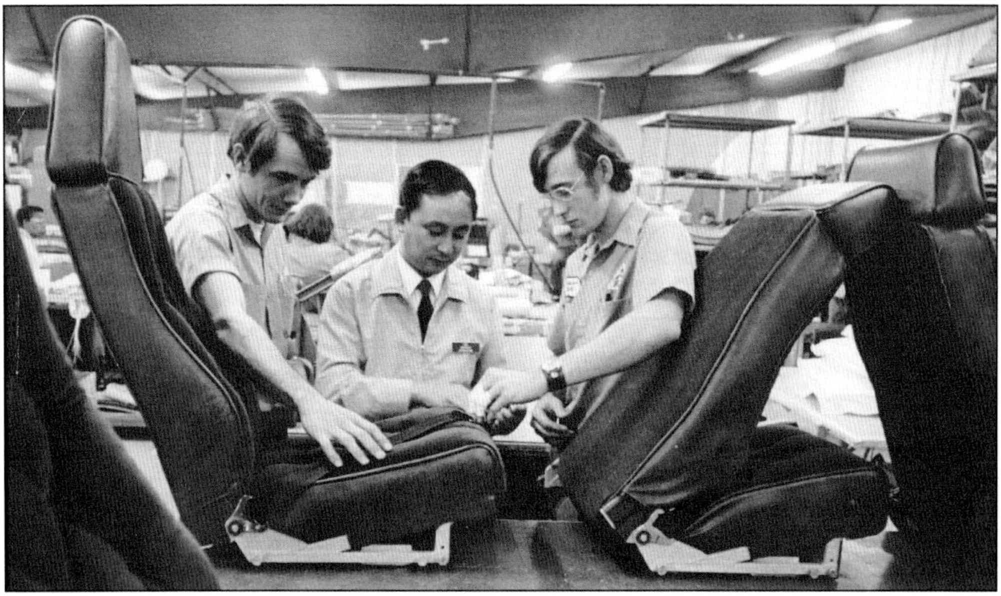

Mitsubishi Aircraft. Mitsubishi Aircraft International, Inc., built a hangar at Mathis Field to assemble the MU-2. This 1974 photograph shows engineer Hal Kawachi (center), Jackie Beane (left), and Marvin Belt (right) discussing a design to meet NASA specifications for a special order deep-cranberry fabric requested by the purchaser. (Private collection.)

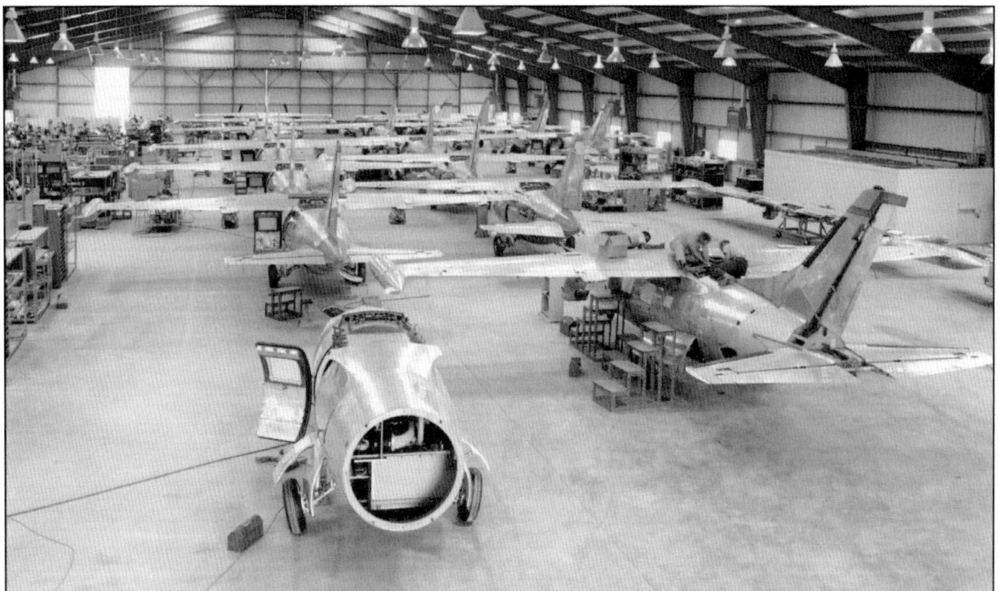

Assembly Line for Mitsubishi Aircraft. This picture shows the assembly line of the MU-2B-25 seven place and MU-2B-35 eight to ten place turboprop aircraft, located at Mathis Field. An agreement finalized in 1964–1965 between Mitsubishi Aircraft International, Inc., and Mooney Aircraft led to the assembly and marketing of the MU-2. Mitsubishi's first postwar aircraft design suitable for civil defense forces in Japan was converted to civilian use in the United States. Mooney filed for bankruptcy in 1969, and the facility was taken over by Mitsubishi, which continued to assemble planes. (WTC.)

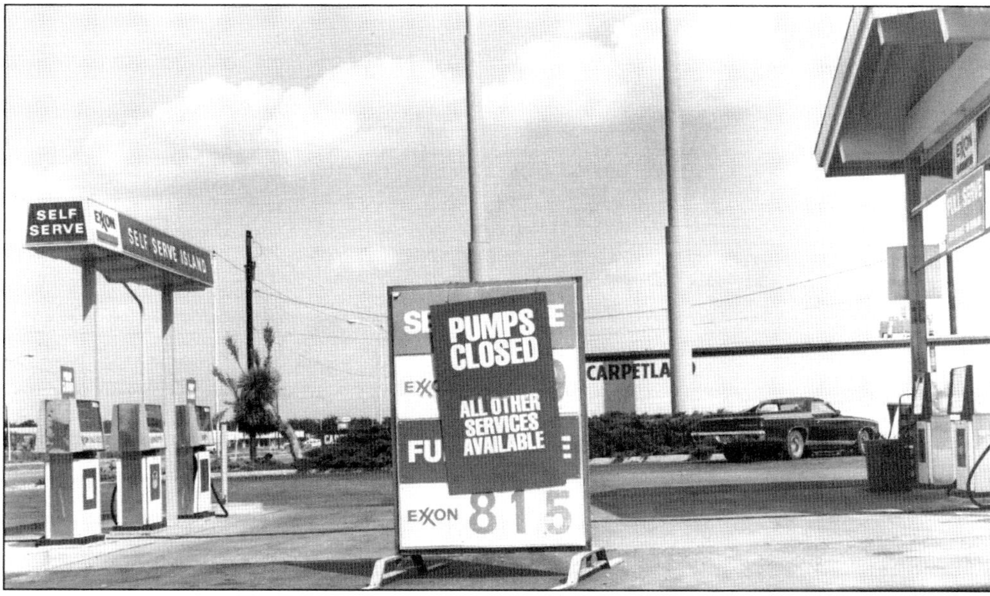

OIL CRISIS. The 1979 oil crisis occurred as a result of the turmoil in Iran. Production of Iranian oil was interrupted; as a result, Organization of the Petroleum Exporting Countries (OPEC) increased production. However, panic resulted, and as in 1973, long lines and a lack of gasoline at the pump followed. (WTC.)

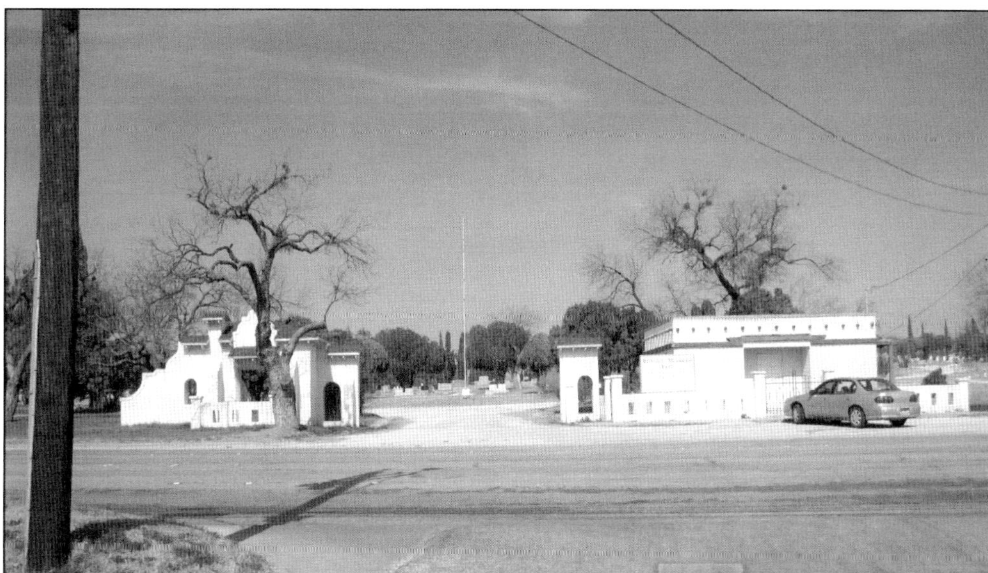

BELVEDERE MEMORIAL PARK. The cemetery was established in 1927 on Arden Road, three miles from downtown. The landscaping plan called for Bermuda grass, 1,000 evergreen shrubs, and an entrance structure. Designed by Swartz and Hamberlin, local architects, the Mission-style structure contained the office and restrooms and featured asymmetrical parapets, tile roofs, overhanging eaves, niches, decorative ironwork, and a porch roof supported by square piers. The drought of the 1950s caused the cemetery to fall into disrepair, and Harold Gibbs and his wife, Norma, helped bring it back to its earlier appearance. In 1975, Burt Terrill removed the entrance structure and rebuilt it in the spirit of the original design. (Photograph by author.)

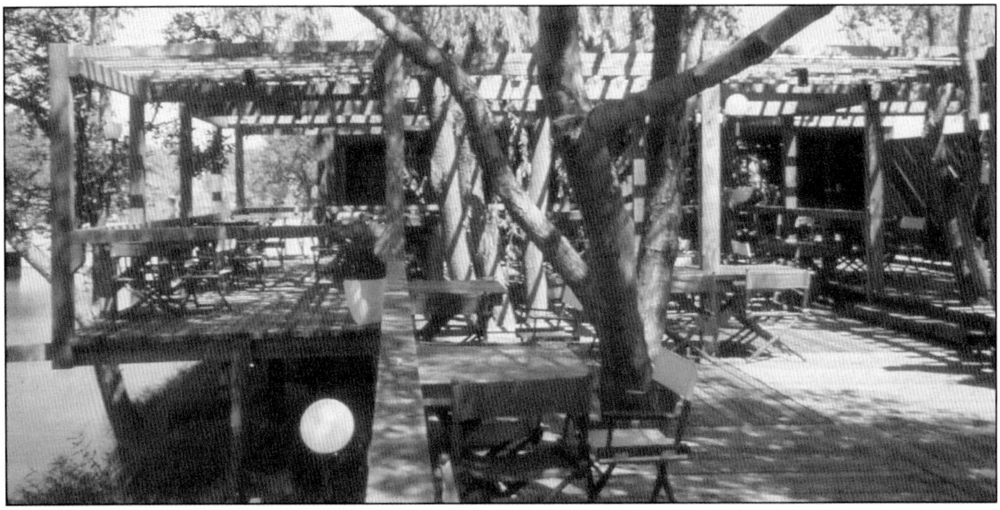

Beer Garden on the Concho River. In 1974, local architect Jack E. Meek was hired to design a beer garden on the banks of the Concho River, east of the low-water crossing on South Irving Street. The 4,000-square-foot structure cost $50,000 to construct. Meek took advantage of the downtown river setting that served as a catalyst for future development on the river. In 1974, it received an award of merit from the Texas Society of Architects. Unfortunately, subsequent owners changed the original concept of the six-to-nine-month business, first designed without air-conditioning, by enclosing spaces and losing the original design concept. (Courtesy of Jack E. Meek, AIA emeritus.)

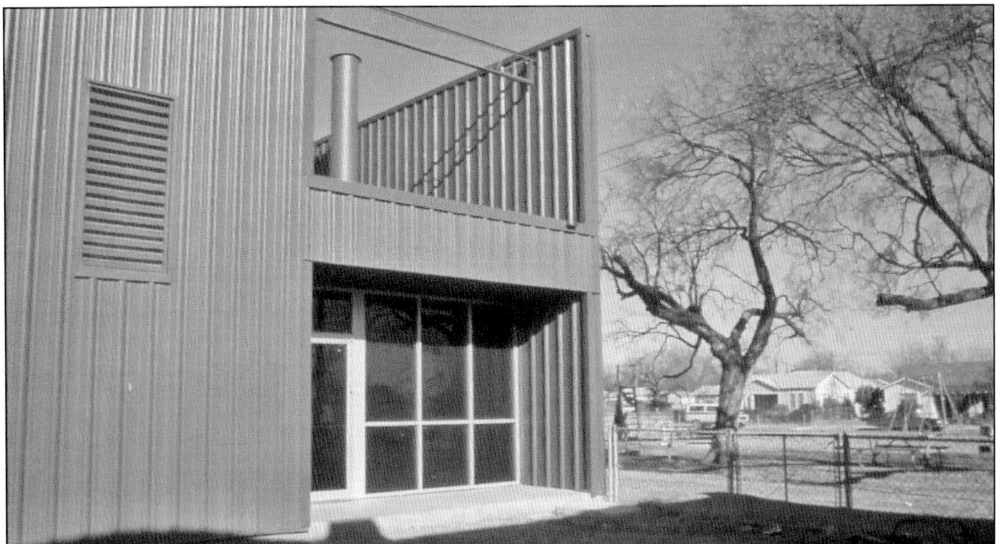

Prototype Neighborhood Recreation Center. Jack E. Meek, local architect, was hired by the City of San Angelo to design a prototype neighborhood recreational center with a budget of $200,000. The steel-frame structural system with brightly painted metal panel skins was successful in that more than one was built, and Meek received the 1977 Honor Award from the Texas Society of Architects. The three centers were built at 2750 Ben Fickin Road, 1103 North Farr Street, and 2722 Magdalen Street. Red and blue colors were selected to make the building a fun place to be, and it proved to be successful, as it remains a neighborhood hub. (Courtesy of Jack Meek, AIA emeritus.)

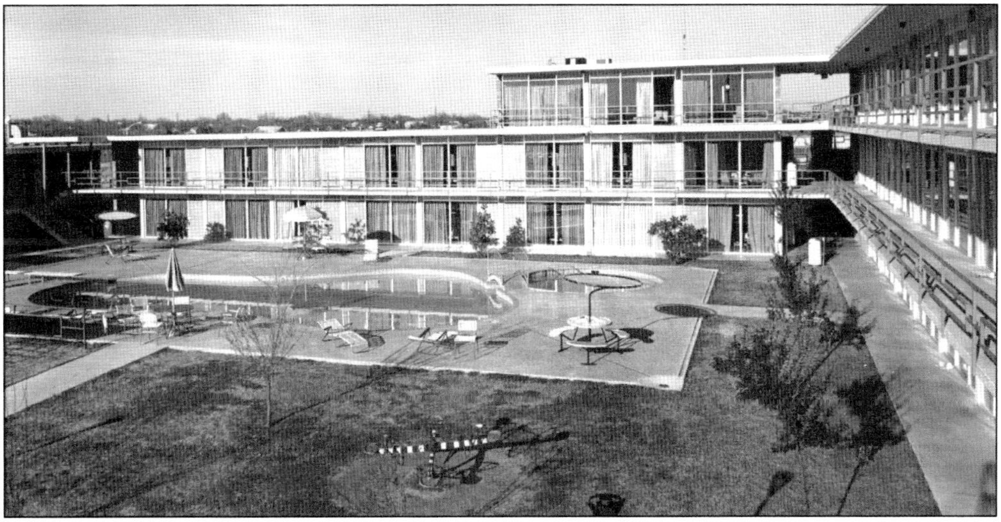

Holiday Inn. The first Holiday Inn, built in Memphis, Tennessee, in 1952, was designed by architect Eddie Bluestein initially for Kemmons Wilson. Bluestein is credited with the hotel's name, a reference to the popular 1942 musical film of the same name. By the end of the 1950s, the company had built 100 motels around the country, and by 1968, the number had increased to 1,000. Completion of the San Angelo location at 333 Rio Concho Drive occurred in 1965. Around 1978, the swimming pool area was roofed over to create what the company called a "holidome," an attempt to turn the hotels into roadside resorts. Holiday Inn and many other motel chains were built in this period to meet the new demand created after World War II, when families started taking to the road in significantly increasing numbers in what has been called "the golden age of family travel." (WTC.)

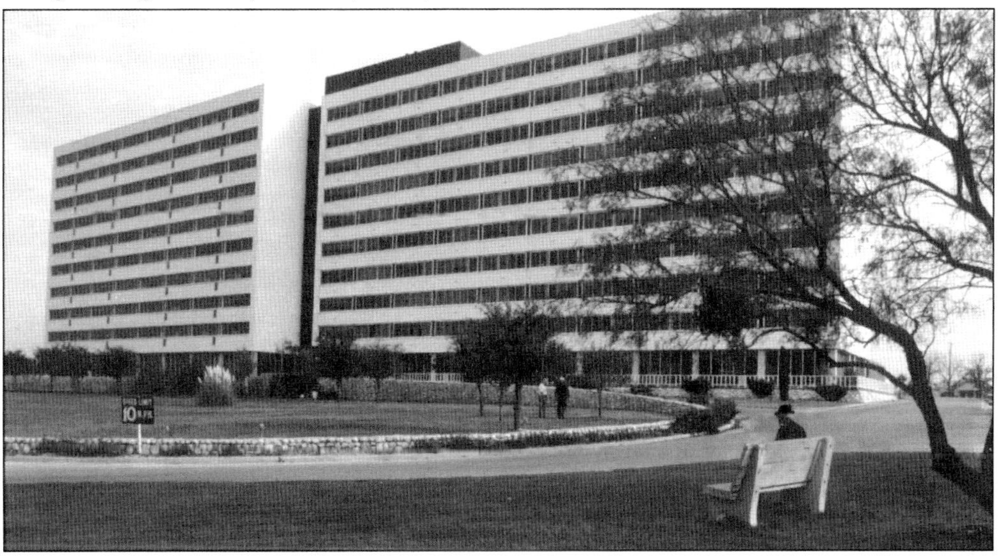

Rio Concho Manor. During the late 1950s, a group of retired officers from Goodfellow Air Force Base approached some city leaders, including Houston Harte and Col. Robert Augustinus, regarding a need for low-cost housing for seniors. This group formed the Rio Concho Trust, which built Rio Concho Manor just south of the Concho River along a deep river bend. In 1972, the trust added an east wing to Rio Concho Manor, which provided a total of 226 low-cost apartments for senior citizens. (WTC.)

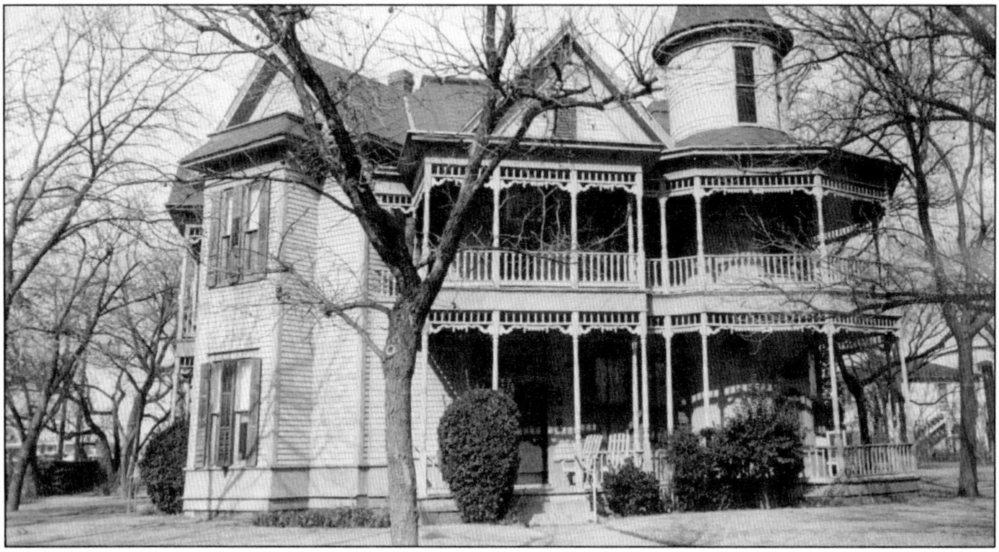

DeBerry Mansion. The DeBerry house was built in 1885 and located at 338 West Twohig Avenue. The local newspaper reported in 1955 that the house had been recently painted for the first time in many years and that it took 100 gallons of paint to complete the project. At one time, the color scheme featured two shades of pink, with gray trim and a black shingle roof. The Queen Anne–style house became the property of the San Angelo National Bank in July 1971 in settlement of the DeBerry estate. The bank offered to give the structure away, but it was eventually razed. During the demolition of the house, workers discovered human bones in the attic. The San Angelo police were called to the scene, and their subsequent investigations revealed that one of the DeBerry children, John, was fascinated with a box of bones originally belonging to a neighbor, Dr. John A. March. The young boy brought some of the bones home with him, and they somehow ended up in the attic. John DeBerry eventually became a doctor himself and practiced in Sonora. (WTC.)

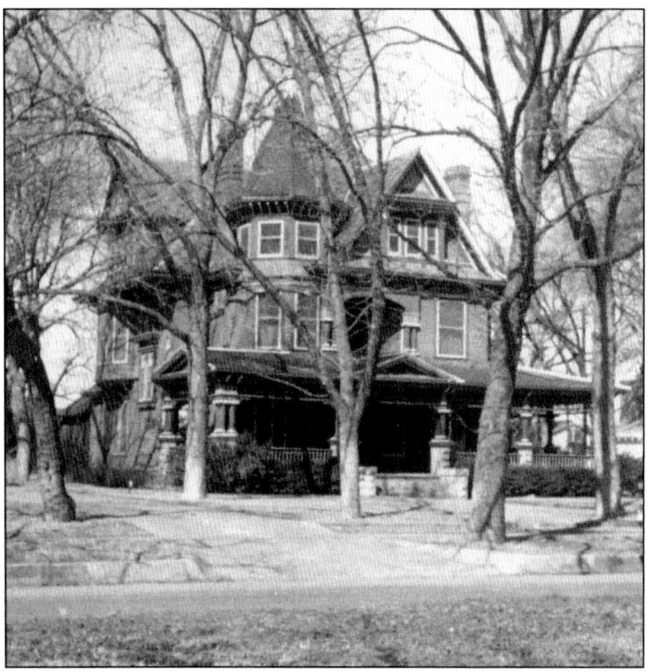

Welge House. Among the many historic houses lost from this period was the Welge House at 220 Twohig Avenue. This Queen Anne–style house, likely built for Richard Nails, dates to around 1900. In 1918, Henry Welge purchased the house. As late as 1955, his unmarried daughters, Alma and Matilda, still lived in the house. In 1954, the owners had the home painted with four shades of green as well as aluminum and black, with the scrollwork outlined in white. It is not known if these colors matched the original color scheme, but they certainly emphasized the architectural details. (WTC.)

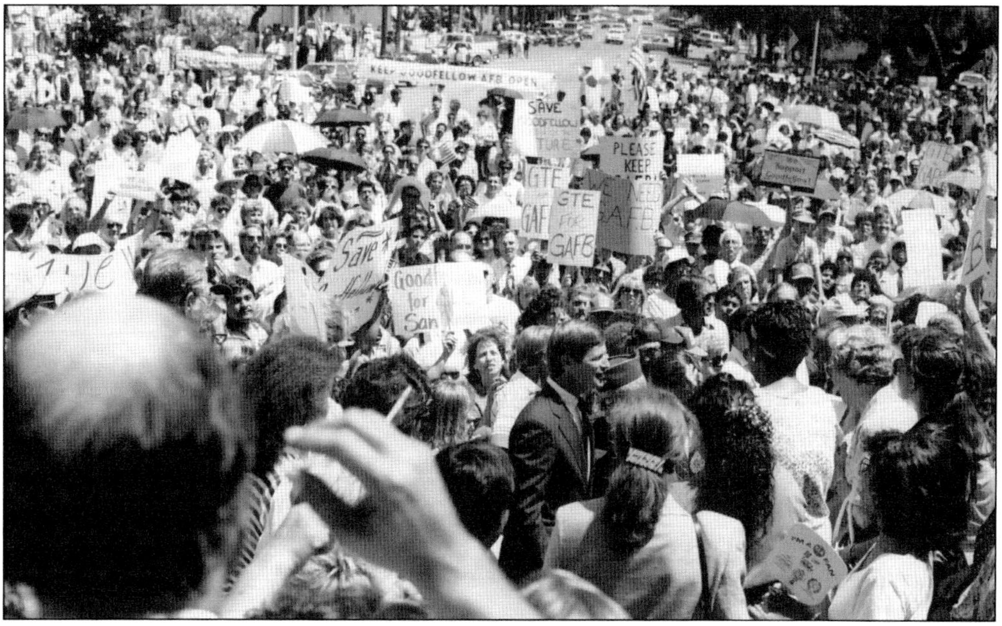

Goodfellow Closing Protest. After 38 years of pilot and intelligence training, Goodfellow's mission had apparently come to an end with the announcement in 1978 that the base would revert to air training command and was a candidate for closure. The local protest to the proposed closure was overwhelming, and the base was eventually taken off the closure list in 1981 and assigned to different duties. (WTC.)

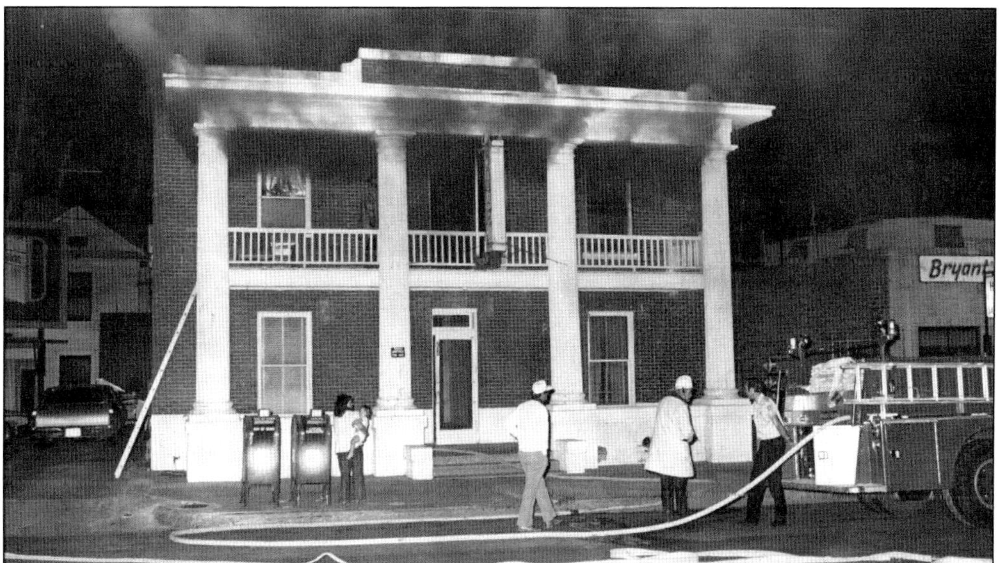

Sealy Flats. The redbrick, two-story hotel, located at 204 South Oakes Street, was built in 1908. A fire broke out in the hotel in 1977, but five units quickly responded to limit the damage. In 1999, Rod and Dennise Bridgman purchased the hotel, which had been vacant for many years. With the help of Johnny Mayo, they rehabilitated the building room by room. Sealy Flats is connected to the Jimmy Reed Courtyard, featuring both live blues music and food. The Bridgmans were some of the first people to experience a revival of urban living. (WTC.)

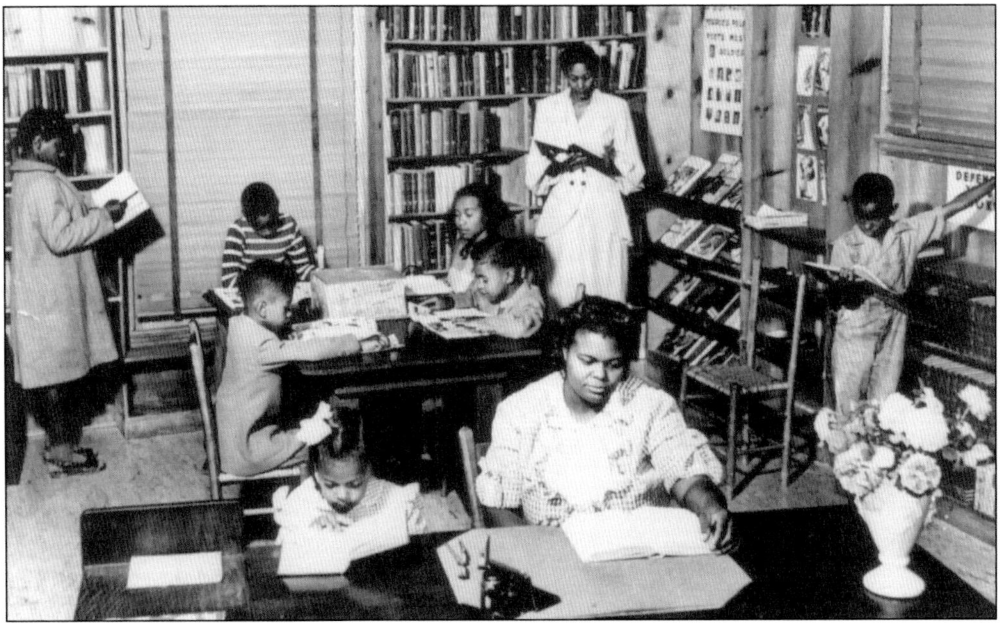

DUNBAR LIBRARY. The Dunbar Branch Library was established in 1933 at 903 North Randolph Street (later Martin Luther King Boulevard) and was in operation until 1975, when the north San Angelo branch opened at 3001 Chadbourne Street. Ethel Lavert served as the Dunbar librarian from about 1943 until the facility closed. The structure is presently used by the San Angelo North by Northwest Lions Club for its weekly meetings. (WTC.)

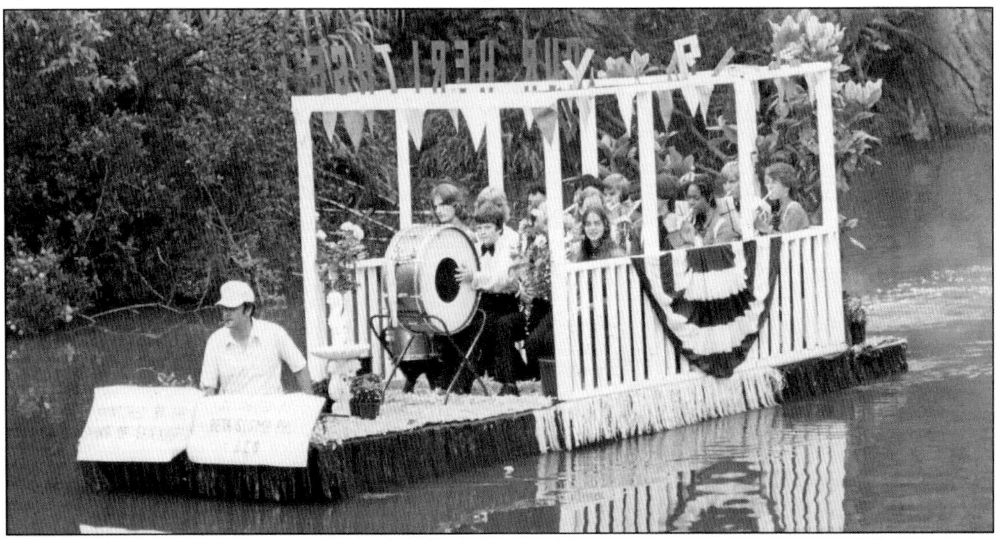

FIESTA DEL CONCHO. A new festival called Fiesta del Concho began in 1973, following the withdrawal of support for the Miss Wool of America pageant the previous year. F.L. Stephens chaired the first few festivals, and then his wife, Pollyanna, took over, followed by Roger Allen. Originally located at Santa Fe Park, the event later moved to El Paseo de Santa Angela Park, as well as on both sides of the Concho River. The initial festival included a river parade, food booths, street dances, Fort Concho events, style shows, and a tractor pull. Over the years, the parade moved downtown, with RiverStage concerts and armadillo races added as new events. The last festival took place in 2001. (WTC.)

Four

1980 AND BEYOND

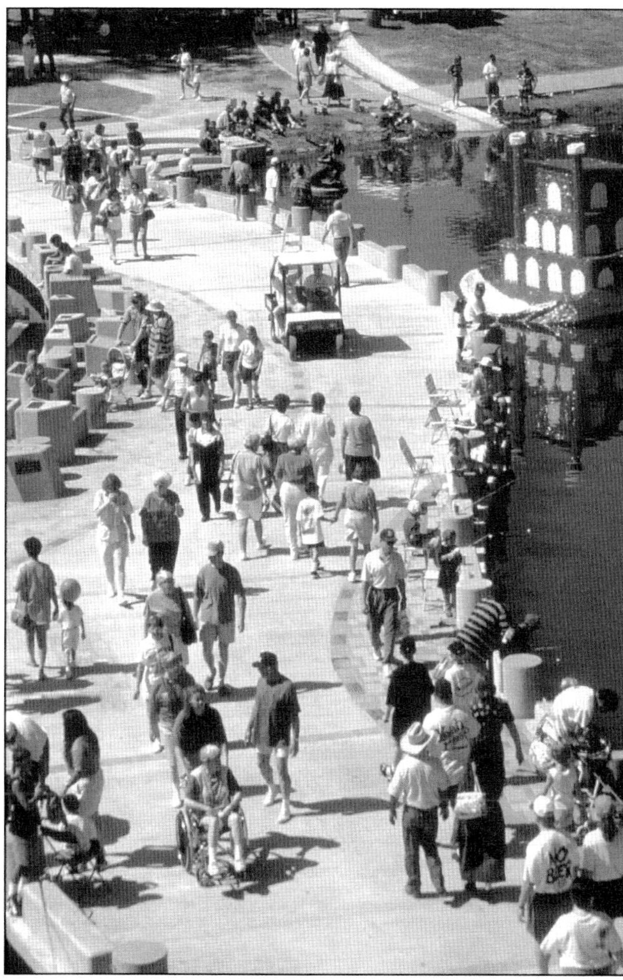

CELEBRATION BRIDGE. The R/UDAT team proposed a plan "connecting the past to the future" for the revitalization of the historic city center. The team also recommended short-term goals like the design and construction of the pedestrian bridge, linking the historic downtown with Fort Concho, the depot, and other new construction to follow. Within eight days, the public-private joint venture plan was submitted to the city council to construct a pedestrian bridge across the Concho River. The plan was approved, and the bridge was dedicated on July 3, 1993, and named Celebration Bridge. (Courtesy of Downtown San Angelo, Inc.)

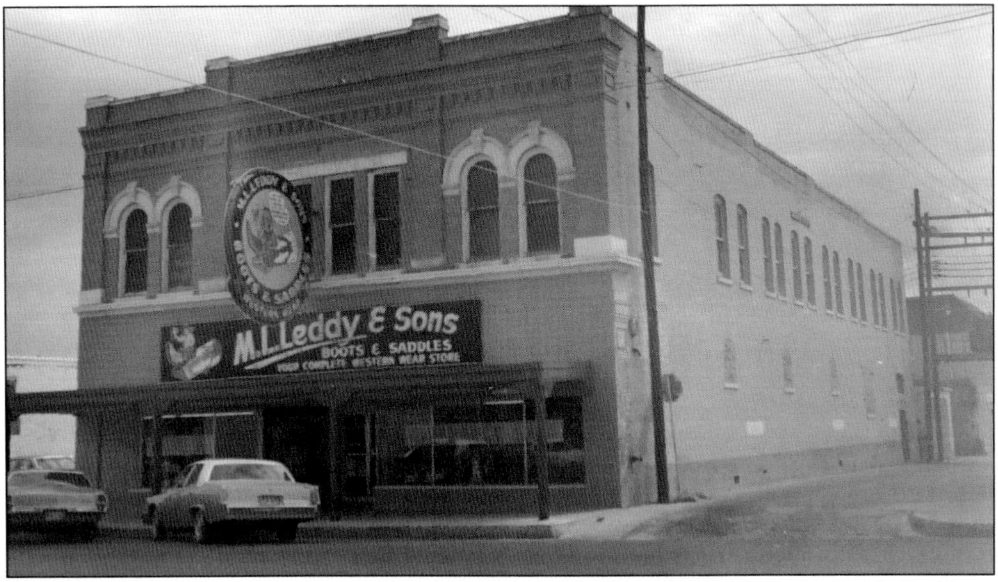

Old Leddy Building. The year 1984 marked the demolition of the former M.L. Leddy Building, located at 14 South Chadbourne Street. The building was designed by local architect Oscar Ruffini for Dr. T.W. Connerly. It featured brick with a stone-trim facade; paired, arched flank sash windows with a single lintel in the center; and four pilasters extending to the pressed brick cornice. M.L. Leddy & Sons moved from downtown to the Village Shopping Center. Many remember the animated neon sign with a cowboy riding a rocking boot. The word balloon proclaimed, "Tough as a bronco, neat as a pen, easy as a rocking chair." The First Baptist Church purchased the building as part of a five-year expansion plan, with the purpose of leveling the building to construct a playground for its Montessori kindergarten. Letters to the editor pleaded for saving the building as well as for constructing a proper playground. (Courtesy of the Texas Historical Commission.)

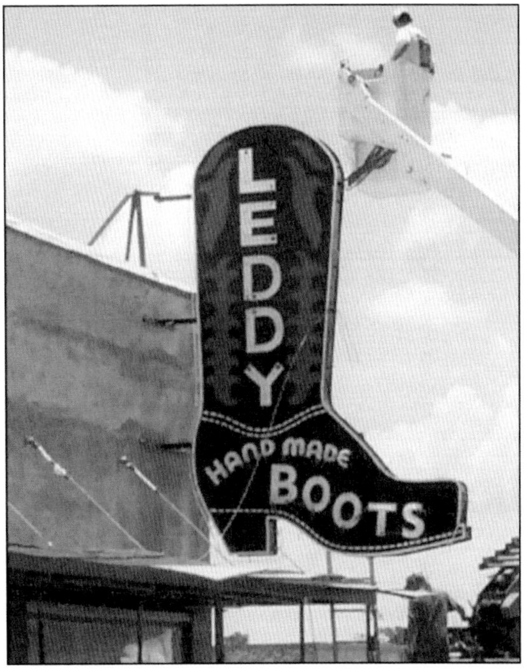

Installing the Leddy Boots Sign. M.L. Leddy's Boots and Saddlery returned to downtown San Angelo in 2007 after being located in the Village Shopping Center since 1987. The original neon sign on their building on South Chadbourne Street was removed and lost over time. The neon sign shown here is new, but matches the one installed at the M.L. Leddy's store located in Fort Worth Stockyards. That sign has become a symbol of the business in Fort Worth, and so, its look was also used on the store in San Angelo. (Courtesy of Downtown San Angelo, Inc.)

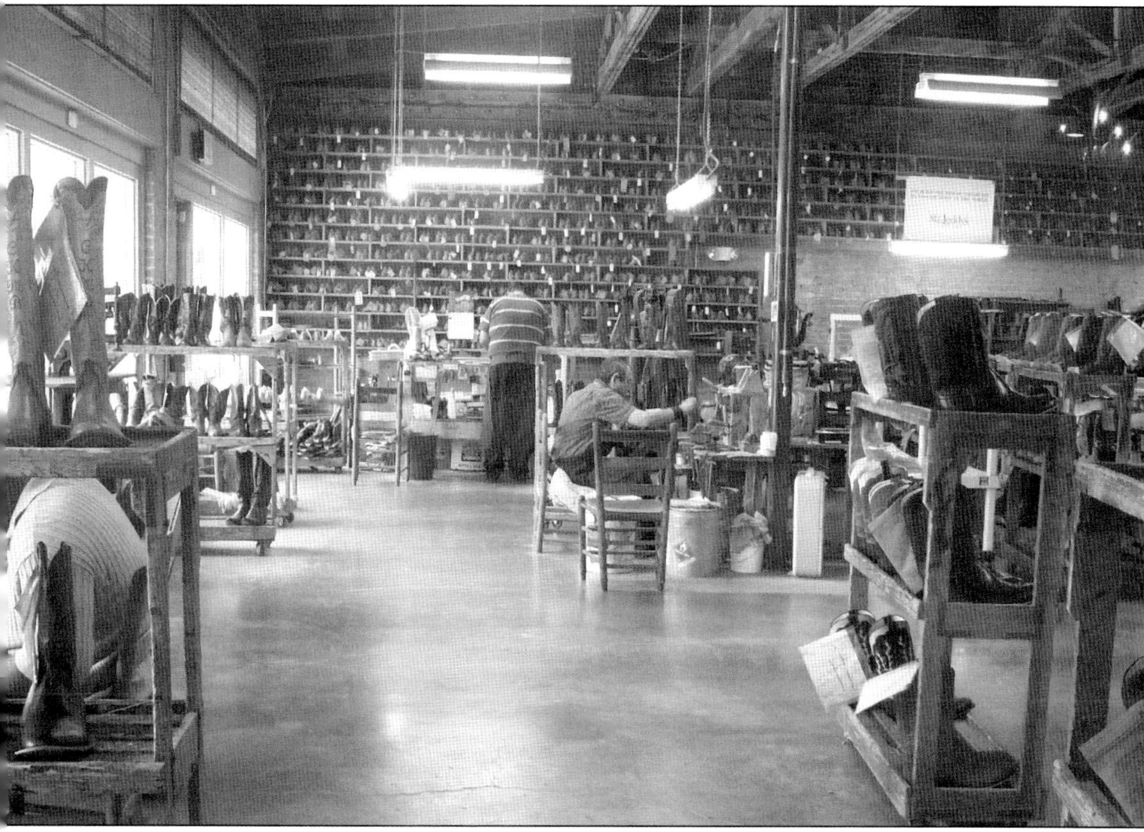

Leddy Boots Workroom. M.L. Leddy's Boots and Saddlery moved into an 11,000-square-foot building at 222 South Oakes Street in 2007. The layout of the building is unique, allowing the public to view the boot-making process through picture windows. At present, the 15 employees have a combined 190 years of work experience in making boots. Also of interest is the wall of old wooden lasts, shaped for each individual foot and used to make the custom boots. In the display room is the reassembled stone front porch of the family house, originally located at 2905 Lake Drive. (Courtesy of Downtown San Angelo, Inc.)

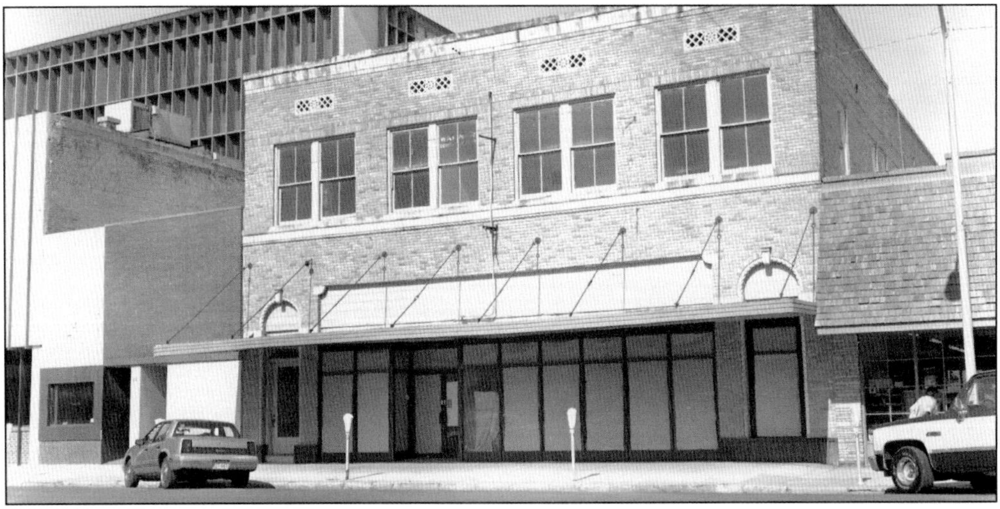

Holcomb-Blanton Print Shop. In 1992, the historic Holcomb-Blanton Print Shop was demolished along with two other buildings to create a landscaped 39-vehicle parking lot east of the Central National Branch of the First National Bank of Lubbock. The building was listed in the National Register of Historic Places in 1988. The bank was asked to go through the federal review process, which requires that options be explored other than demolition. The continued need for more parking to keep business downtown was cited as the reason for the demolition by the bank. (Photograph by author.)

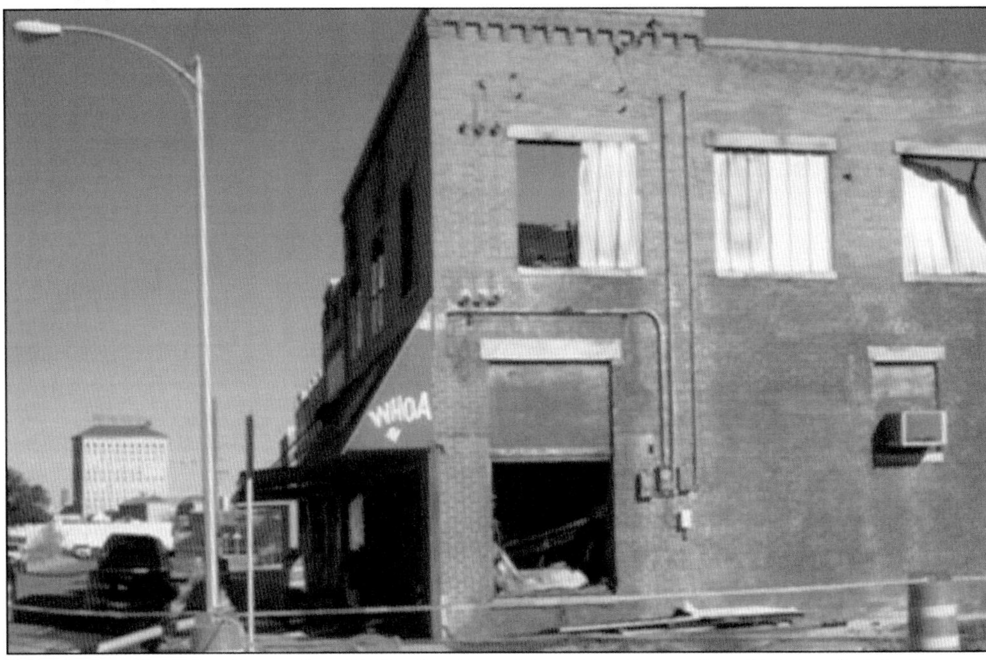

Boot Shop Fire. In December 2008, the Brest Boot Co., located at 512 South Chadbourne Street, caught fire, and the roof and second floor were destroyed. The boot business started in this building in 1923. The brick shell is all that is left. Options for its preservation and reuse should be considered due to its important corner orientation and its c. 1890 date of construction. Fires have destroyed several buildings in the downtown area, and many have been lost forever. (Courtesy of Downtown San Angelo, Inc.)

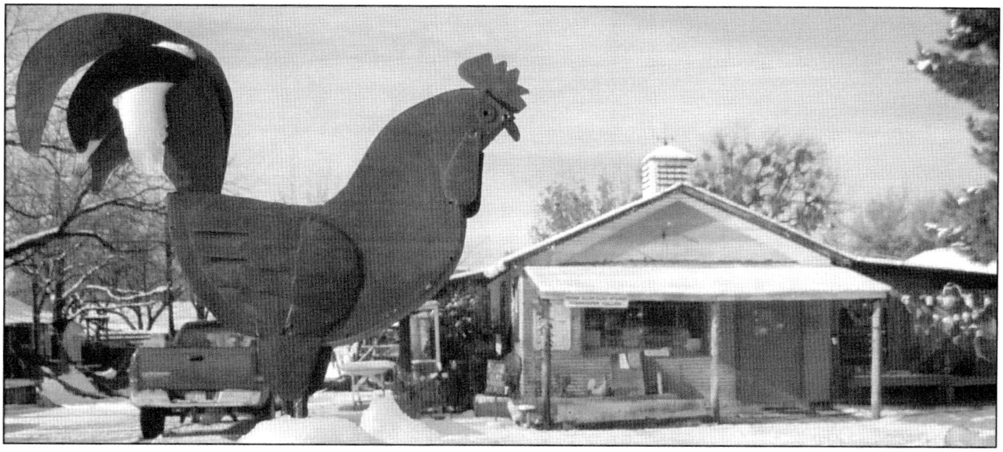

Chicken Farm Art Center. Roger Allen, with Richard Ramirez and Bill Rich, two former partners who, like Allen, were potters, purchased an old chicken processing plant in 1971 at 2505 Randolph Street (present-day Martin Luther King Boulevard). By 1974, the site was called Chicken Farm Art Center, and more existing buildings were converted to artist studios, a restaurant, and bed-and-breakfast lodging. The first Saturday monthly event sees all the studios opened, with vendors displaying their wares and local musicians performing throughout the day. (Photograph by author.)

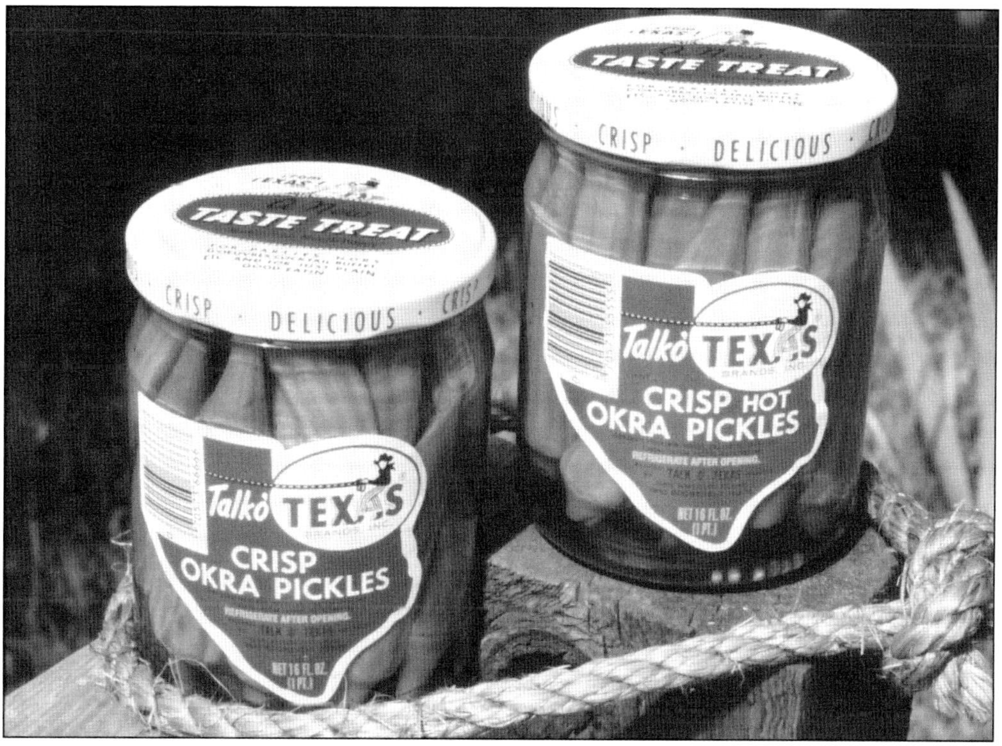

Pickled Okra. These jars of pickled okra were likely canned in the early 1980s. In 1950, the company began in the San Angelo kitchen of Dick and Mitzi Grimes. It expanded over the years, first following purchase by Al Ricci in the mid-1950s and then later in the years after the 1986 relocation to the present location at 1610 Roosevelt Street. Despite its expansion through the years, the okra pods are still placed in the glass jars by hand. (Courtesy of Barney's Studio.)

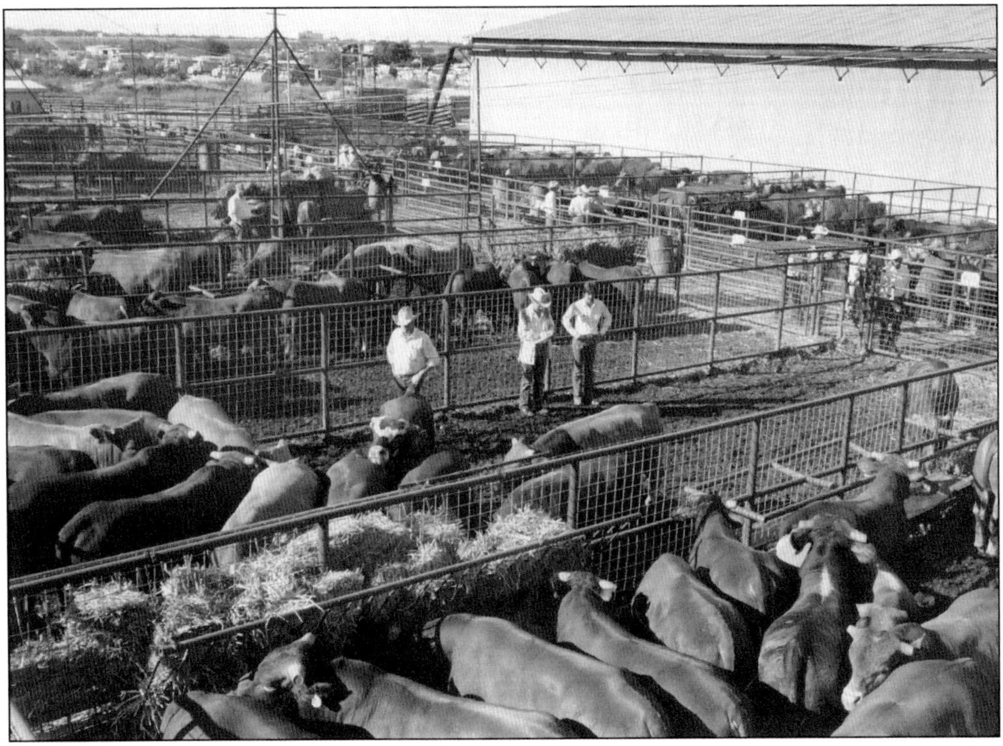

Feed Lot. Buyers examine cattle at the Isa Bulls at Producers Livestock in October 1987. Other agriculturally oriented companies that have been located on Bell Street include Handy Packing Co., Boyd & Clark Feed Yards, Midwest Feed Yards, and Armour & Co. (WTC.)

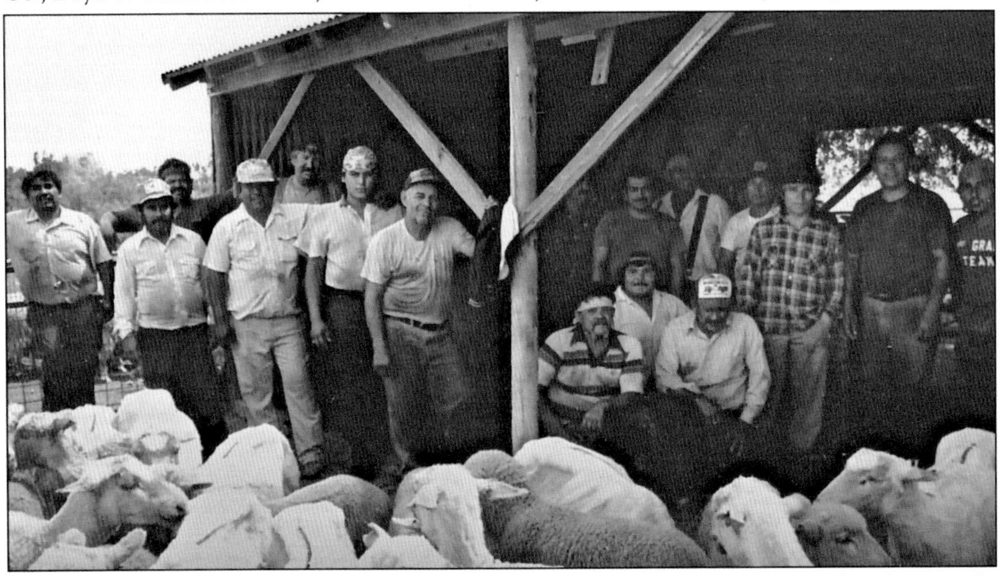

Sheep-shearing Crew. Each member of the Santiago Sr. shearing crew, shown in this photograph, received an advance before shearing commenced the next year in order to provide their families with a "good Christmas." After Santiago Sr.'s death in January 1990, each of these men returned to work under Santiago Jr. to ensure the contracts were fulfilled. Upon completion of the job, each man repaid his advance in full to Santiago Jr. (WTC.)

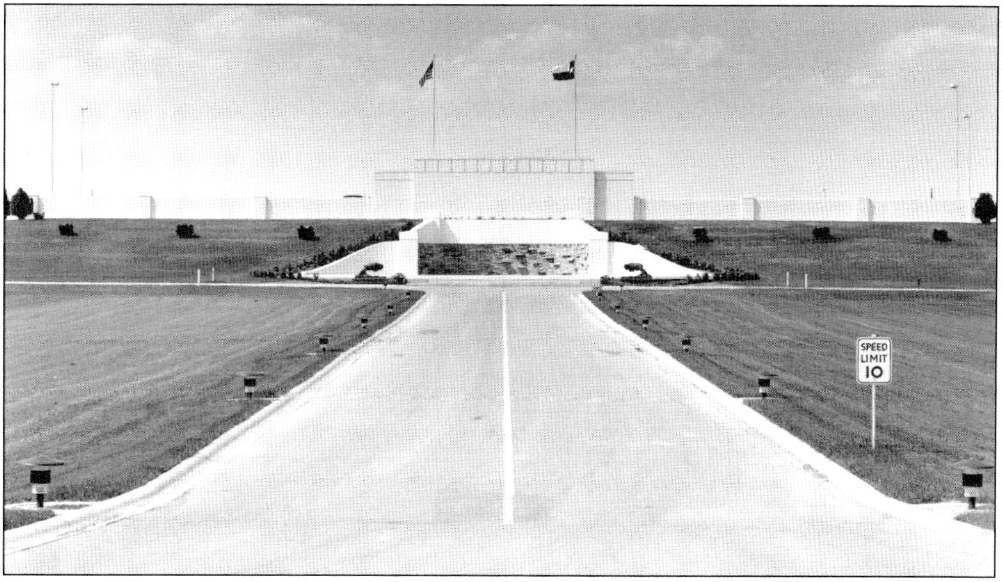

ETHICON. This underground plant is located at 3348 Pulliam Street. It is owned and operated by Johnson & Johnson Co. and has over 600 employees. It was constructed by Templeton Construction Co. (WTC.)

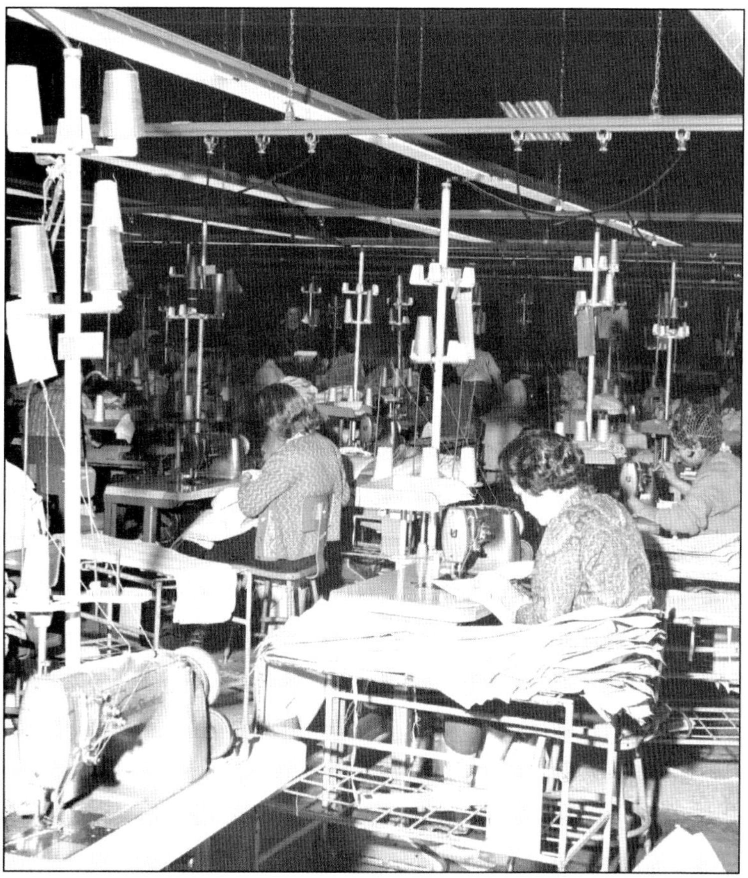

LEVI'S INTERIOR. In 1972, Levi's built a million dollar plant, located in the industrial park off Loop 306. At that time, it employed 450 individuals. In 1984, the company reported that men's straight-leg and boot-let blue jeans were produced in this plant. With the increase in competition from high-end designers as well as retail giants, such as Sears, the plant was closed in 1997. (WTC.)

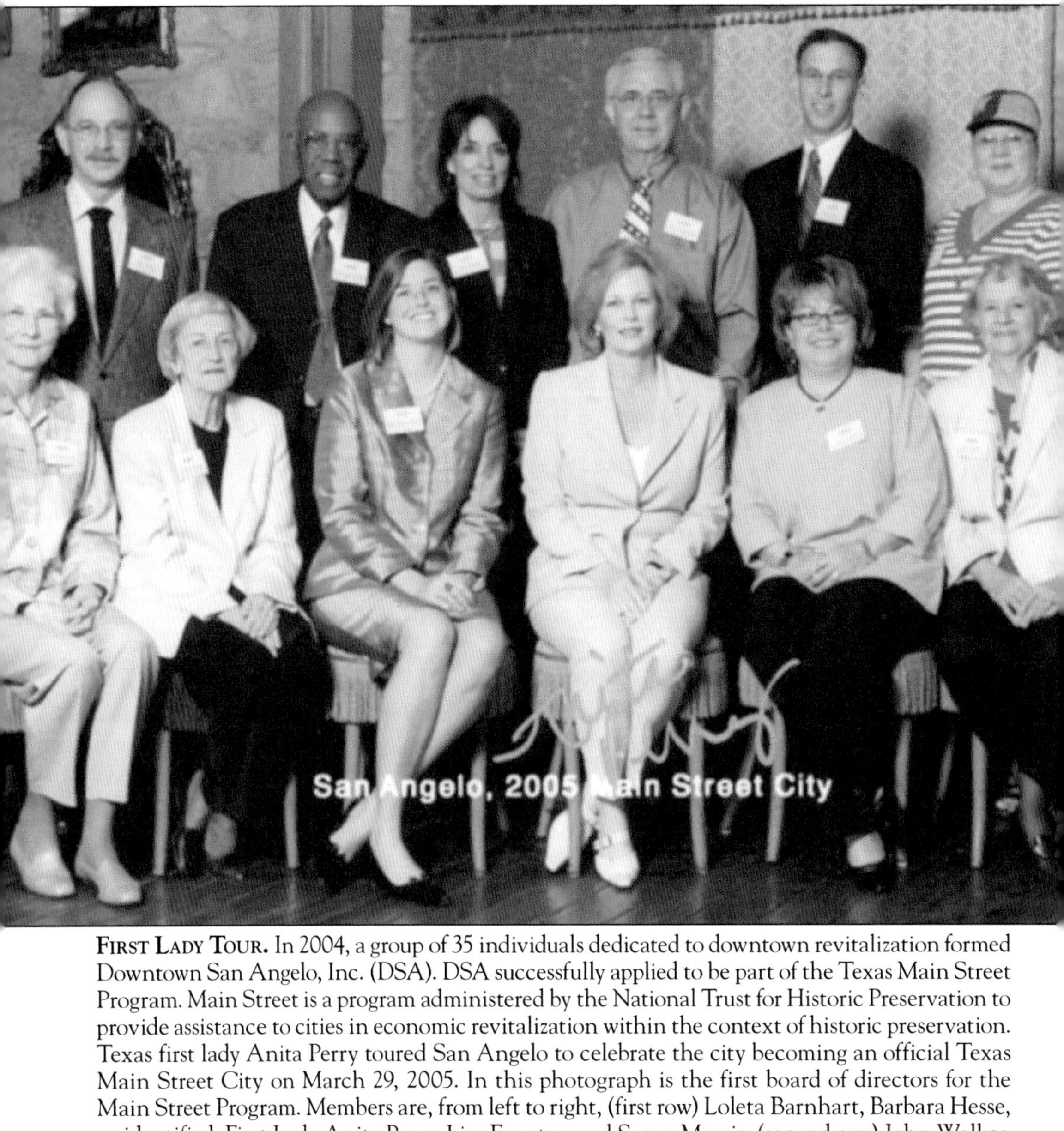

First Lady Tour. In 2004, a group of 35 individuals dedicated to downtown revitalization formed Downtown San Angelo, Inc. (DSA). DSA successfully applied to be part of the Texas Main Street Program. Main Street is a program administered by the National Trust for Historic Preservation to provide assistance to cities in economic revitalization within the context of historic preservation. Texas first lady Anita Perry toured San Angelo to celebrate the city becoming an official Texas Main Street City on March 29, 2005. In this photograph is the first board of directors for the Main Street Program. Members are, from left to right, (first row) Loleta Barnhart, Barbara Hesse, unidentified, First Lady Anita Perry, Lisa Fuentes, and Susan Morris; (second row) John Walker, Rev. Nathaniel "Hank" Hankins, Joyce Wilde, Bobby Eggemeyer, Rick Wise, and Debbie Cross. (Courtesy of Downtown San Angelo, Inc.)

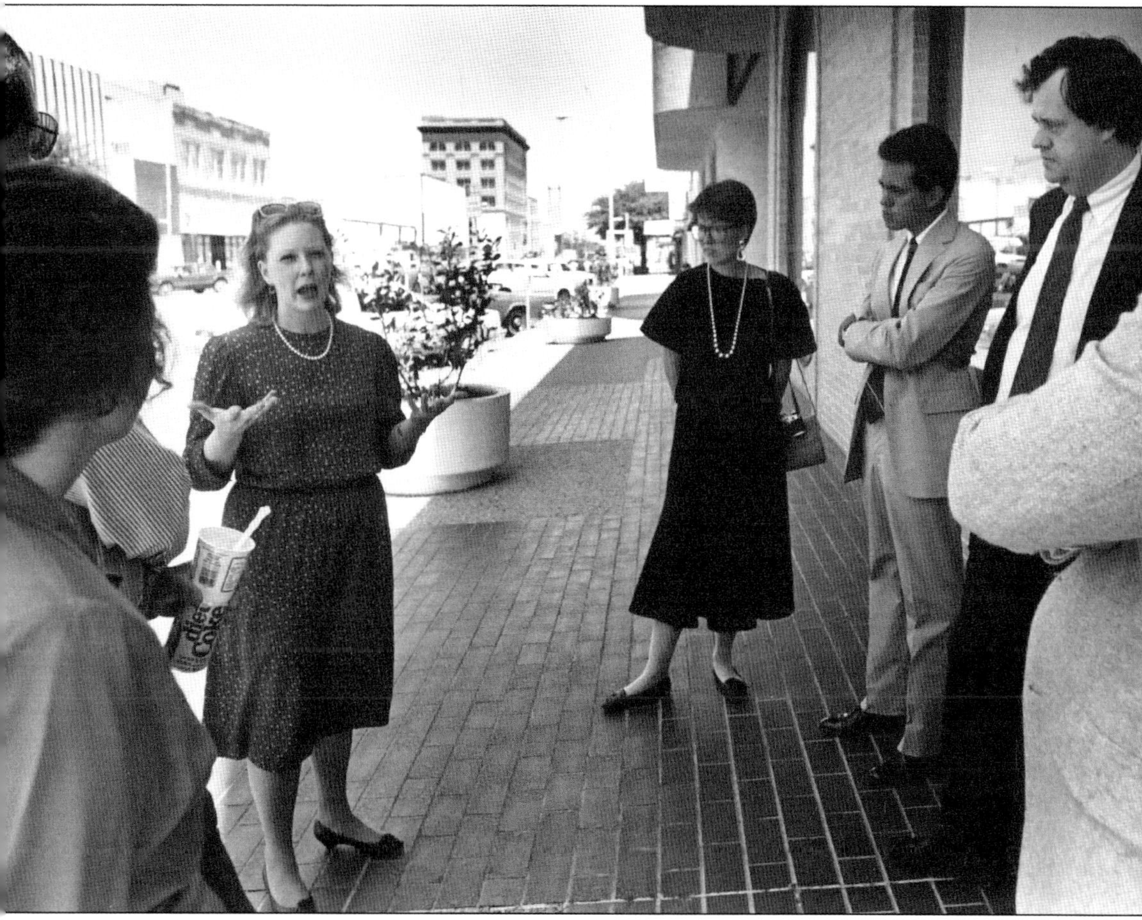

HISTORIC PRESERVATION. In May 1988, Libby Barker Willis (left of center), field officer for the Fort Worth office of the National Trust for Historic Preservation, toured downtown with Howard Taylor (far right), director of the San Angelo Museum of Fine Arts, and next to him, Gary Acevedo, county commissioner. The local preservationists listened to her advice on how to preserve historic downtown San Angelo. Ironically, the old Holcomb-Blanton Building, visible behind Willis's head, would be demolished four years later. Four years before her visit, in 1984, the demolition of the M.L. Leddy Building (see page 80), designed by Oscar Ruffini, drew a lot of attention. Discussions on saving downtown can be read in editorials at least as far back as 1962. A combination of many incidents and the hard work of countless individuals and organizations resulted in the historic downtown enjoyed today. (WTC.)

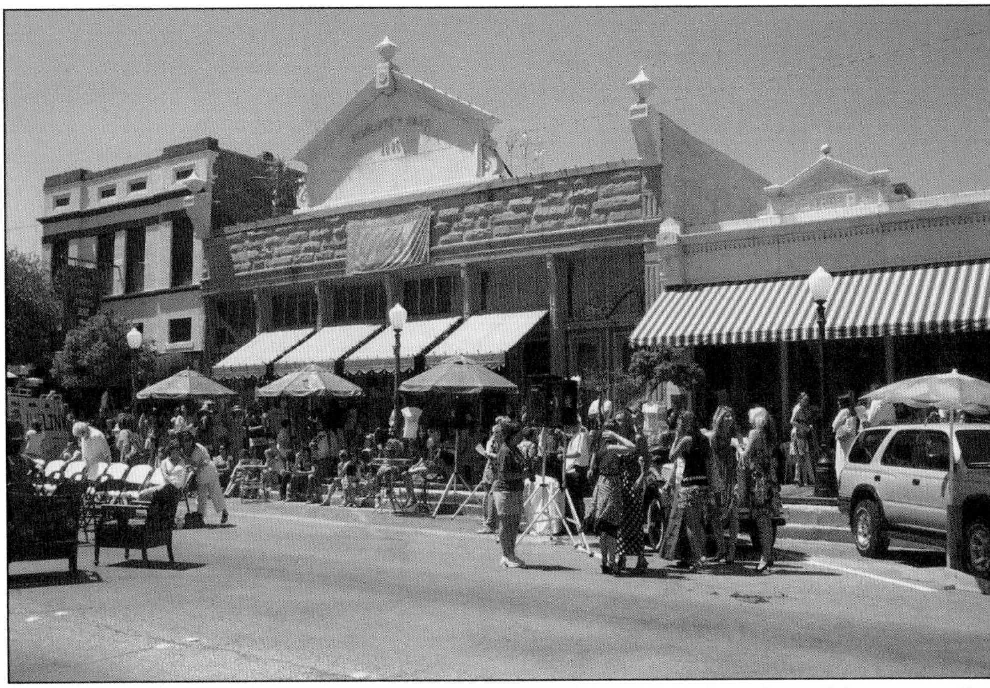

STREET FESTIVAL. Street festivals are important to the continued vitality of downtown San Angelo, and closing part of Concho Avenue on a Saturday in the spring draws a good public crowd. The event pictured occurred on April 28, 2007, and included a fashion show. (Courtesy of Downtown San Angelo, Inc.)

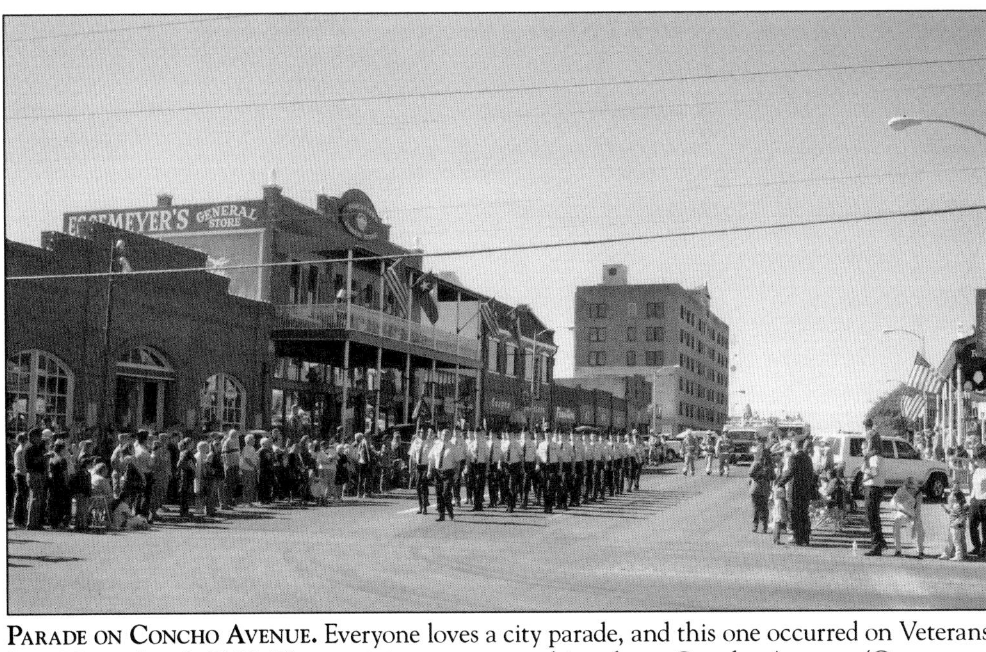

PARADE ON CONCHO AVENUE. Everyone loves a city parade, and this one occurred on Veterans' Day, November 8, 2008. The participants are marching down Concho Avenue. (Courtesy of Downtown San Angelo, Inc.)

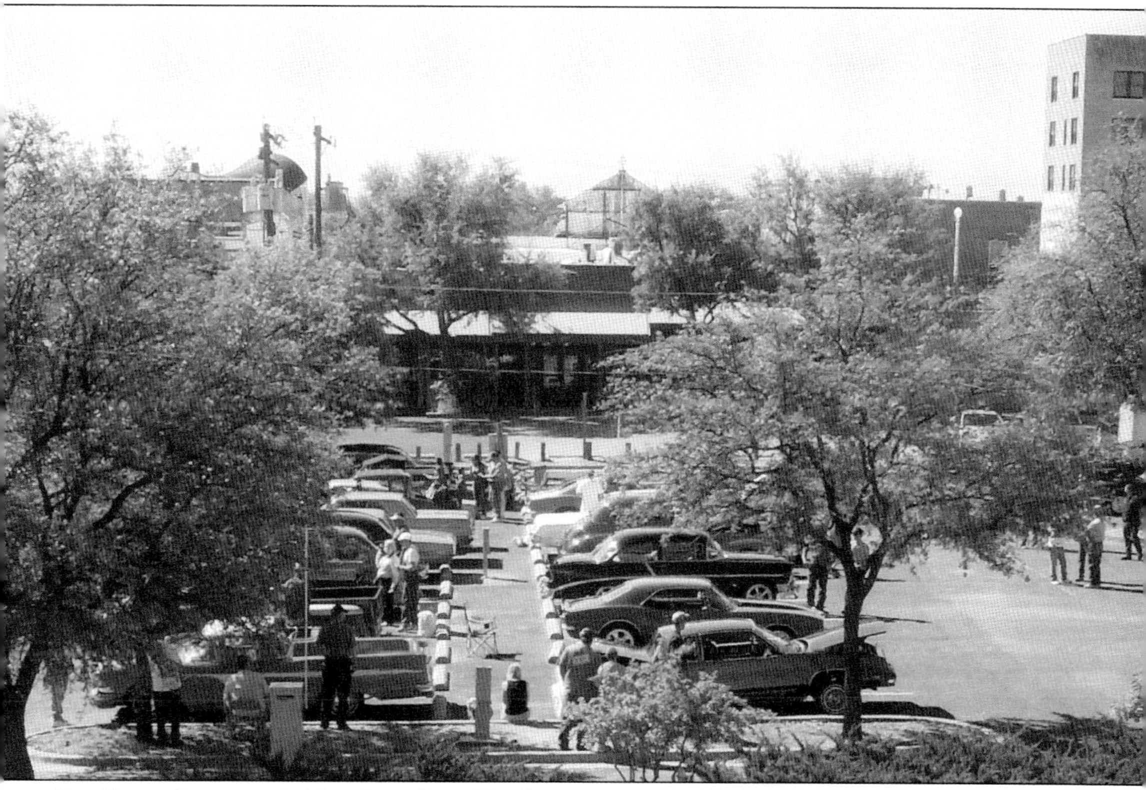

CAR SHOW. Events are held to draw the public downtown to benefit the community and businesses in town. This annual car show, located next to the Federal Building, is a popular event. (Courtesy of Downtown San Angelo, Inc.)

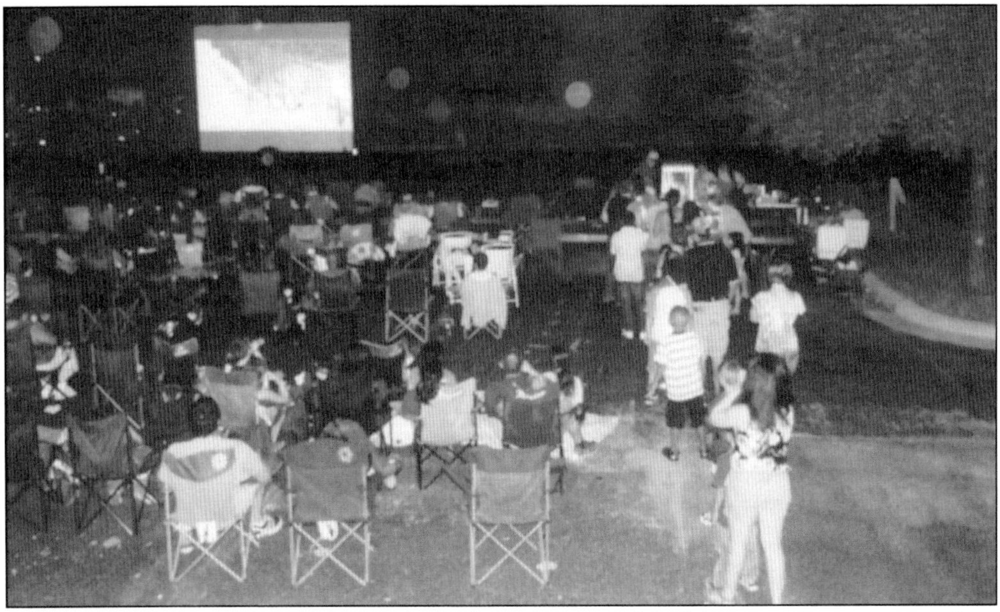

Outdoor Movies. In 2009, outdoor movie nights were initiated in the parking lot catercorner from the Cactus Hotel at 17 East Twohig Avenue. This is another example where downtown activities reinforce the sense of people and place. In 2012, 8,000 people attended the movies. Other outdoor movie series, like the one used at Sugar Land Town Square, were previously examined. Many local people, along with sponsors, underwriters, and partner stations, including KCSA radio station, pitched in to make this happen. (Courtesy of Downtown San Angelo, Inc.)

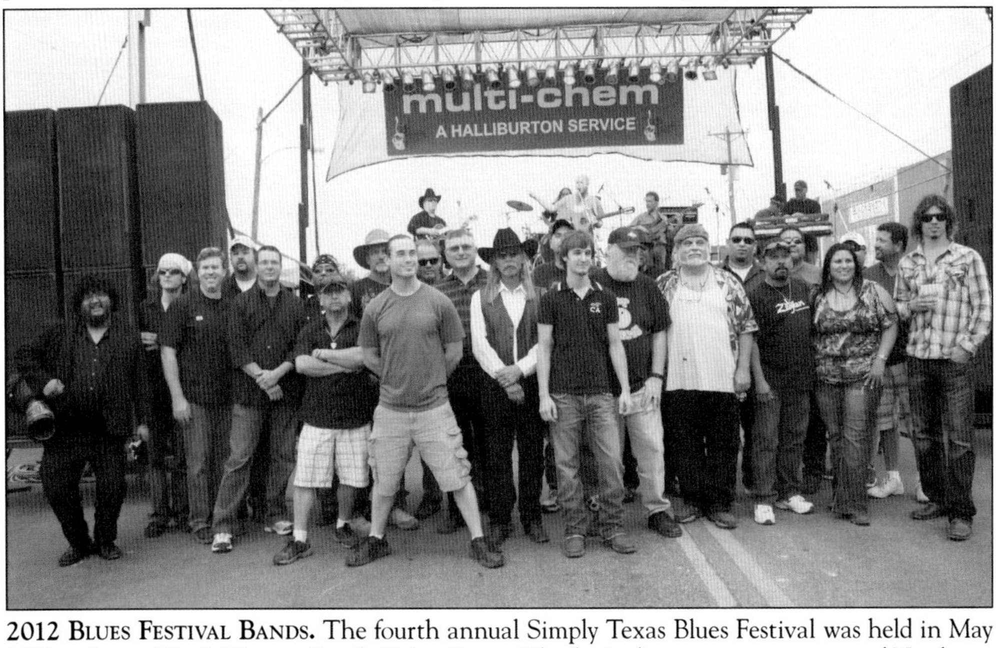

2012 Blues Festival Bands. The fourth annual Simply Texas Blues Festival was held in May 2012 in front of Sealy Flats on South Oakes Street. The festival was a great success, and Newberry Stafford won the solo/duo contest, and Mike Mulligan and the Altar Boyz won the band contest to represent the San Angelo Blues Society at the national blues festival contest in Nashville. (Courtesy of Debra Oresko.)

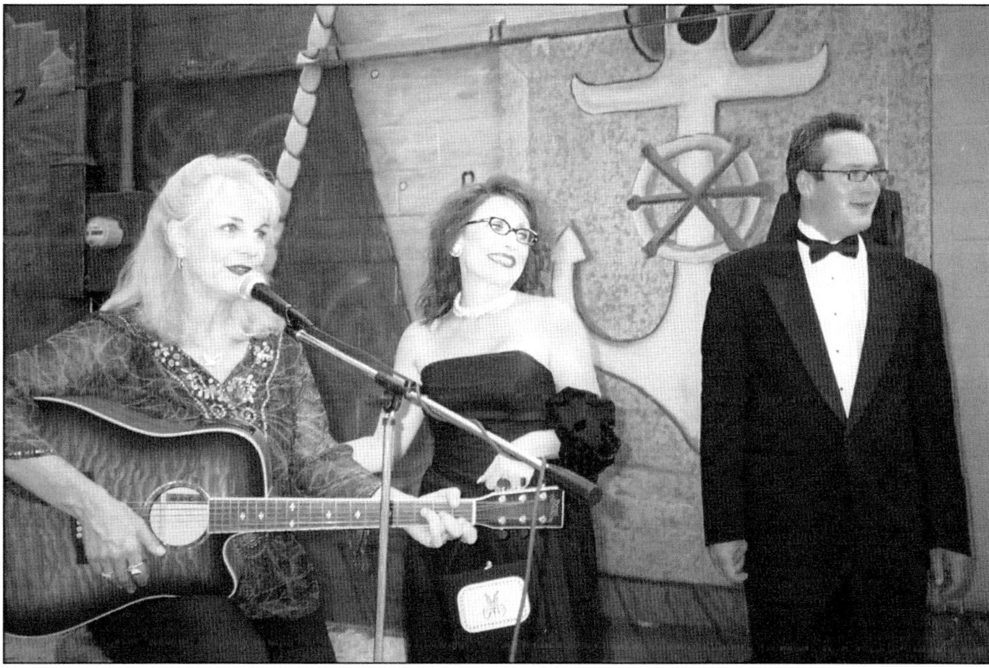

The Black Tie Alley Event. The Black Tie Alley Event, held on October 14, 2006, introduced Paintbrush Alley, located between Twohig and Concho Avenues and from Irving Street to Chadbourne Street, behind the Texas Theater. The paintings on the buildings go from whimsy to nostalgia. The individuals in the photograph are, from left to right, Cynthia Jordan, Vicki Milam, and Mayor J.W. Lown. (Courtesy of Downtown San Angelo, Inc.)

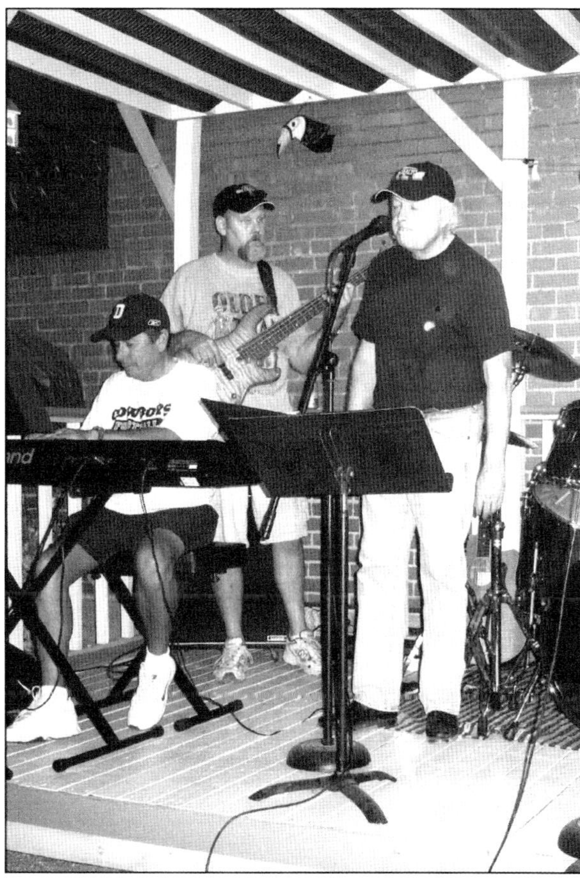

First Performance at Sealy Flats. The first performance at Sealy Flats was by Jimmy "Slim Jim" Rose Band. This image of the Santa Rita Boys Band was taken shortly after the restaurant opened. Rod and Dennise Bridgman worked to keep blues music alive in San Angelo. Other live music clubs exist in town, and more have opened. Some of the oldest clubs are Blaines Pub, Fat Boss's Pub, House of FiFi DuBois, and the Deadhorse. (Courtesy of Downtown San Angelo, Inc.)

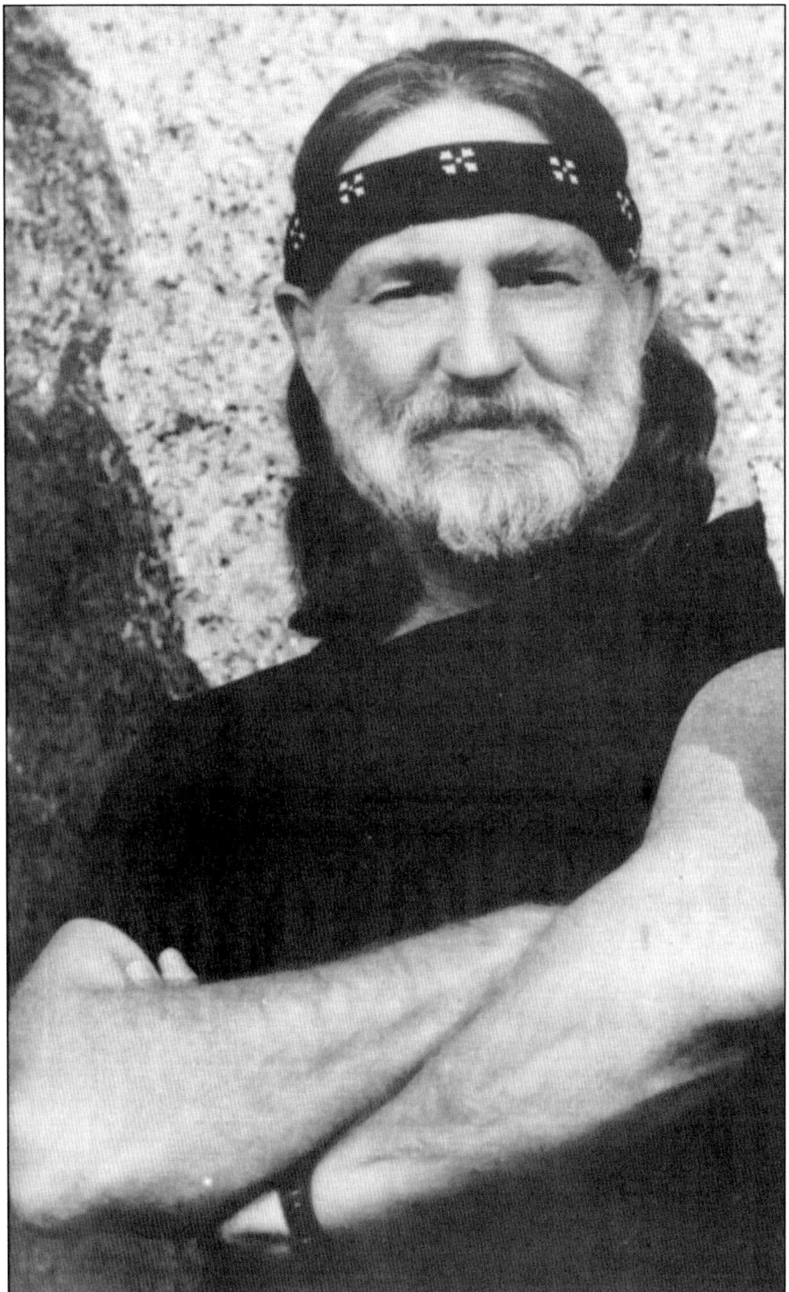

WILLIE NELSON. Through the efforts of Sam Lewis, president of the World Armadillo Breeding and Racing Association, the San Angelo Chamber of Commerce contacted Willie Nelson to stage a benefit performance, at no cost to the city, in Lima, Ohio. A March 1982 *Wall Street Journal* article contrasted the two cities, with statistics such as Lima's 15.4-percent unemployment rate versus San Angelo's 4.2 percent. Nelson performed on July 30, 1982. Mayor Moyer of Lima, Ohio, said, "If San Angelo ever runs into trouble with their water, Lima has lots of water if you need some." In April 1991, Nelson was in financial difficulty due to back taxes, and Lima held a festival to help repay its debt to him. (WTC.)

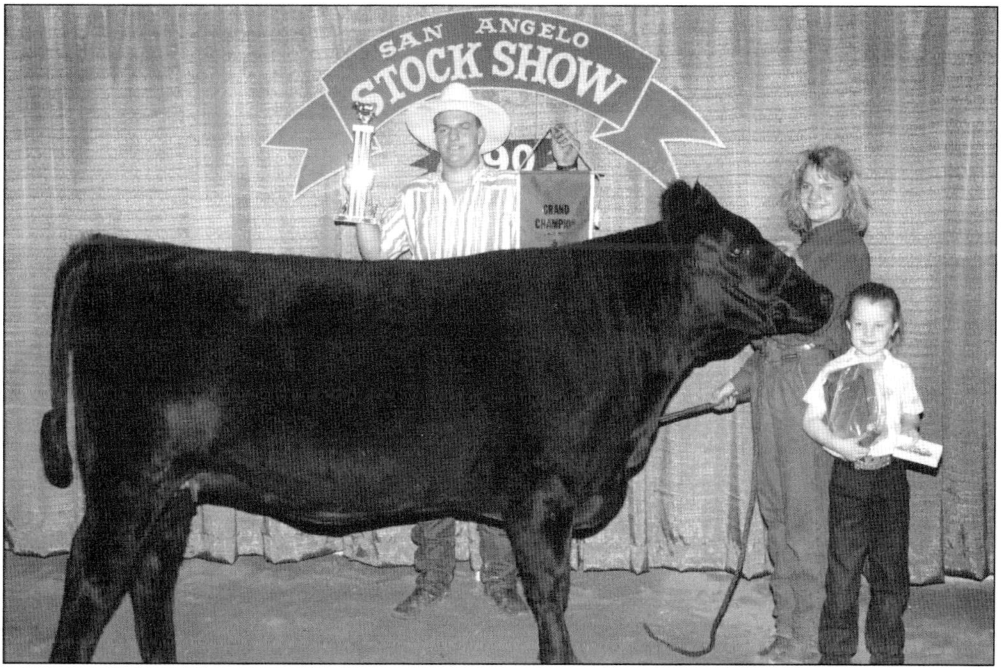

ANGUS HEIFER CHAMPION. The idea of a San Angelo Fat Stock Show and Rodeo was credited to J. Culberson "Cub" Deal, serving as the elected manager of the San Angelo Board of City Development (Chamber of Commerce). The first event was held in 1932. In the 1970s, an increased concern by consumers about high blood pressure and heart disease caused the beef industry to develop leaner meat. That resulted in the San Angelo Fat Stock Show and Rodeo and other stock shows removing the word "fat" from its name. Shannon Grote (center) won the grand championship at the 1990 stock show. Her brother Will and sister Ashley are seen helping to hold the trophy, plaque, and ribbon. (WTC.)

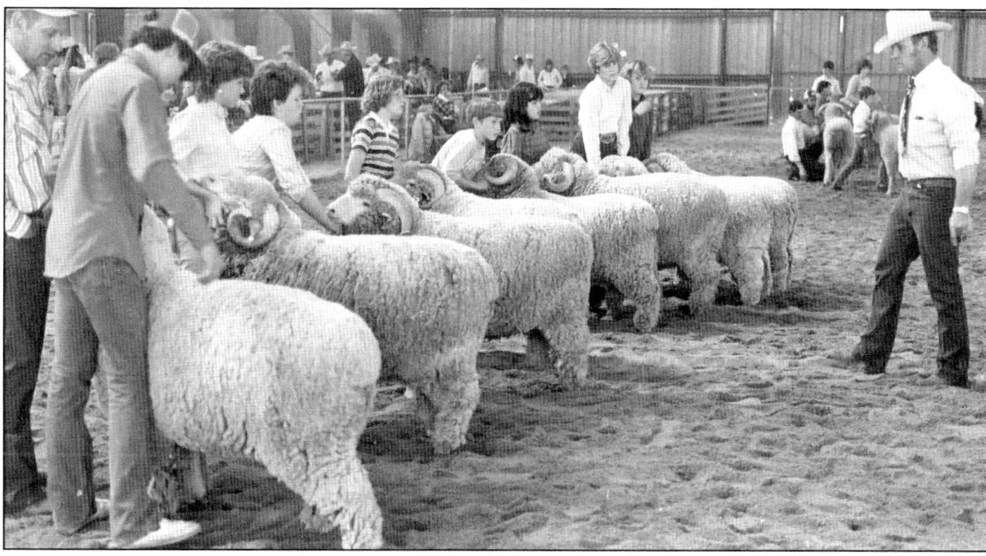

JUDGING RAMS. Judge Jerry Swift is seen during early judging of rams for wool and confirmation at the San Angelo Stock Show in 1984. The breeding sheep show and method of judging have not changed since this photograph was taken. (WTC.)

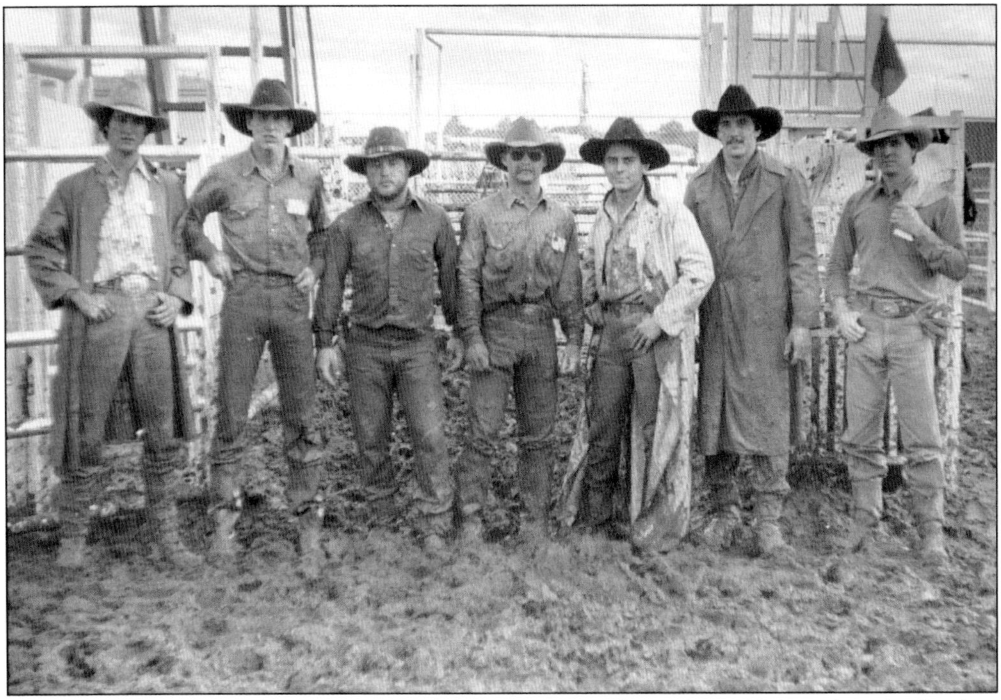

Roping Fiesta. Shown here are some of the contestants from the 1983 San Angelo Cowboy Roping Fiesta, held at the San Angelo Fairgrounds. As can be seen in the photograph, the grounds were muddy. Despite drizzling rain, 5,000 people attended Saturday's calf-roping contest. Hosted at the same time but by a different sponsor, the barrel races were cancelled—just too much mud in the Concho Riders Arena. (WTC.)

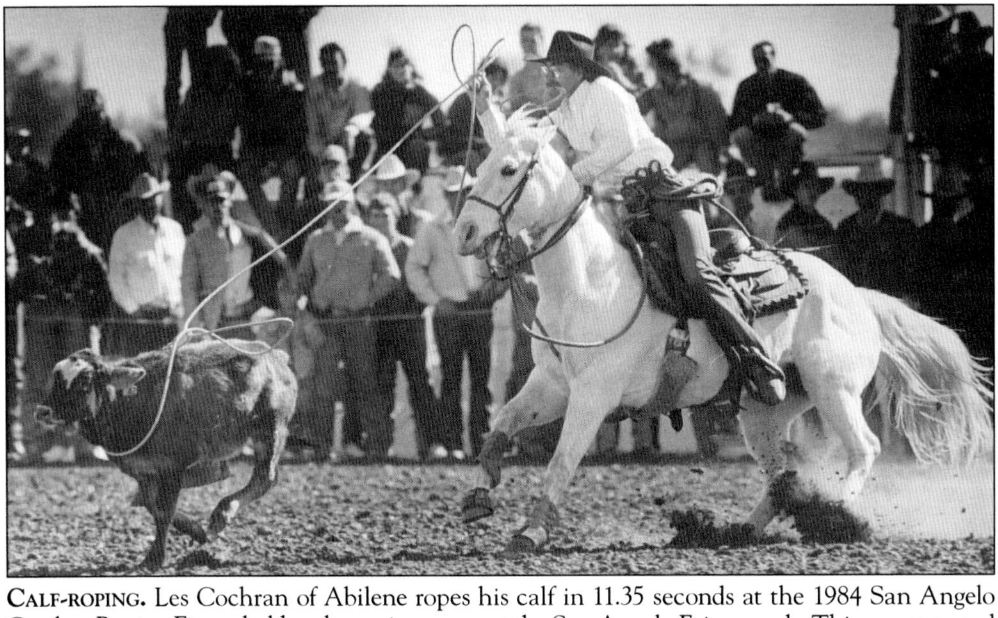

Calf-roping. Les Cochran of Abilene ropes his calf in 11.35 seconds at the 1984 San Angelo Cowboy Roping Fiesta, held at the roping arena at the San Angelo Fairgrounds. This event started in 1954 as a fall draw to the stock show and rodeo fairgrounds. In 1962, the association began what has become a crowd favorite, the match calf-roping. (WTC.)

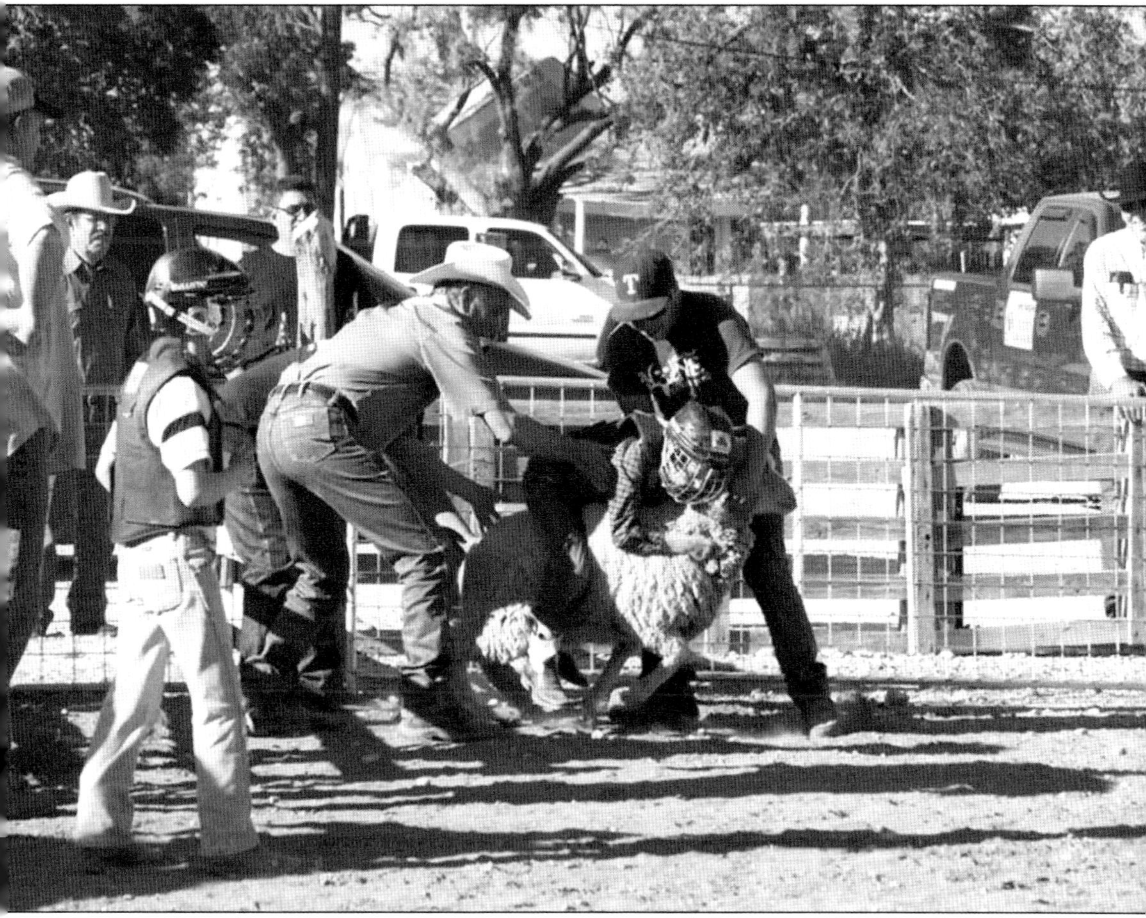

The Wooly Bully Kids' Rodeo. The Wooly Bully Kids' Rodeo at the "Stockee Yards," 120 East Concho Avenue, is an annual event held in conjunction with the Art-O-Ber-Fest. This event is a great family activity that relates back to the sheep industry, which was an important part of San Angelo. The action is very quick, as the mutton-busting child is usually on and off the sheep in a split second. This is sometimes punctuated by the contestant having second thoughts about the whole matter and parents reinsuring them that they will enjoy it. This photograph is from the October 2011 event. (Courtesy of Downtown San Angelo, Inc.)

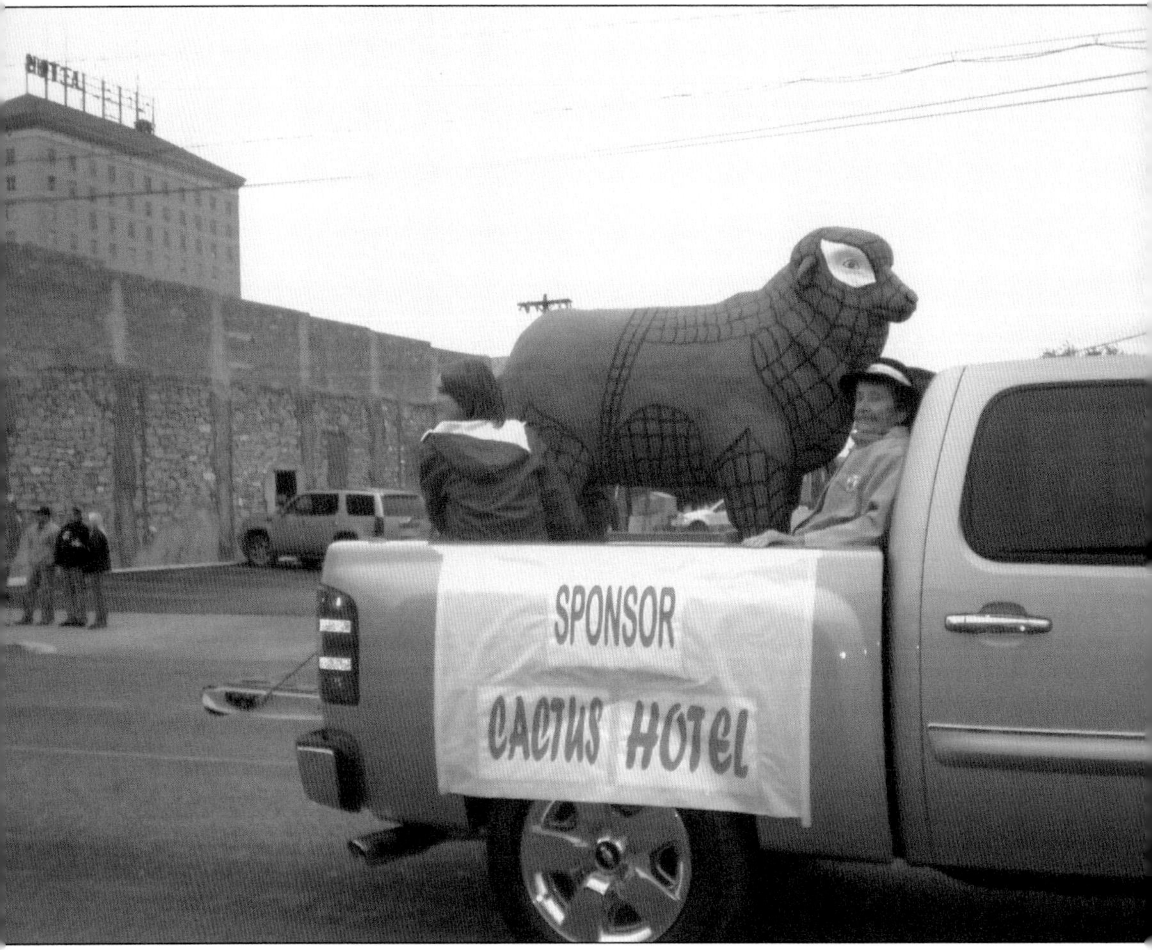

Miss Wool Sheep Spectacular Parade. One of the Art-O-Ber-Fest events is the "Miss Wool" Sheep Spectacular Parade, making reference to earlier Miss Wool and Angelo State University (ASU) homecoming parades that were well-attended downtown events. The sheep industry had a great impact on San Angelo financially and brought national recognition through the Miss Wool pageant. It also provided ASU with its distinctive ram mascot. In the current event, businesses or individuals purchase the fiberglass sheep, and then artists paint or create designs on the iconic animals. The sheep are then permanently displayed in the downtown area, and people are allowed to vote on their favorite sheep in the Miss Wool contest. (Courtesy of Downtown San Angelo, Inc.)

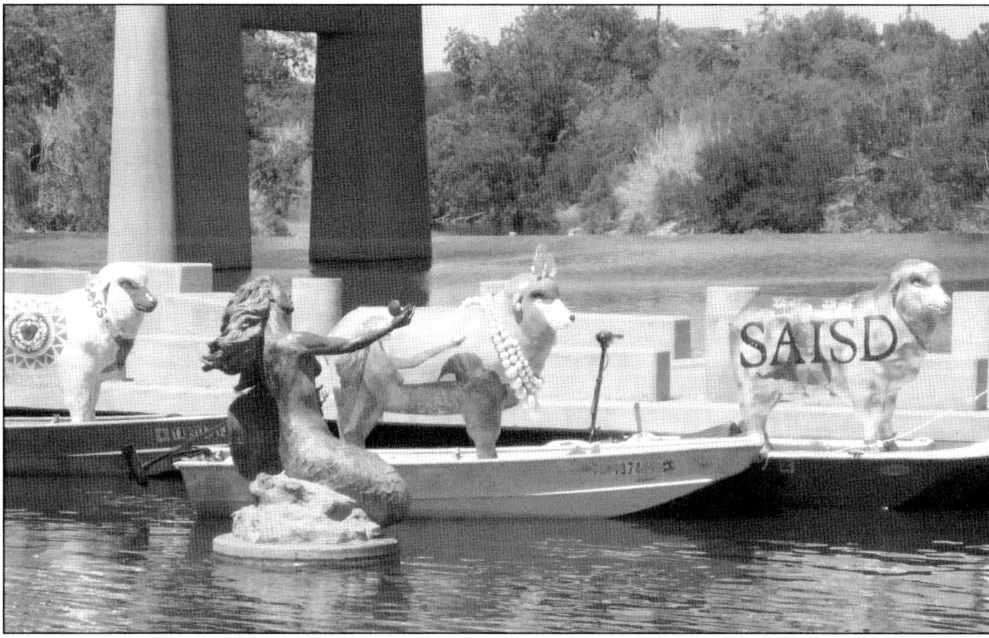

MISS WOOL PARADE. In 1966, the annual Miss Wool pageant was held in June, but the traditional downtown parade with school participation was not possible, so the idea of a river parade was created. It continued until 1972, when the American Sheep Producers Council withdrew its support. Fiesta del Concho recreated the river parade for several years before deciding on a simpler street parade. In 2011, the Miss Wool River Parade again took place. (Courtesy of Downtown San Angelo, Inc.)

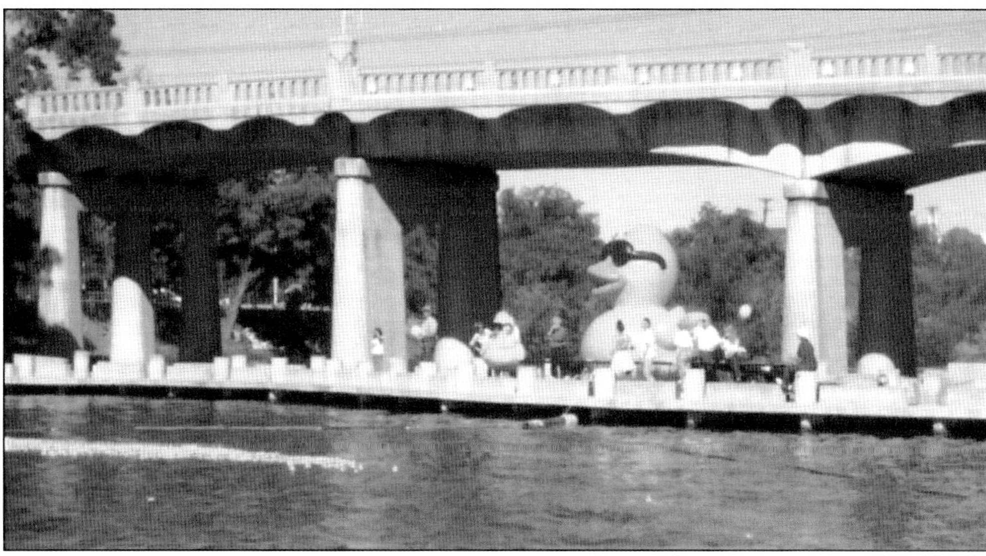

DUCK RACE FINISH LINE. For the Waddlin' on da Wiver fundraising event in October 2006, 10,000 yellow plastic ducks were released into the Concho River from a dump truck on the low-water crossing. Individuals adopted the ducks and paid for the chance to win prizes. The photograph shows the finish line at Celebration Bridge. The current in the river was not strong, despite the encouragement of several personal watercrafts, and the journey down the river took two hours before the winning ducks could be determined. (Courtesy of Downtown San Angelo, Inc.)

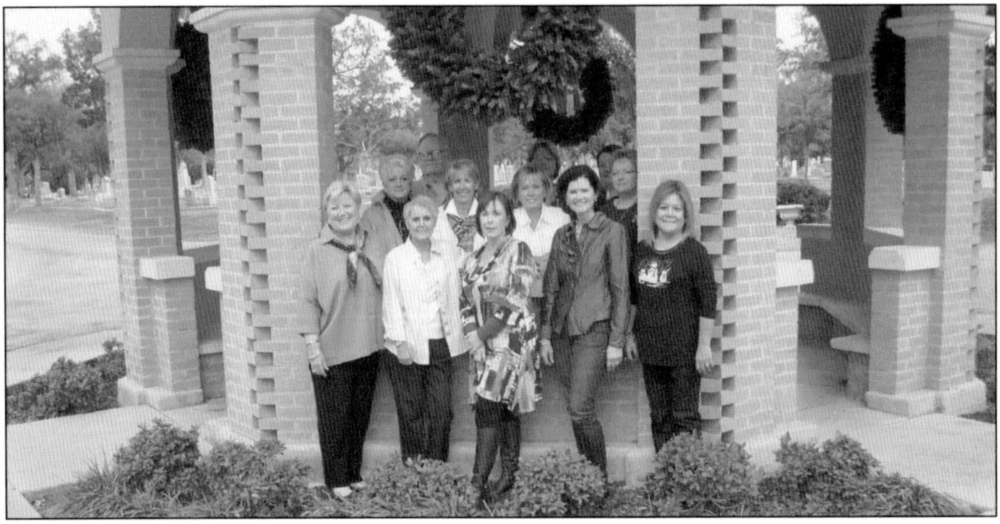

Gazebo at Fairmount Cemetery. Fairmount Cemetery was established in 1890, mainly because the old city cemetery on East Fourth Street, between Magdalen and North Oakes Streets, was nearly full. Over the years, improvements have been made to the 57-acre site, including the construction of a gazebo. The Fairmount Cemetery Board and Friends of Fairmount Cemetery decided to celebrate the 100th anniversary of the gazebo and also to enhance the site during the Christmas season with wreaths. Members are, from left to right, (first row) Beverly Stribling, Jean Johnson, Eva Moutos-Choate, Cora McGowan, and Martha Visney; (second row) Ann West, Angela Williams, Jackie Martin, and Susan Ball; (third row) Richard Round, Eva Horton, and Candice Brewer. (Photograph by author.)

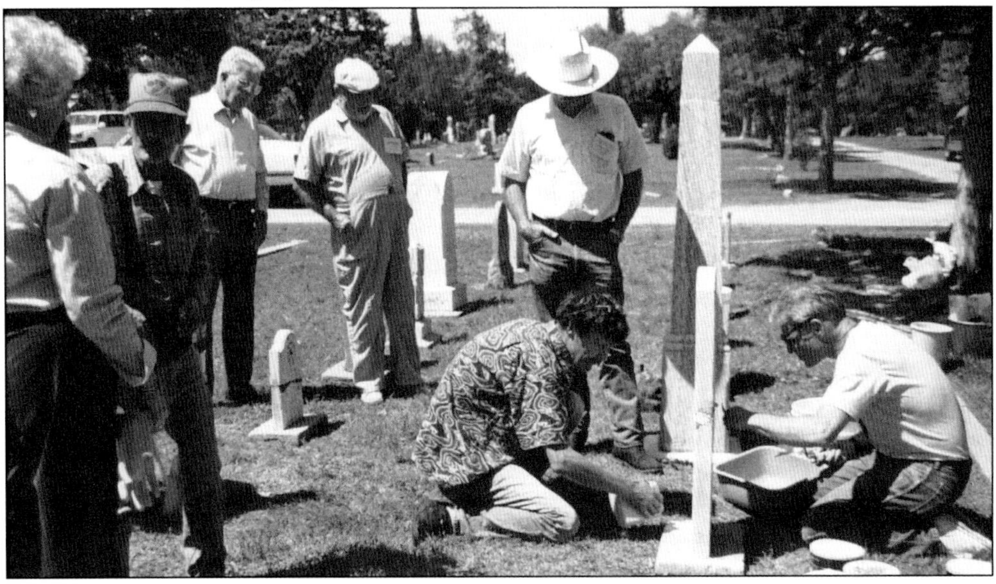

Fairmount Cemetery Workshop. In 1994, the Tom Green Historical Commission sponsored a cemetery workshop at Fairmount Cemetery. Kneeling from left to right, John Dennis, conservator at the Dallas Museum of Art, and the author, who was then working for the Texas Historical Commission, are shown demonstrating correct methods for repairing historic grave markers. This section of the cemetery, located in the southeast corner, contains some of the oldest markers. Most of these graves and markers were moved from the original city cemetery. (Private collection.)

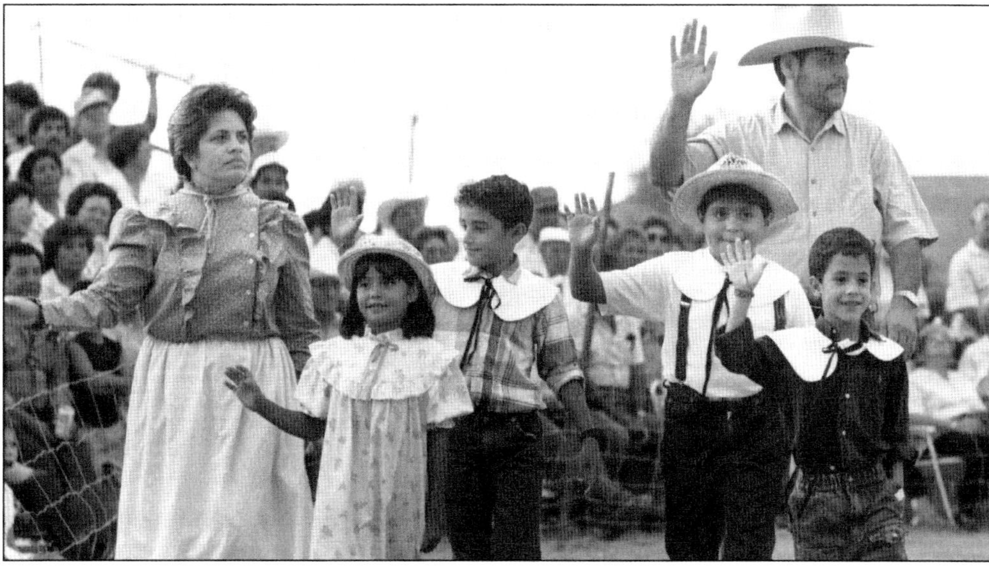

Fiestas Patrias Pageant. San Angelo has a long tradition of Fiestas Partrias celebrations, dating back to 1910. In 1946, the celebration was held in the front yard of Estanislado Sedeno's home at 113 West Avenue North. Sedeno Plaza was subsequently the site of the Fiestas Patrias in San Angelo for 27 years. On September 5, 1972, Estanislado Sedeno returned to Sedeno Plaza, and Mayor C.S. "Chic" Conrad proclaimed the date Estanislado Sedeno Day. In this photograph, the Alderette family represents a pioneer family during the Fiestas Partrias pageant in September 1988. Seen here are, from left to right, Dolores DeLeon; children Tana Hermandez, Jose Antonio Contreras, Andrew Hermandez, and Gabriel Contreras; and Arnoldo DeLeon. Arnoldo is the author of the pageant, and Dolores is the great-great-granddaughter of Pablo Alderette. (WTC.)

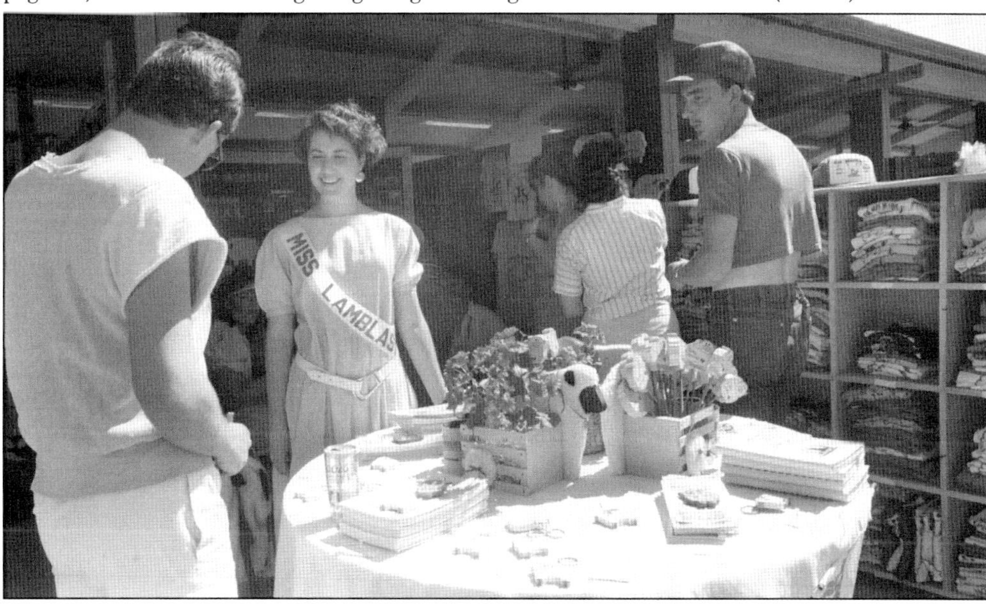

Miss Lamblast. Miss Lamblast, Shaun Smith, helps at the arts-and-crafts booth at the ninth annual Lamblast, held at the Goodfellow Air Force Base Recreation Camp at Lake Nasworthy in April 1987. Approximately 2,300 people attended the event. That year, 29 cooking teams competed for the World Championship Lamb Cook-off; the Outhouse Cookers of Stratford won. (WTC.)

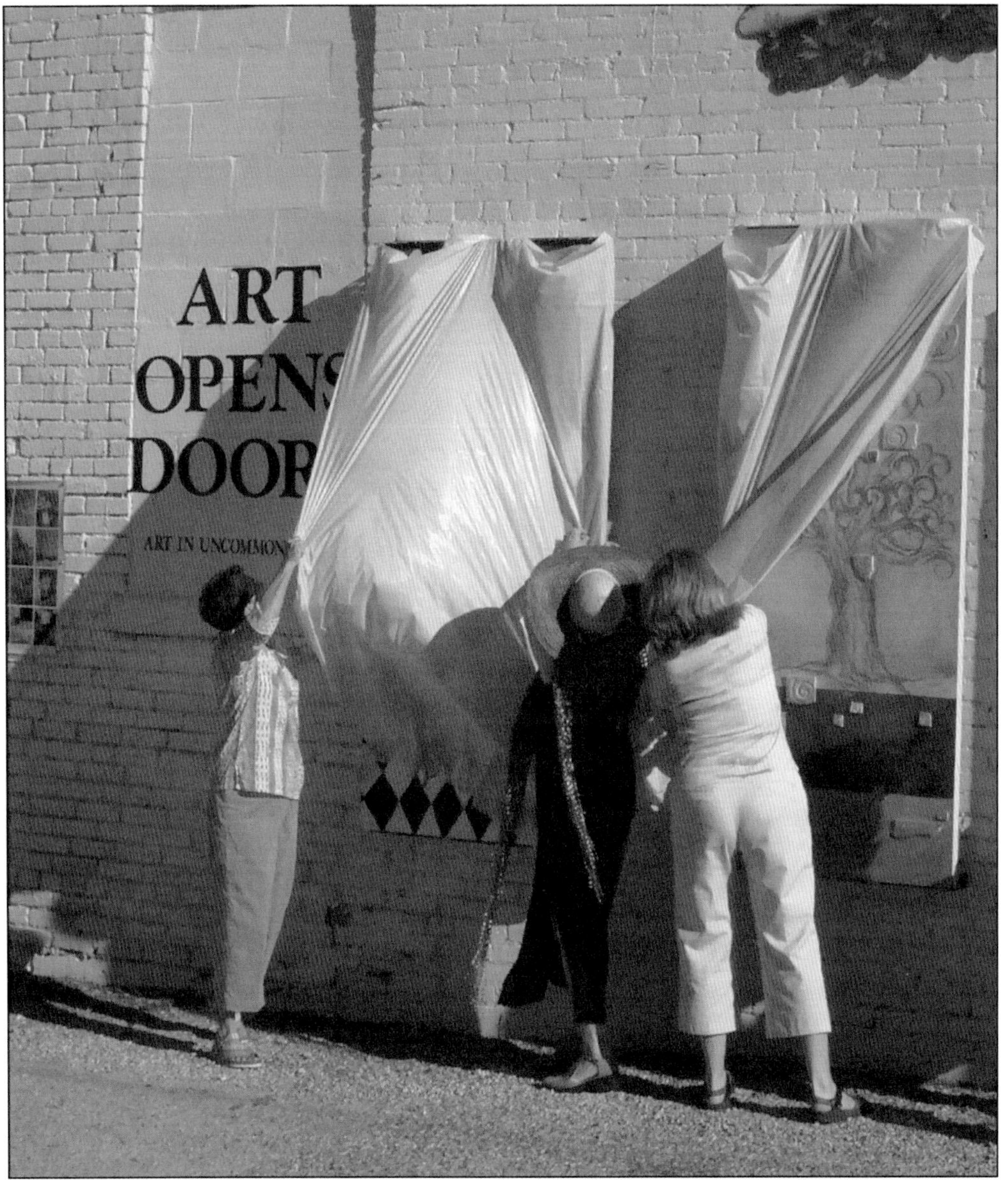

Art Opens Doors Unveiling. Here is the unveiling of the new "Art Opens Doors," an Art in Uncommon Places project. Painted by a local artist, it is a display of doors at 215 South Oakes Street in the alley behind the Federal Building. Also, in the alley is a portrait of benefactor Eva Tucker painted on the balcony overlooking the alley. (Courtesy of Downtown San Angelo, Inc.)

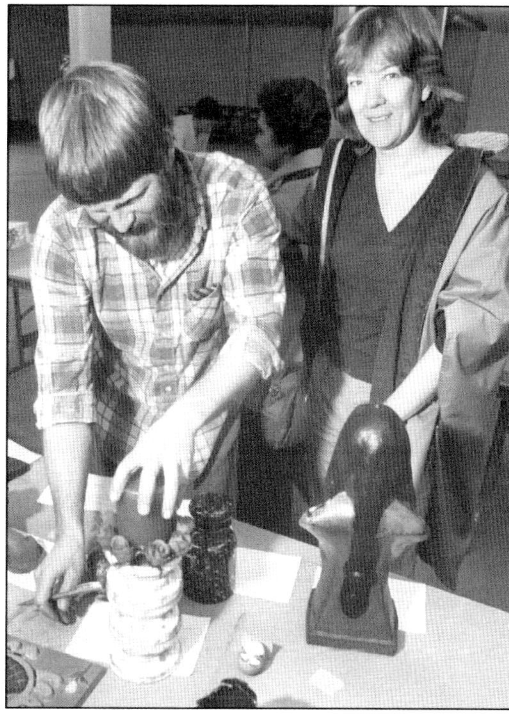

JUDGING AT THE LIVESTOCK SHOW. Roger Allen and Beth Evans, now Beth King, of the Chicken Farm Art Center, judged ceramics and other artworks for the arts-and-crafts division of the Tom Green County Fair and Junior Livestock Show in January 1983. (WTC.)

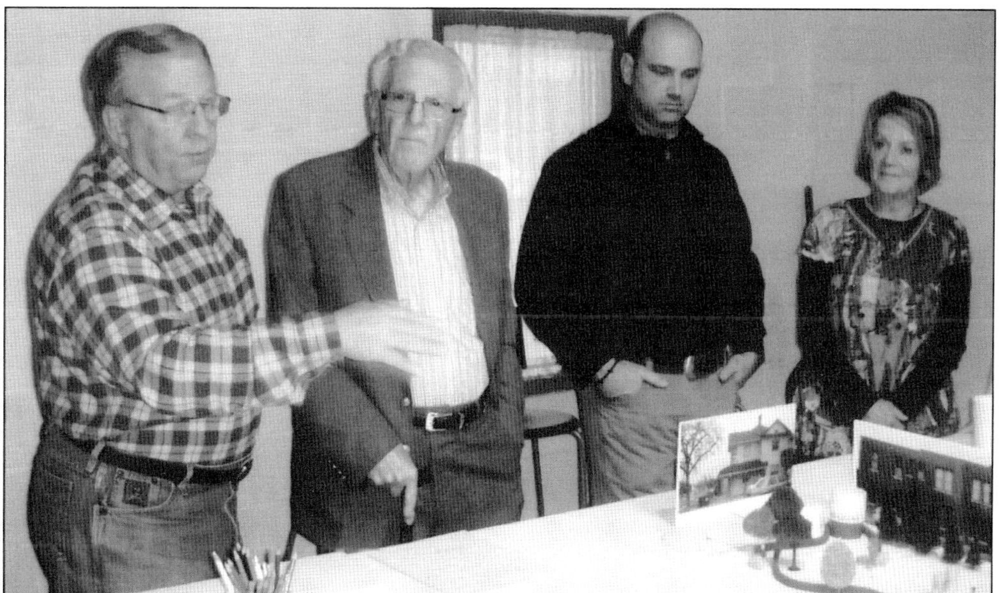

HERITAGE PARK. The vision for the pocket park began with the owner of the vacant lot, J. Willis Johnson, and his desire to see the lot, found at the southeast corner of South Oakes Street and Twohig Avenue, transformed into a welcoming oasis. The lot has been leased to Downtown San Angelo, Inc., to be used as a park. In this photograph, some of the members of the committee attend a design brainstorming session held on February 7, 2012. Shown are, from left to right, Lee Pfluger, chairman; J. Willis Johnson, owner; Scott Sustek, sculptor; and Julie Raymond, from Art in Uncommon Places. (Courtesy of Downtown San Angelo, Inc.)

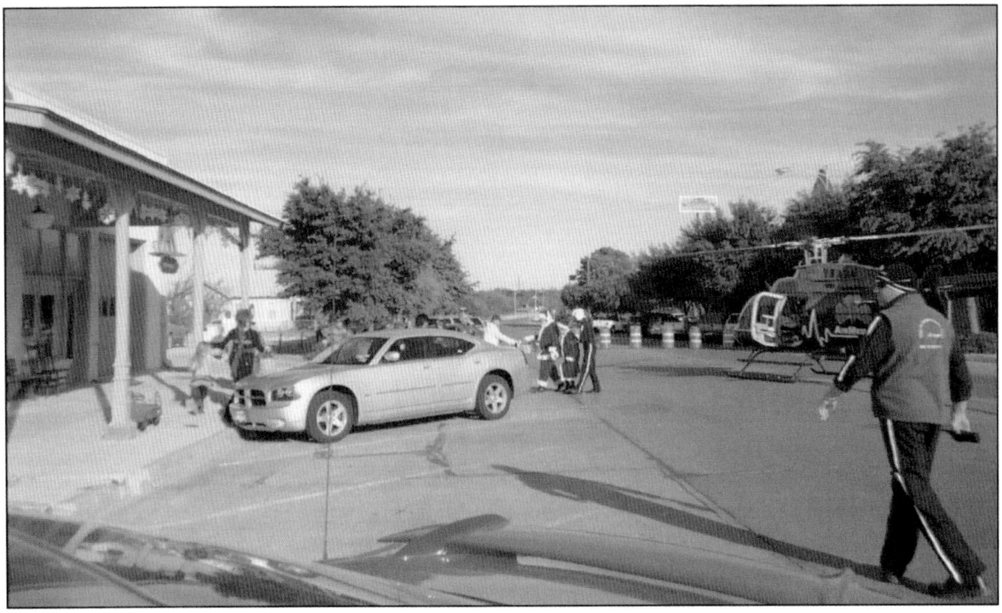

ARRIVAL OF MR. AND MRS. SANTA CLAUS. The tradition of Santa arriving before Christmas in a helicopter continues today on East Concho Avenue. The first time Santa officially arrived in San Angelo in a helicopter was in 1954, and he landed on the roof of the Standard-Times Building during the annual pre-Christmas party. The local newspaper reported that between 8,000 and 10,000 people waited his arrival. John Boles, former Hollywood movie and singing star, led the singing of "Jingle Bells." Santa, with help from the staff of the *Standard-Times*, took 15 minutes to toss bags of candy to the crowd. Before he left town, he made a visit to the pediatrics ward at Shannon Hospital. The helicopter was owned by T.W. Murray of Murray Petroleum Co. of San Angelo and piloted by W.N. Bradshaw. (Courtesy of Downtown San Angelo, Inc.)

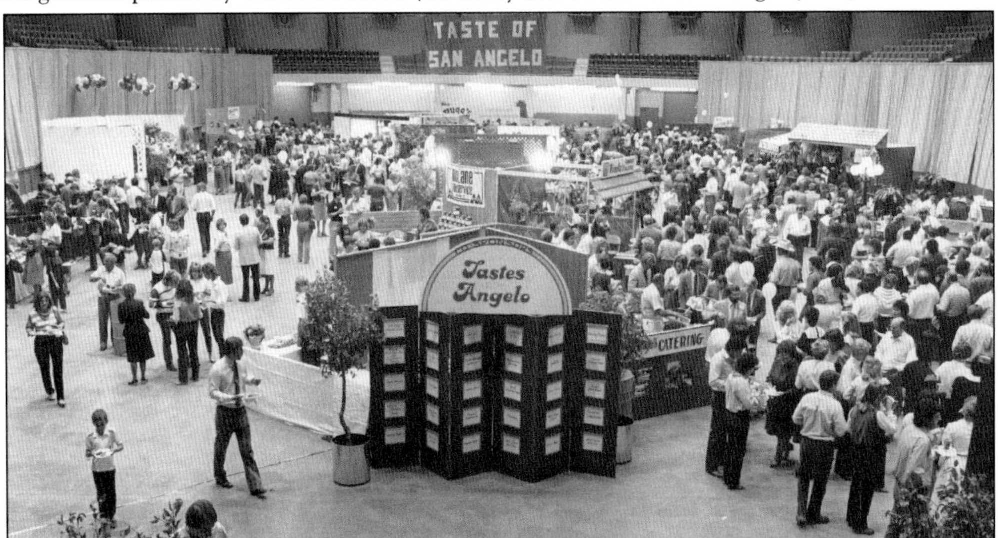

TASTE OF SAN ANGELO. In October 1984, a good crowd gathered for the Taste of San Angelo, later called the San Angelo Wine and Food Festival, held at the coliseum. The festival benefits the nonprofit San Angelo Cultural Affairs Council in its mission to enhance the arts and culture of San Angelo. (WTC.)

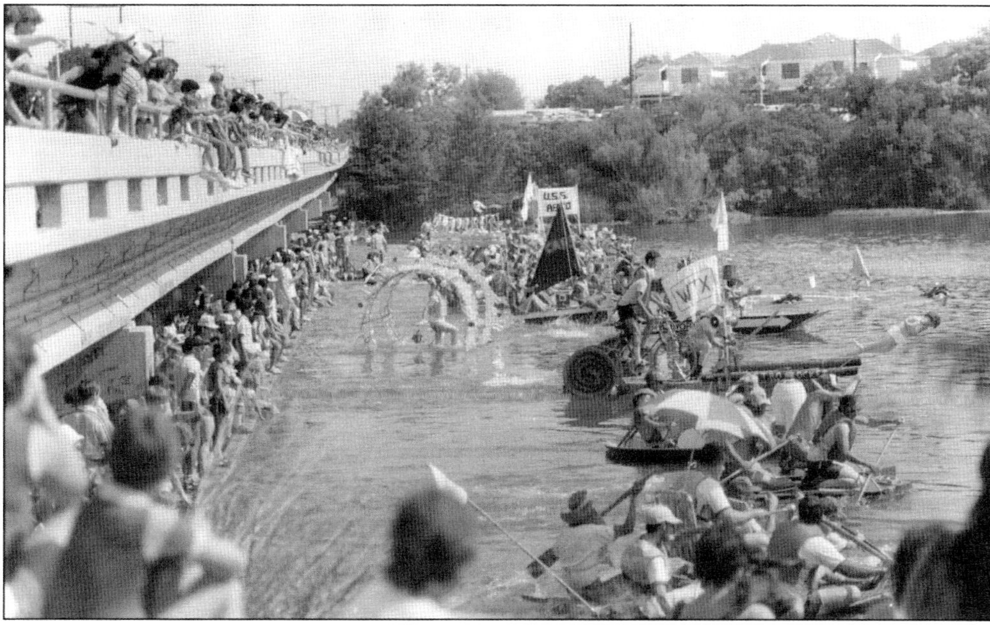

START OF RIVER RAFT RACES. Participants and spectators gather along the Concho River in June 1986 at the Bell Street Bridge, the official starting line for the annual River Raft Races. This was the beginning of the 14th annual Fiesta del Concho. (Courtesy of Downtown San Angelo.)

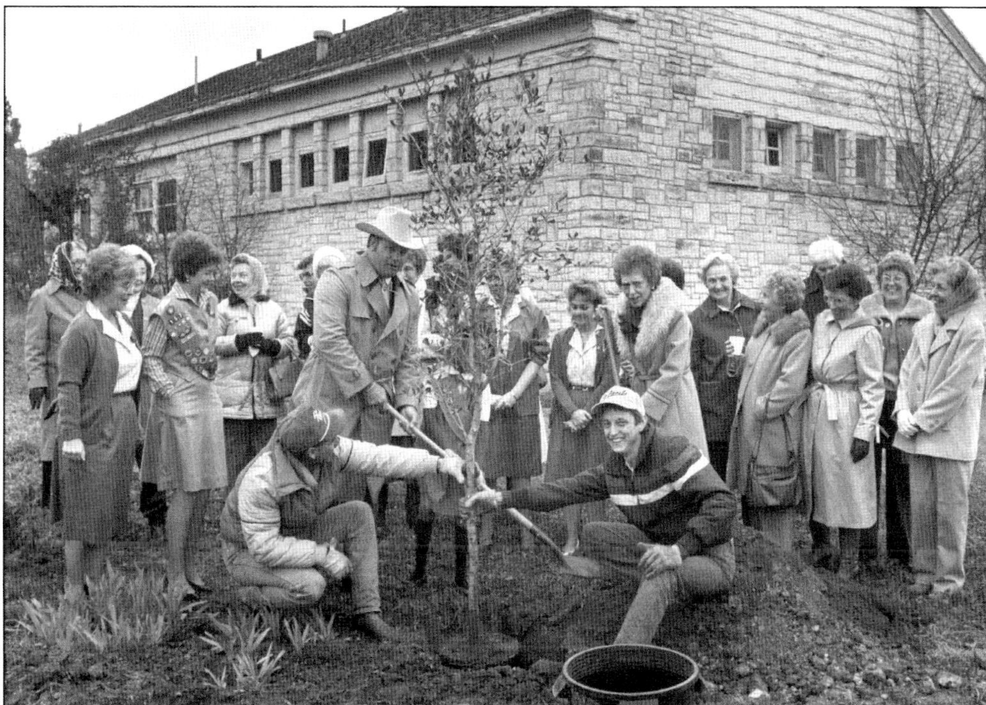

TREE PLANTING AT GIRL SCOUT HEADQUARTERS. Mayor Burt Terrill (at left with the shovel) gathers with Girl Scouts, Scout leaders, and friends to plant a tree on the grounds on the Girl Scout headquarters. (WTC.)

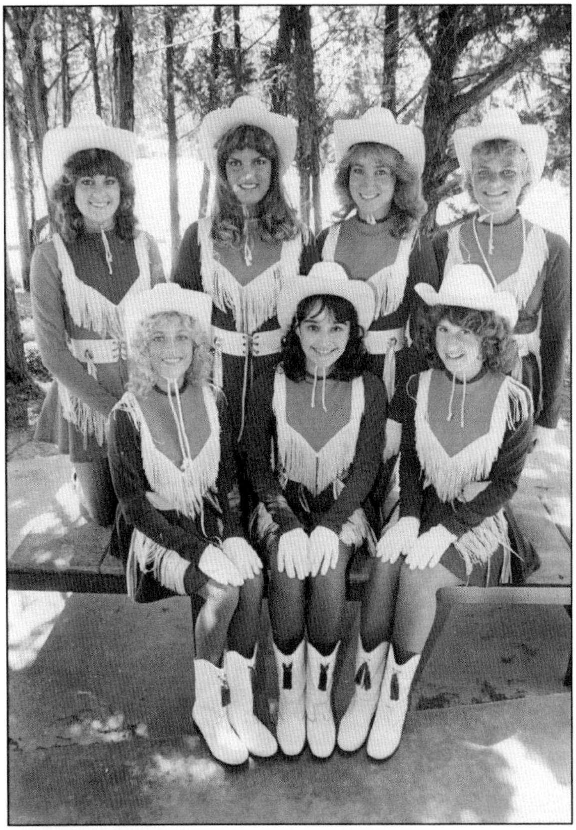

Tex-Anns. The Tex-Anns at the San Angelo Central High were created in 1957 to promote school spirit. The members perform and attend all football and basketball games and most other sporting events. Pictured in June 1983 are, from left to right, (first row) Cheryl Hones, second lieutenant; Hilda Perez, second lieutenant; and Paige Parry, second lieutenant; (second row) Patty Young, alternate; Whitney Smith, captain; Christy Bartlett; first lieutenant; and Margie West, captain. (WTC.)

Pecan Judging. Pecan judges, from left to right, E.O. "Dusty" Nevills, Arthur Barlemann Jr., and Olvier Werst check the quality of the entries at the December 1991 Tom Green County Pecan Show. In 1991, Texas lead the nation in the number of acres of pecan orchards at approximately 150,000. (WTC.)

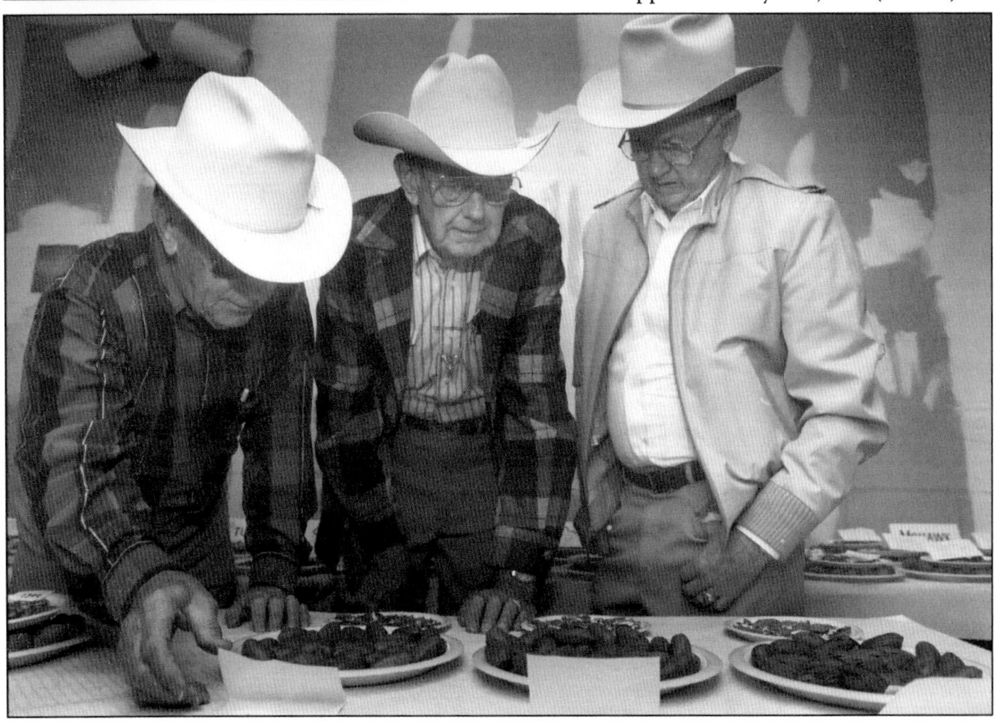

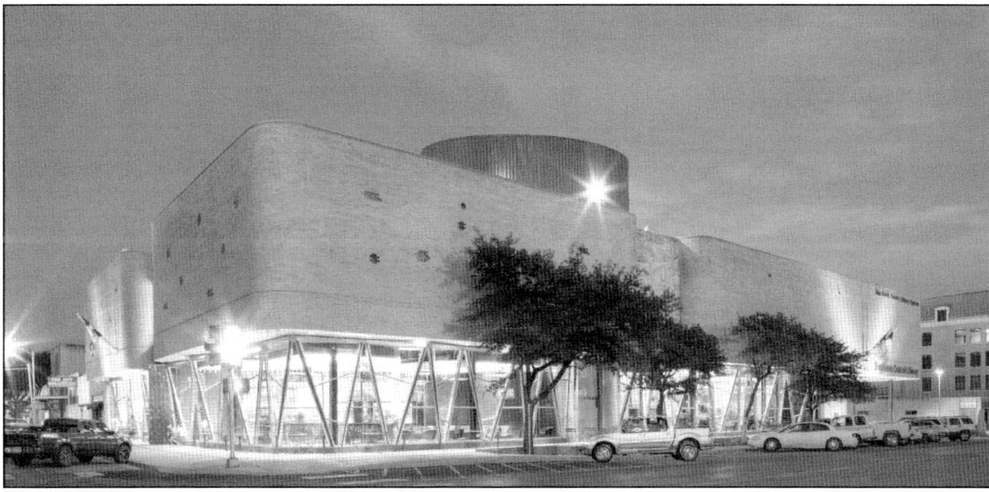

STEPHENS CENTRAL LIBRARY. When Hemphill-Wells department store closed, it left an important corner at Beauregard Avenue and Irving Street empty. The Tom Green County Library was then housed down the street in the old Sears Building. Ralph Hoelscher, county commissioner, came up with the idea of using the old Hemphill-Wells Building as a library. This proposal strongly supported revitalization of downtown, tripled the space for the library, and gave back the space the library was previously using to the county. After renovations, the library moved in and has been well received and well used, bringing more people downtown. (Courtesy of Downtown San Angelo, Inc.)

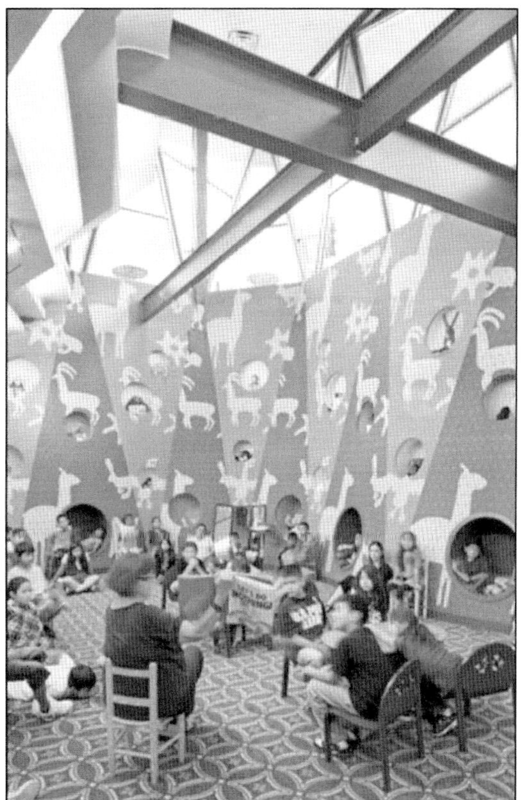

INTERIOR OF STEPHENS CENTRAL LIBRARY. Holzman Moss Bottino Architecture of NYT with associate architect Craig Kinney worked on this project. The use of bright colors on the walls, patterned carpet, natural light, and large circular features on the ceiling to represent lily pads give the interior a unique experience to the visitor. The library received the Texas Downtown Association 2011 President Award for the Best Rehabilitation and Renovation. The award recognized excellence in rehabilitation of the interior/exterior of an existing building. (Courtesy of Downtown San Angelo, Inc.)

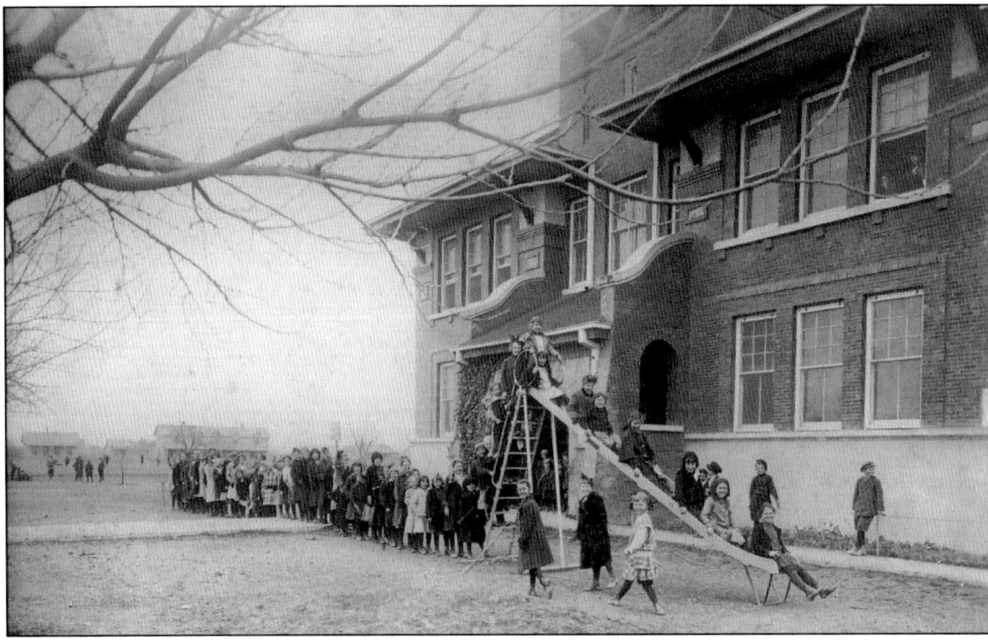

Fort Concho School. During the 1980s, the old Southern Ward School, built in 1905 on the parade grounds, was torn down, and a new school was constructed nearby. With the removal of the old school and other business buildings that had been constructed along South Oakes Street, the fort's original parade grounds was open for the first time in nearly a century. (FC.)

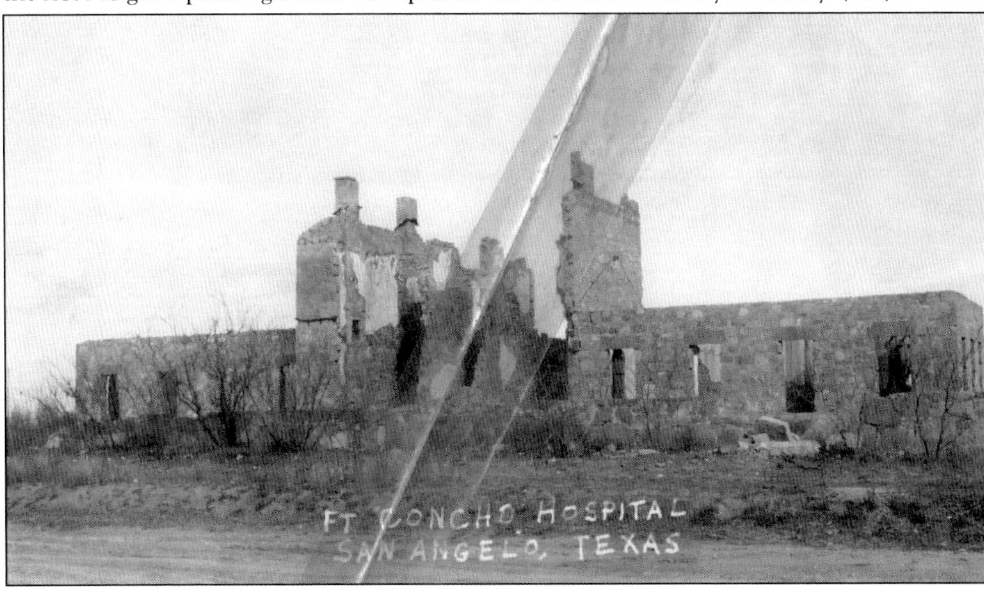

Fort Concho Hospital Ruins. One of the major elements missing from Fort Concho was the Post Hospital. Three projects were interwoven to accomplish this reconstruction: removal of the old ward school on the parade grounds, construction of a new elementary school at the fort's southeast corner, and reconstruction of the Post Hospital. Fortunately, the foundation stones and photographs were able to aid in the reconstruction that occurred in 1986–1987. The Post Hospital Building tells the story of medical care at the fort in the 1880s. The south ward of the reconstructed hospital is the library for the new elementary school. (FC.)

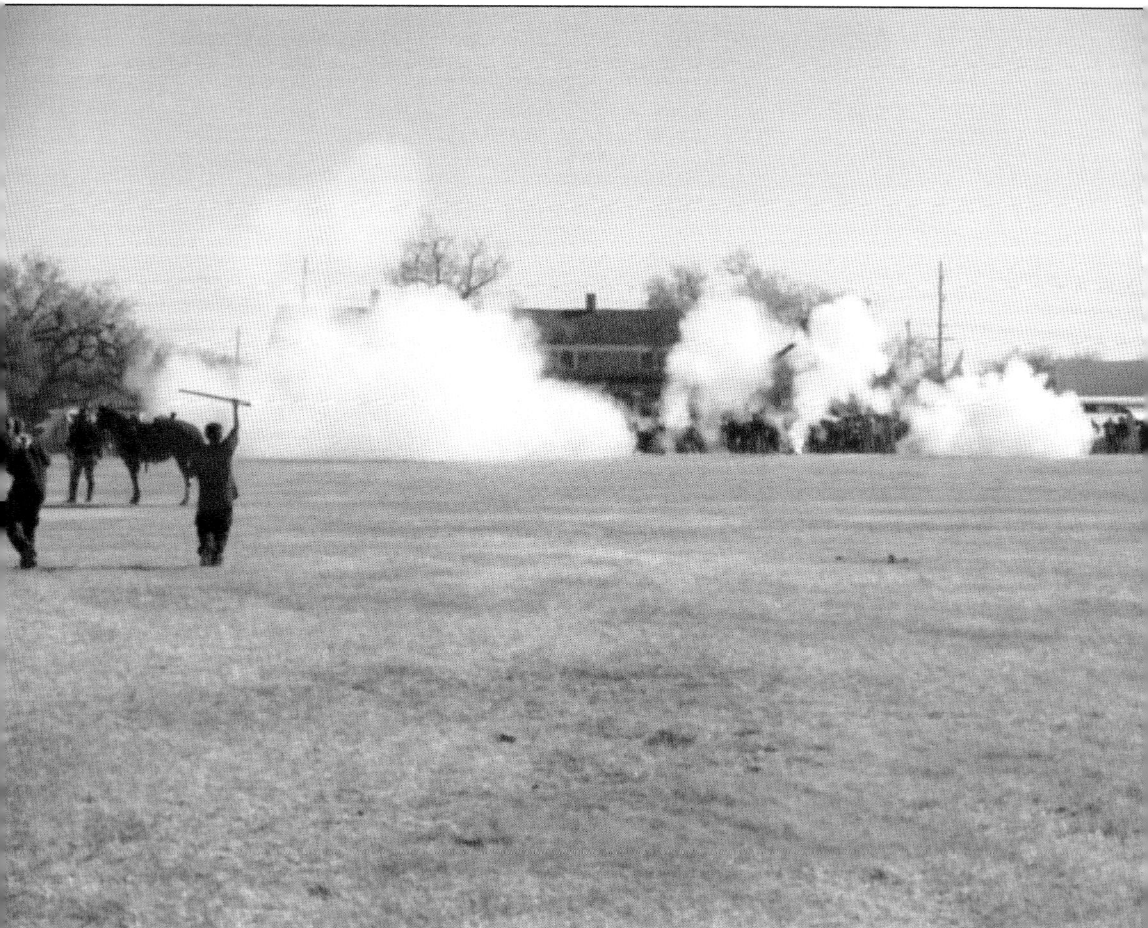

Fort Concho Activities. Cannon volleys can be seen in the distance in front of the headquarters at Fort Concho during Christmas. Other special events at the fort during the year include Buffalo Soldier Heritage Day, Texas Mesquite Arts Festival, Fort Concho Frontier Day, Armed Forces Day, Memorial Day, a quilt-and-needlework vendor market, Independence Day, National Cowboy Day, National Museum Day, Concho Valley Archaeology Fair, and night tours of Fort Concho. Fort Concho received the National Historic Landmark (NHL) designation in 1961. NHL is only given to nationally significant historic places by the secretary of the interior because they possess exceptional value or quality in illustrating or interpreting the heritage of the United States. Today, fewer than 2,500 historic places bear this designation. (WTC.)

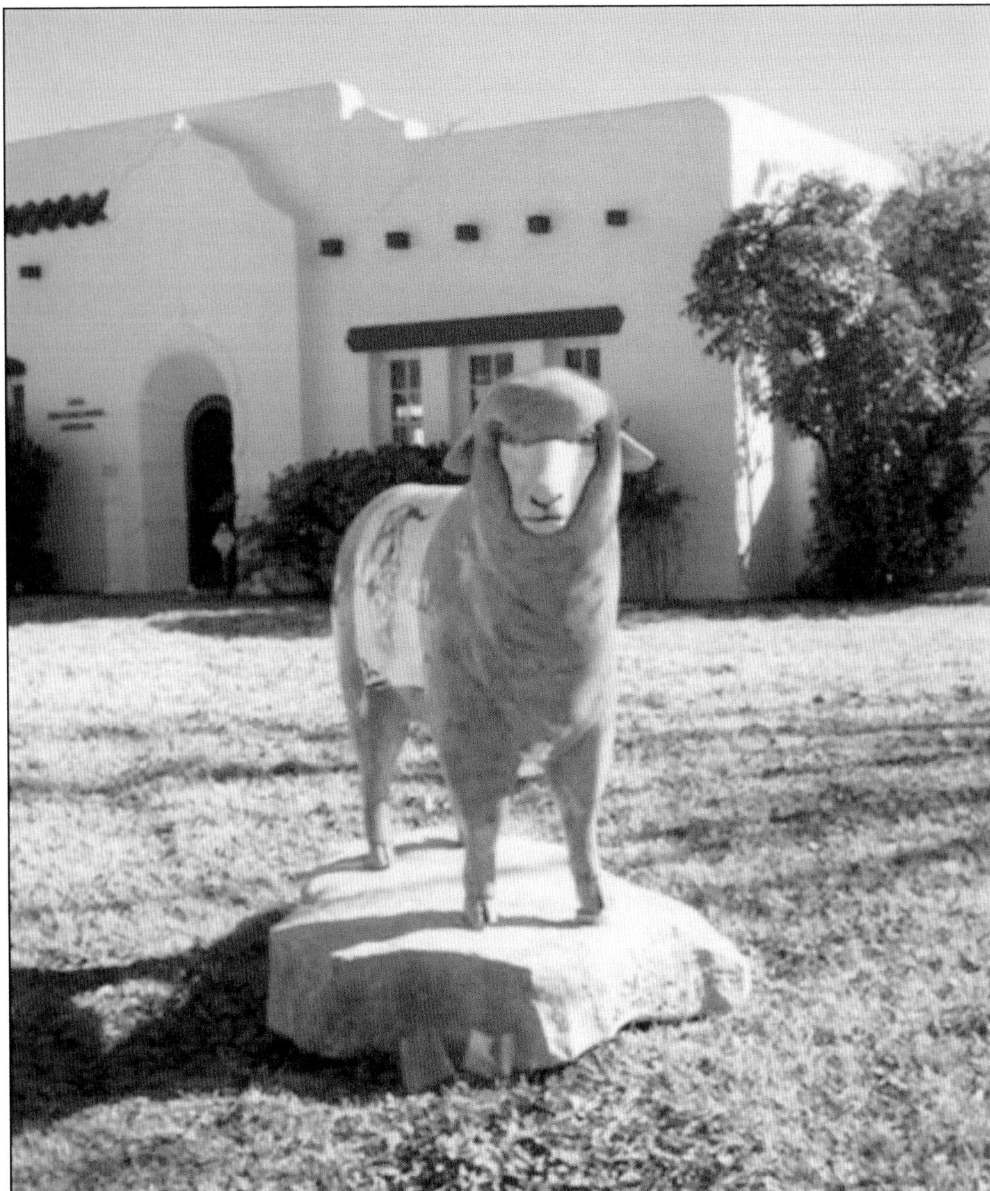

Wool Ewe in Front of TS&GRA Headquarters. Artist Raul Ruiz decorated "Wool Ewe Remember," located in the front yard of the Texas Sheep & Goat Raisers Association headquarters at 233 West Twohig Avenue. This is an example of the various San Angelo Spectacular Sheep scattered around the city. It makes a tongue-in-cheek reference the Miss Wool of America pageant that used to be hosted in San Angelo. (Courtesy of Downtown San Angelo, Inc.)

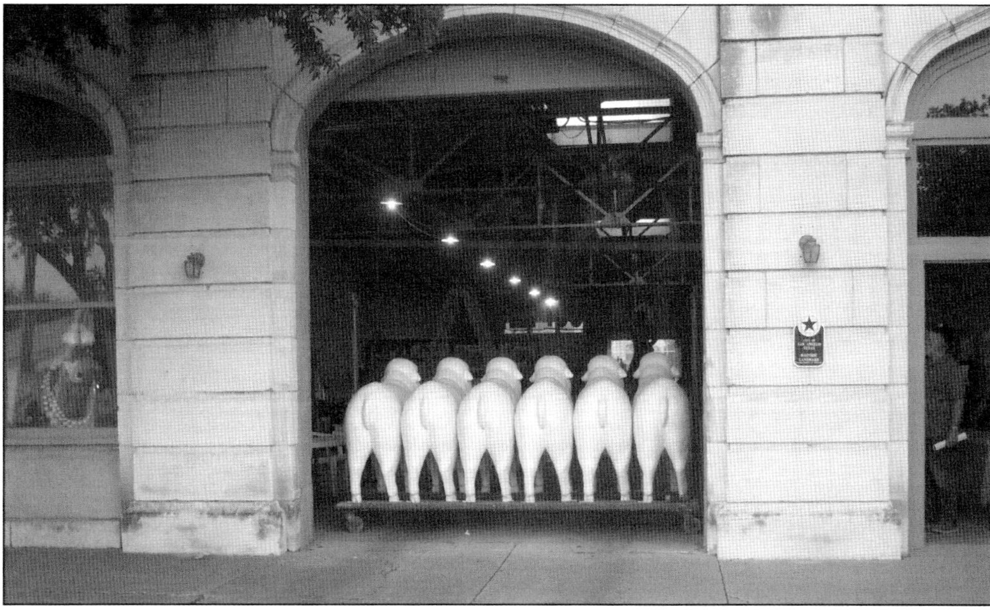

Sheep Ready to be Painted. Six sheep await painting and sponsors for the San Angelo Spectacular Sheep program in the historic Wendland Building at 30 West Concho Avenue. Art in Uncommon Places used the facility to create various art projects around town, including the mosaic vehicles. (Courtesy of Downtown San Angelo, Inc.)

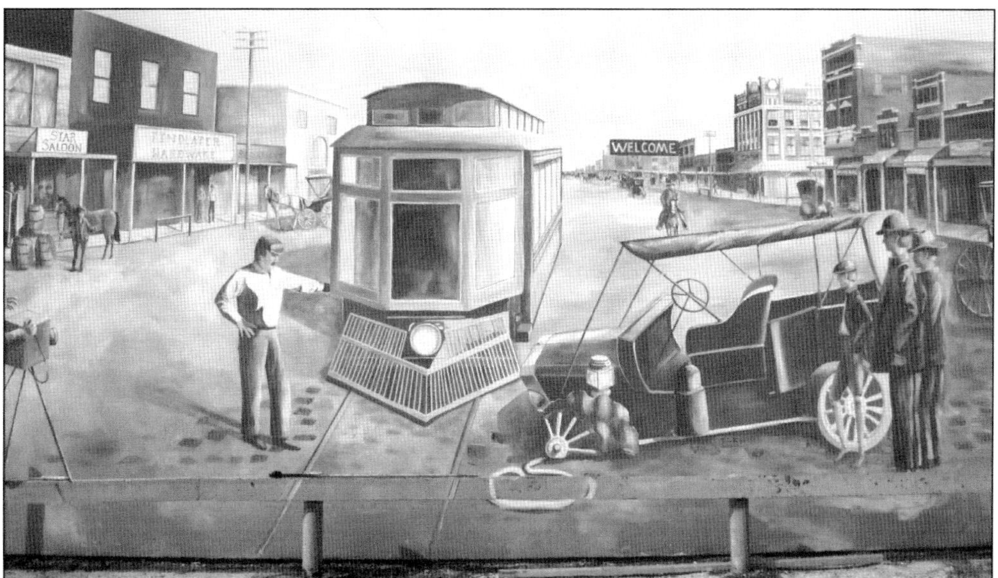

Historic Murals of San Angelo. A portion of the Chadbourne Street mural, depicting the street in 1908, is painted on a wall at the intersection of Concho Avenue and South Chadbourne Street. The Board of Directors of Historic Murals of San Angelo, Inc., has worked tirelessly since planning, and development began in 2002 for the first mural, titled "The History of Transportation in San Angelo." Many other murals have been painted on walls around the downtown area, and more are planned. (Photograph by author.)

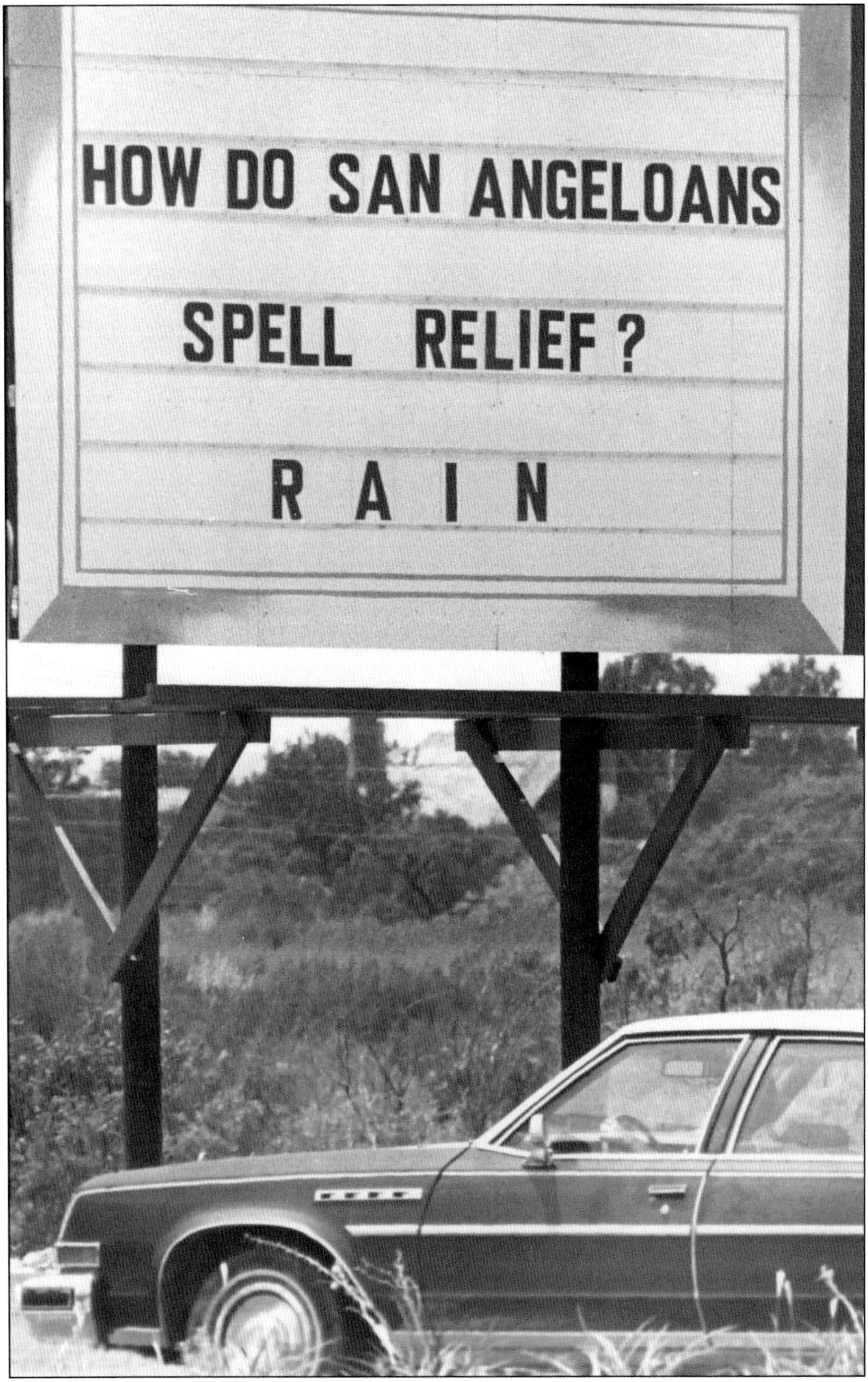

Drought. The drought of 1998–2000 spanned two consecutive winter seasons. The record for La Nina (and El Nino) events, dating back to 1950, shows that back-to-back occurrences of La Nina are not uncommon. (WTC.)

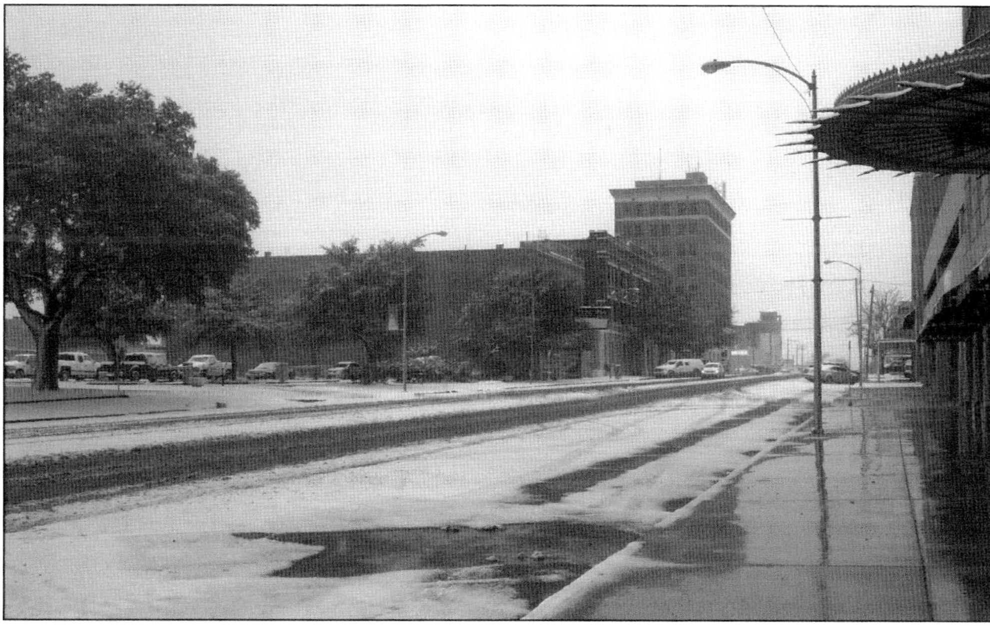

SNOW IN FRONT OF THE CACTUS HOTEL. A trace of snow was captured on film on February 23, 2010, in front of the Cactus Hotel, looking west on Twohig Avenue. The average seasonal snowfall in San Angelo is 2.9 inches. The greatest recorded snowfall of 13 inches occurred in February 1924 and January 1926. (WTC.)

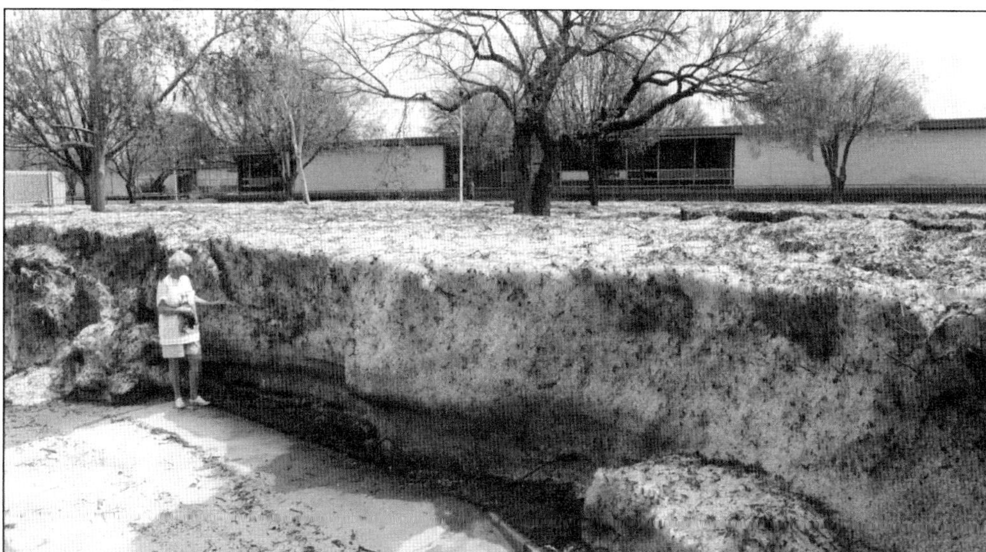

HAILSTORM. The Memorial Day storm on May 28, 1995, certainly is one of the worst storms to hit the San Angelo area since the tornado of 1953. A hailstorm in the early 1960s did damage to windows in the downtown area, but this was the closest to another tornado. Robert Bluthardt recalls working at his office at Fort Concho when the storm ran across the fort and behind Officers Row. The high winds, rain, and hail took their toll on trees, stripping leaves and breaking branches. The photograph was taken at least 10 days after the storm with Johnnie Webster standing by the hail, piled a block from Jim Bean's studio near Central High School. (Courtesy of Jim Bean, photographer.)

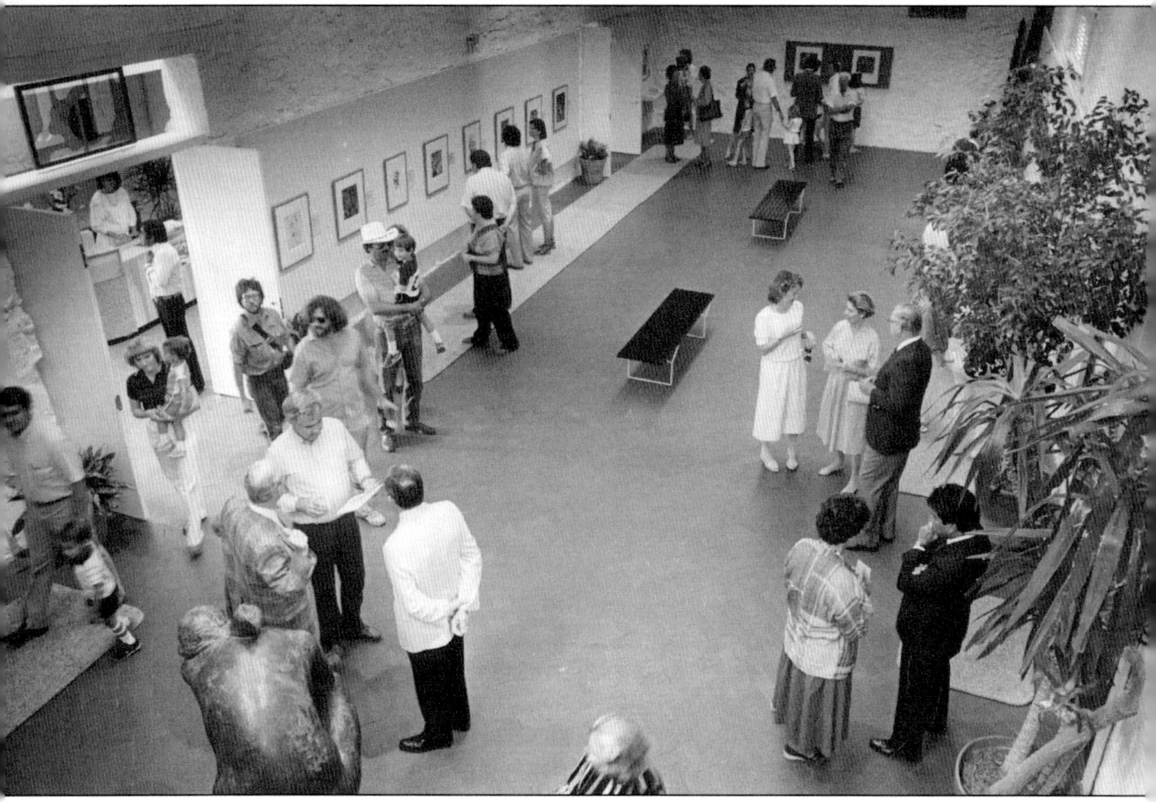

Opening of the First San Angelo Museum of Fine Arts. In 1981, the Concho Valley Fine Arts Council and the Fort Concho Museum Board joined together to plan for the San Angelo Museum of Fine Arts (SAMFA). Architect Bud Oglesby, formerly of San Angelo, designed the museum's first building, and funding came from a combination of public and private money, with the goal of $250,000 from private community contributions. Planning called for the museum to be located in Fort Concho's Quartermaster Storehouse and for it to retain the historical appearance of the exterior. However, its interior was modern and included a mezzanine, open appearance, and ample walls to exhibit art. The grand opening occurred on April 20, 1985. (WTC.)

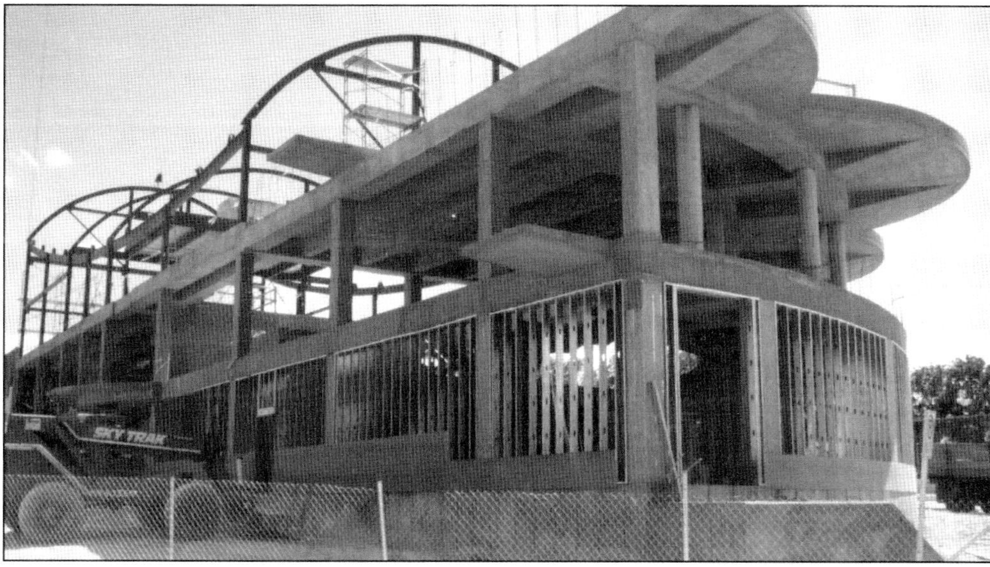

Construction of the Second SAMFA Building. Less than 15 years after the opening of the first SAMFA in an existing building at Fort Concho, San Angelo saw its new SAMFA museum constructed near the river. Hardy Holzman Pfeiffer Associates of New York City was selected to design this museum. The firm's approach was to develop a long, skinny, multicomponent building that ran perpendicular to the Concho River and responded to the sloping site. The hyperbolic, parabolic roof sags in the middle, causing local debate on its inspiration. Some say it is the shape of a saddle; others say a prairie schooner. (Courtesy of San Angelo Museum of Fine Arts.)

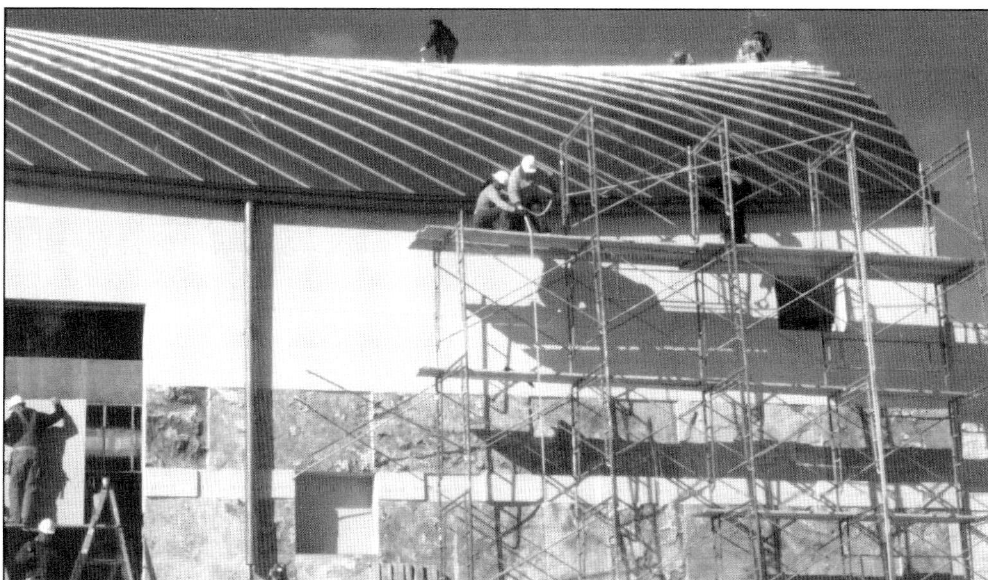

SAMFA Construction. The roof is made out of tongue-and-groove wood supported by glue-laminated wood beams. Natural-faced limestone from a quarry in Garden City was used in the exterior as well as the interior. Mesquite blocks of wood were used as flooring, and exposed clay tiles were installed for the walls. On top of the cantilevered curved roof, "Art Museum," spelled in large, neon, individual, metal-channeled letters, announces the entrance. (Courtesy of San Angelo Museum of Fine Arts.)

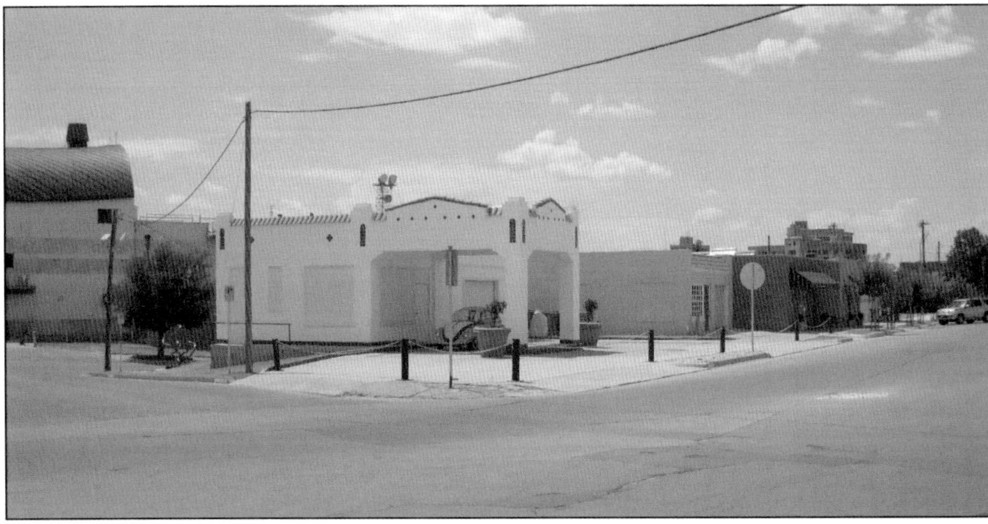

San Angelo Museum Fine Arts Oakes Street Properties. Once the San Angelo Museum of Fine Arts was completed, some opinions were expressed to remove the entire block of empty historically commercial buildings along the west side of South Oakes Street to improve views of the museum. Museum director Howard Taylor felt that the buildings had potential for art-related activities, purchased them in 2003, and worked to preserve them. Starting from the service station at 433 South Oakes Street with "Art Bug" by Melodie McDonald, which is now located on the banks of the Concho River, and going north are COOP Gallery, an artist's studio, an artist's apartment, a vacant lot, and Upper Colorado River Authority Building. (Photograph by author.)

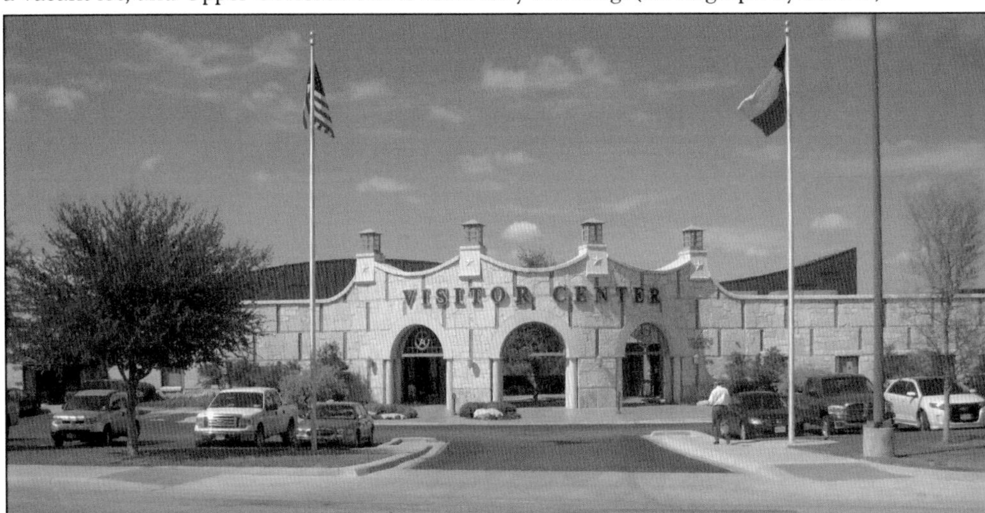

Visitor Center. The San Angelo Visitor Center, completed in 2003 and located on the banks of the Concho River between US Highway 87 North and South, was designed by Craig Kinney of local firm Chakos, Zentner & Marcum, architects. Many building materials from the region were used, including limestone and Austin stone for the walls, mesquite wood for the flooring and benches, and cedar for the hanging trellis. The western half of the building houses the San Angelo Health Foundation, and the eastern half houses the San Angelo Chamber of Commerce and the San Angelo Convention and Visitors Bureau. With the move of the visitors bureau from the second floor of the conference center to the present location, a 1,300-percent increase in visitors has occurred. (Photograph by author.)

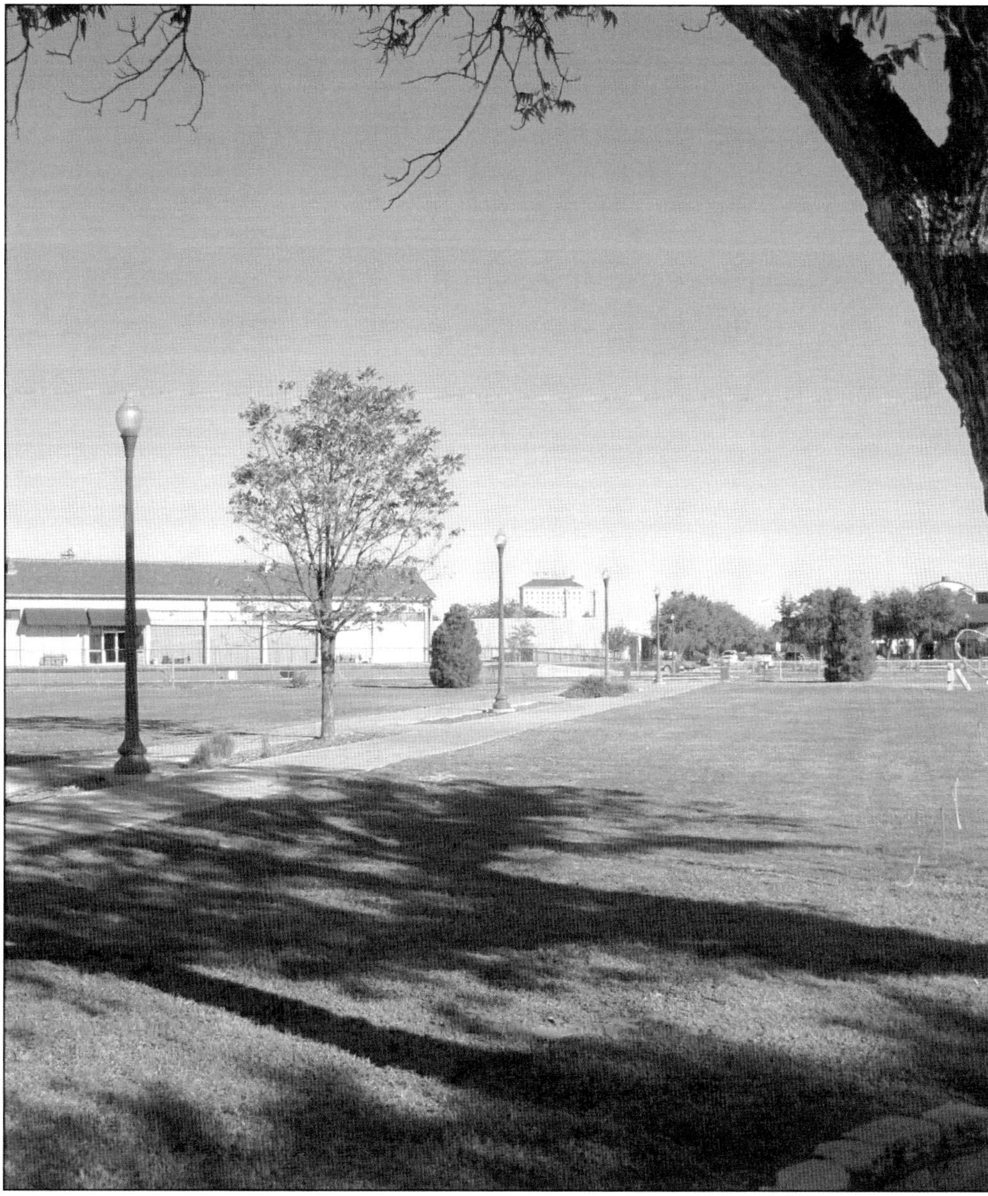

El Paseo de Santa Angela. Part of the recommendations from the February 7–10, 1992, Regional Urban Design Assistance team (R/UDAT) was the construction of El Paseo de Santa Angela Park. The focus of the plan included the historic core on both sides of the river. The area between the Santa Fe depot/warehouse and Fort Concho was developed with twin pavilions, open grass areas, tiered landscaped pedestrian mall leading to the RiverStage, walkways between the historic elements, a covered farmers' market, and parking lots. Twenty years after the R/UDAT report, a sum of $70 million was invested in historic preservation, new construction, and improved infrastructure, all of which has been accomplished on both sides of the river. In 2009, a 200-acre San Angelo Historic City Center Cultural District designation was proposed to the Texas Commission on the Arts from roughly West Washington Drive to the San Angelo Visitor Center, the Concho River, and Rush Street. The cultural district boosts urban revitalization in many ways. (Photograph by author.)

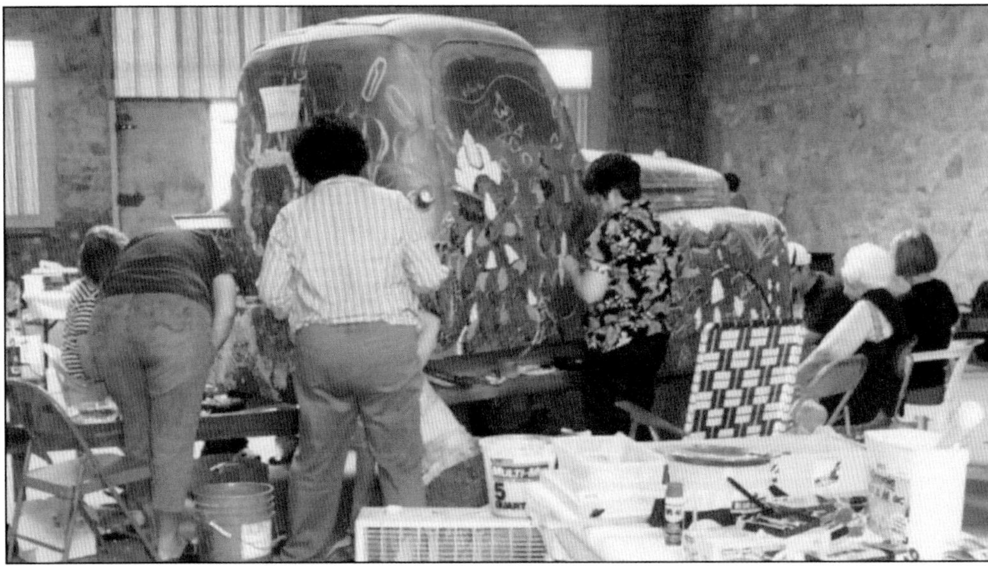

Mosaic Pickup in Progress. Art in Uncommon Places worked for six years to complete the mosaic car sculpture project, which is now located on the banks of the Concho River. With the help of hundreds of community volunteers, it took over 1,000 hours to cover one pickup with mosaics. The original concept was to showcase local artists developing art from recycled materials, such as automobile parts and tiles, to be used as functional pieces in the community. The use of broken tiles hearkens back to when tile-manufacturer Monarch Tile operated in San Angelo from 1946 until 1989 and initially sponsored the National Ceramics Competition for the San Angelo Museum of Fine Arts. Brenda and Kenneth Gunter donated the space in the Wendland Building to work on many art projects. (Courtesy of Downtown San Angelo, Inc.)

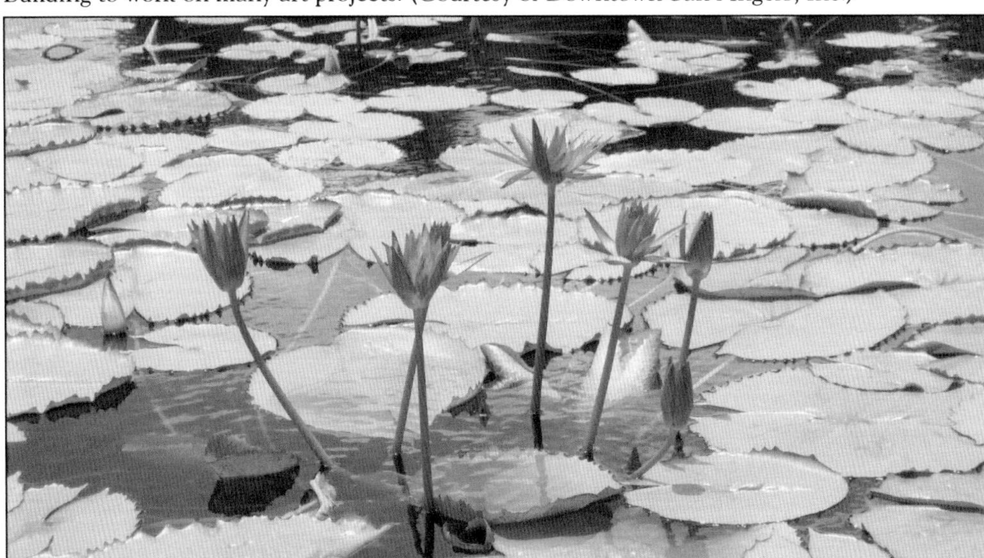

International Water Lily Garden. San Angelo native Ken Landon started growing a variety of lilies in the 1960s. His collection grew in number and reputation as a unique natural resource. Ken is only able to display about one percent of this collection each year at the Civic League Park. From mid-May through October, with the primary month being August, many people visit the ponds, built in 2005 by the city park department. (Photograph by author.)

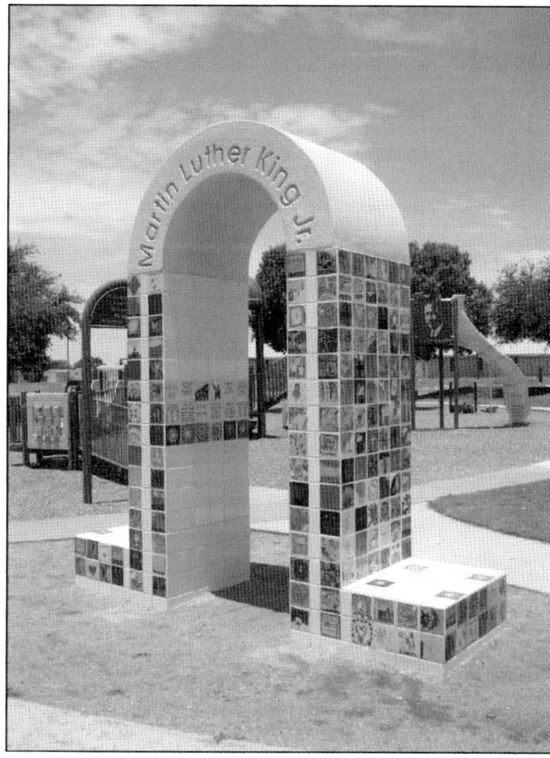

Martin Luther King Jr. Monument. Craig and Sally Meyers were in Atlanta, Georgia, for the Martin Luther King Jr. observance and noticed a monument in front of the Martin Luther King Jr. Elementary School. Upon their return, they talked to Roger Allen, director of the Chicken Farm Art Center, about designing a monument for the Martin Luther King Jr. Memorial Park. Roger designed an arch-shaped monument. Many individuals, such as Jack Meek, architect; John and Darlene Williams of Trinity Ceramic Supply; Stacy Carroll, tile setting; Swain Plastering; and other volunteers, helped to construct the monument. The art students of Ellen Lassiter at Fannin and Reagan Elementary Schools decorated the tiles. It was dedicated on June 19, 2008, as part of the Juneteenth celebration. (Photograph by author.)

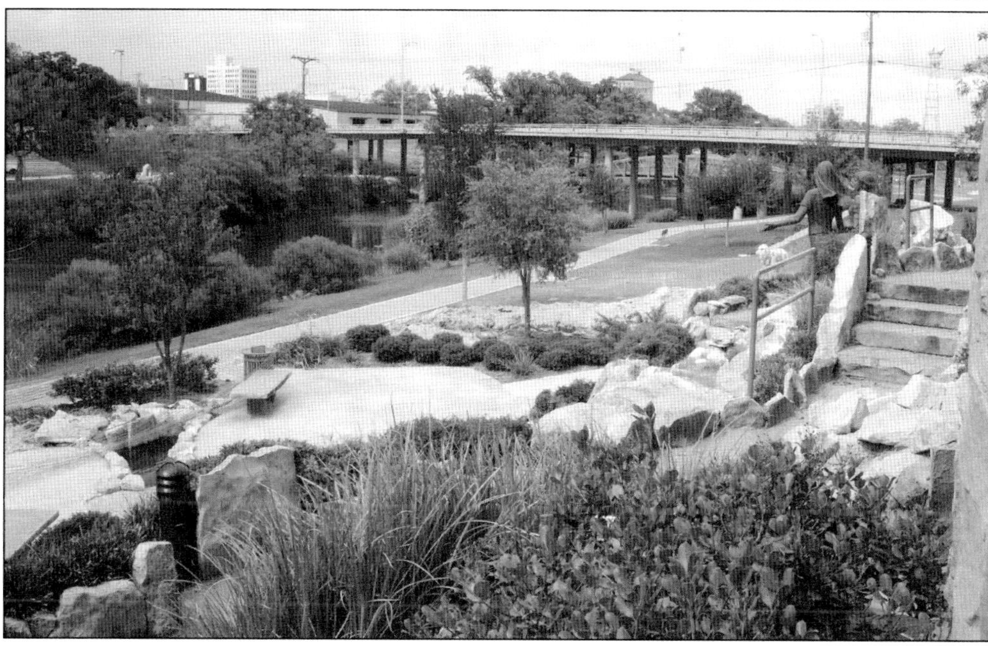

River Landscape. The Concho River and Trails Improvement project was created from the half-cent sales tax to renovate and revive the river. Work included bank stabilization, the design of new trails and renovation of existing trails, and the design of appropriate features/amenities along the trail that would enhance the river experience for all, including the downtown core area. (Courtesy of Downtown San Angelo, Inc.)

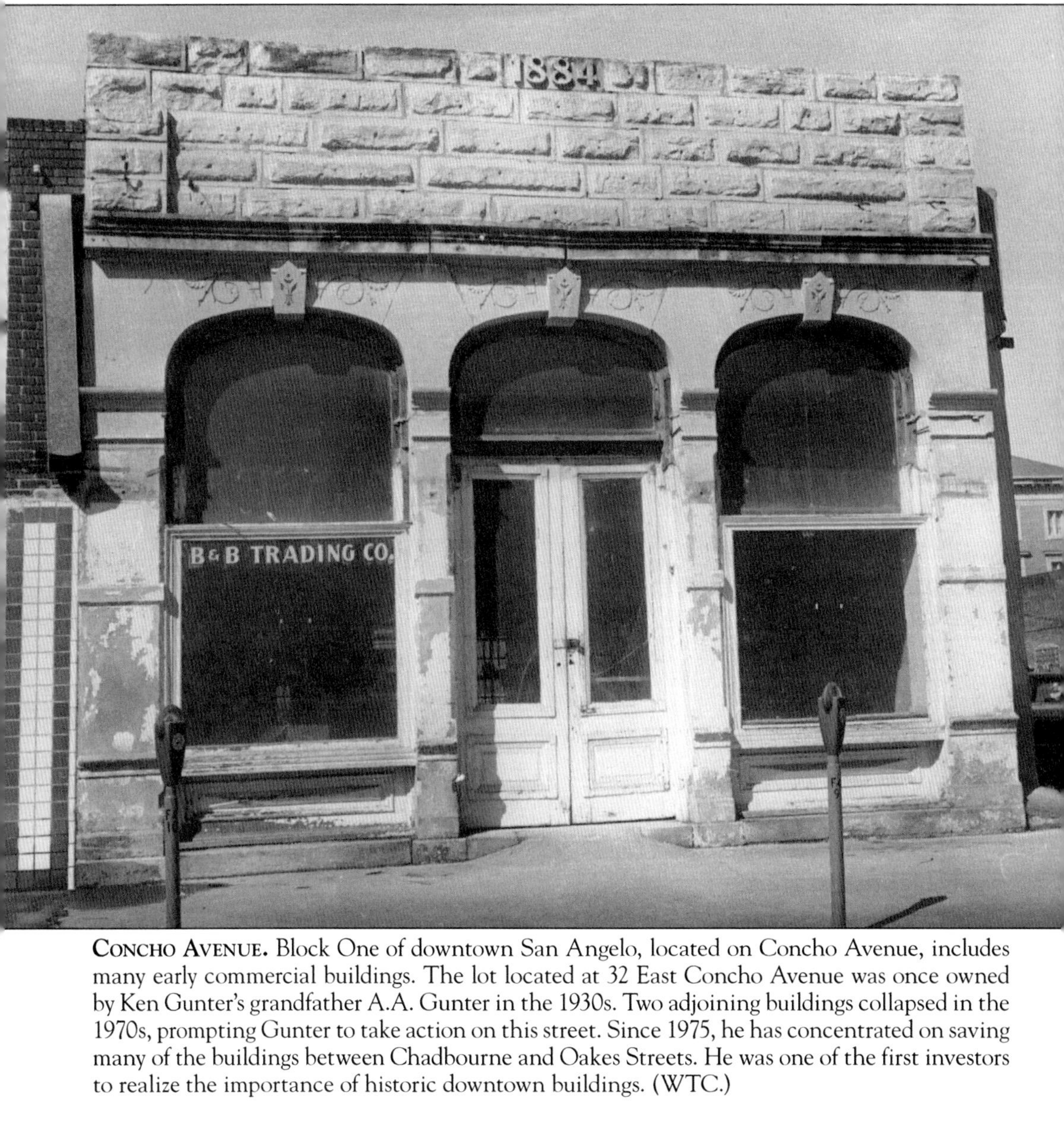

Concho Avenue. Block One of downtown San Angelo, located on Concho Avenue, includes many early commercial buildings. The lot located at 32 East Concho Avenue was once owned by Ken Gunter's grandfather A.A. Gunter in the 1930s. Two adjoining buildings collapsed in the 1970s, prompting Gunter to take action on this street. Since 1975, he has concentrated on saving many of the buildings between Chadbourne and Oakes Streets. He was one of the first investors to realize the importance of historic downtown buildings. (WTC.)

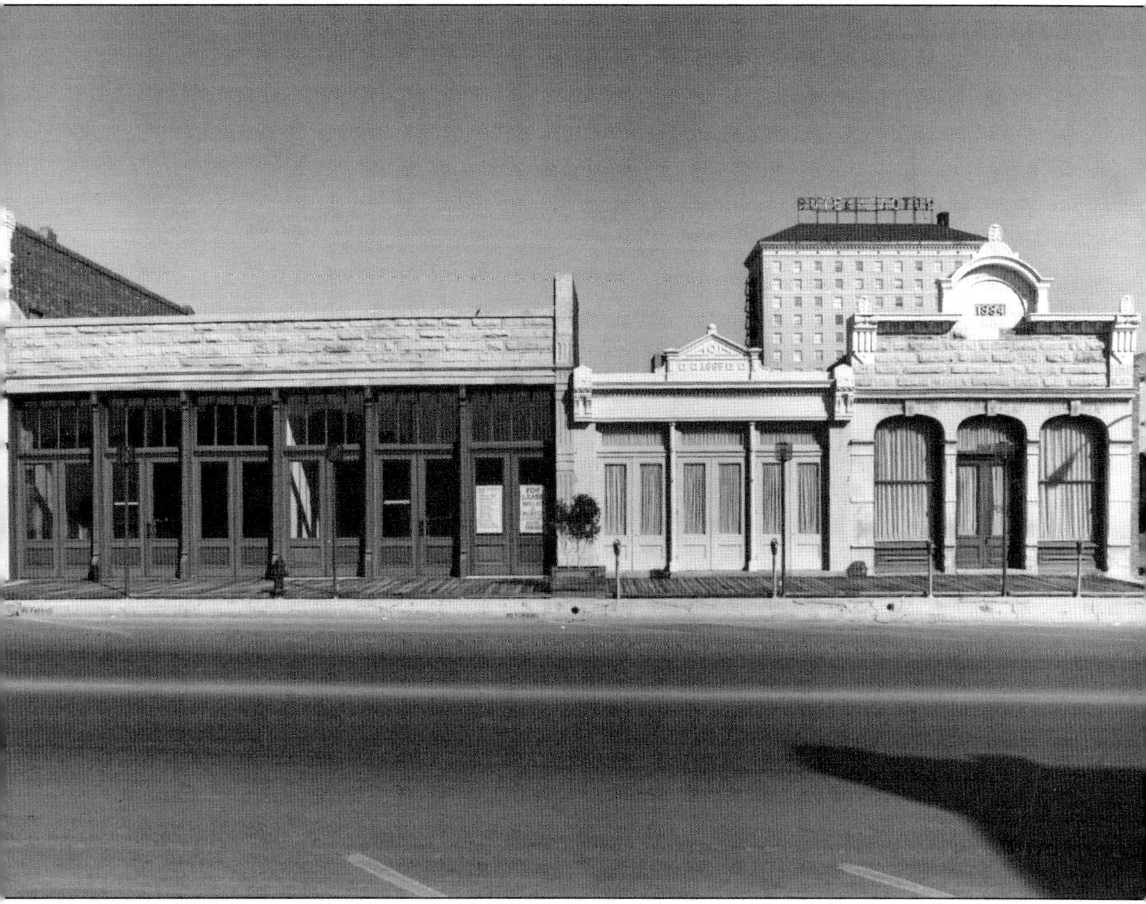

Concho Avenue. Brenda Gunter, whose husband bought and saved Concho Avenue, took up the historic preservation calling in 1998 and became owner of Miss Hattie's Café and Saloon. An arts advocate and president of Downtown San Angelo, Inc., Brenda has also been the force behind the Main Street Program, Art Walk, the Sheep Spectacular program, and other downtown events. As a result, the city has been designated a Preserve America Community, one of America's Dozen Distinctive Destinations by the National Trust for Historic Preservation, and First Lady's Texas Treasures Award. (WTC.)

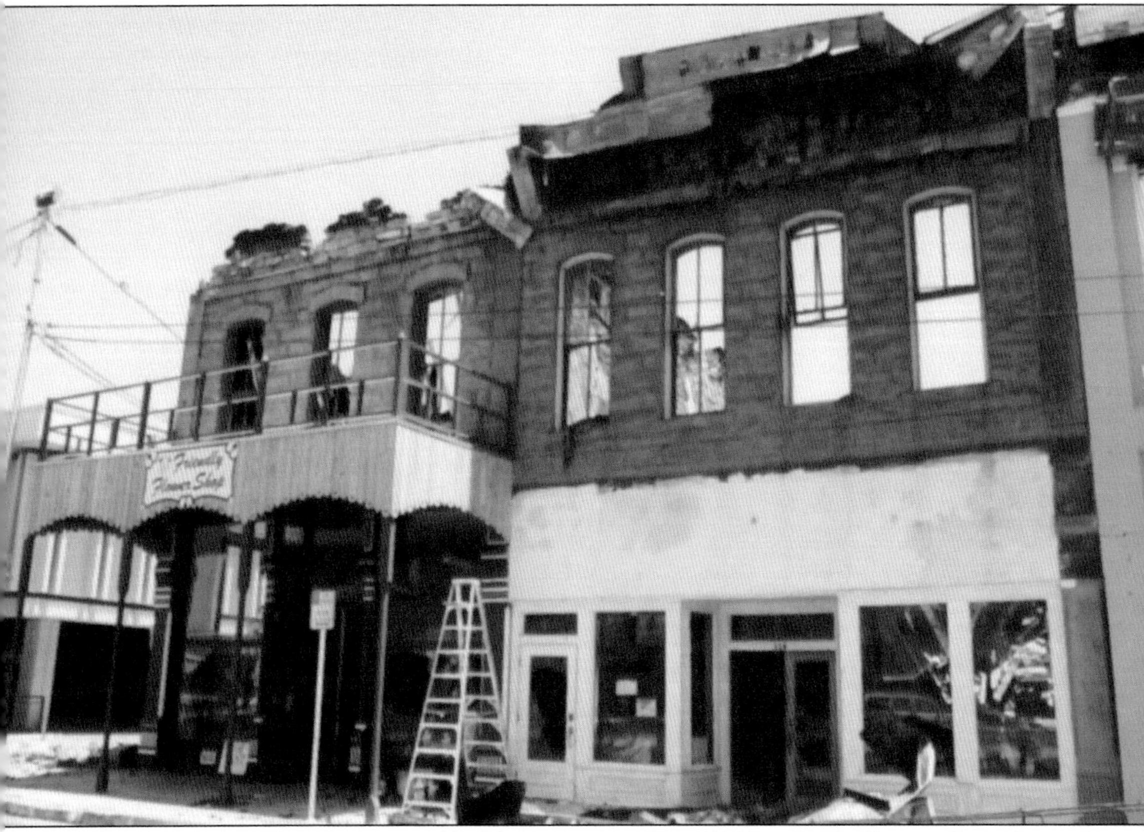

THREE SISTERS. Three commercial buildings at 114, 116, and 118 South Chadbourne Street burned on July 21, 1999. These were dubbed the "three sisters," the Harris, J.J. Rackley, and S.A. Runkles Buildings. At the time of the fire, all three buildings had been restored in the last decade and had active businesses that were forced to move to other locations. There was great concern that all three buildings would be demolished. Great effort by the owners and the preservation community resulted in the buildings being saved. (WTC.)

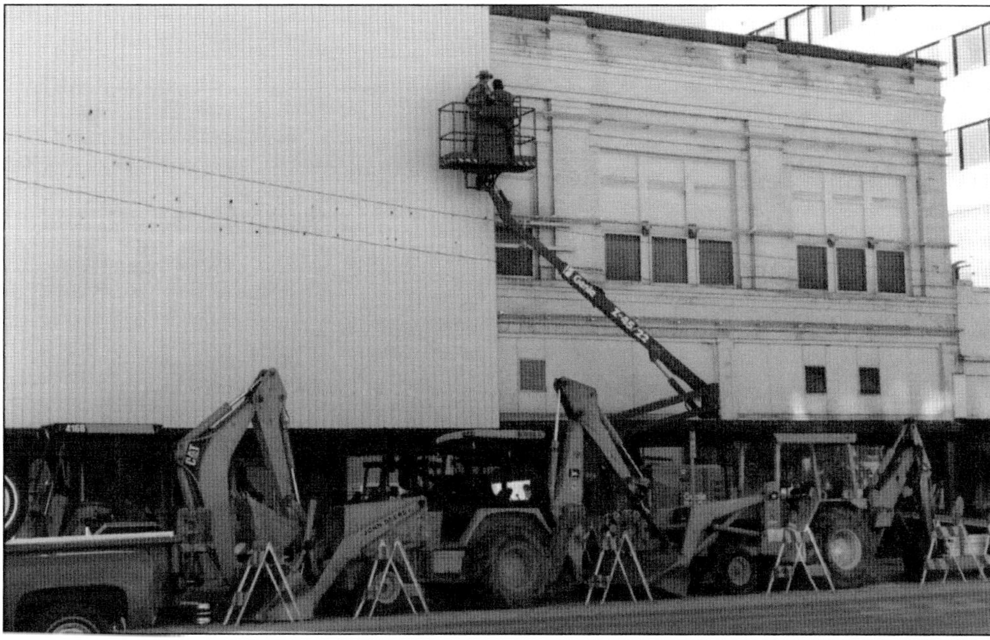

MYERS DRUG. Dale and Joyce Chadwick owned and operated Myers Drug at 22 South Chadbourne Street. When they eventually needed more space, they looked across the street at the old J.C. Penney Building, vacant since 1980. In 1994, the Chadwicks purchased the building for the corner location and not necessarily to preserve the building. Local preservationists Barbara Hesse and Margaret Mallard visited with Dale and told him about the history of the building, including the fact that Oscar Ruffini designed it. The new owners faced many unforeseen challenges, such as removing paint from the brick without permanently damaging the surface, but in the end, they preserved the building and contributed to the historic streetscape, encouraging others to take on similar preservation projects. (Courtesy of Dale Chadwick.)

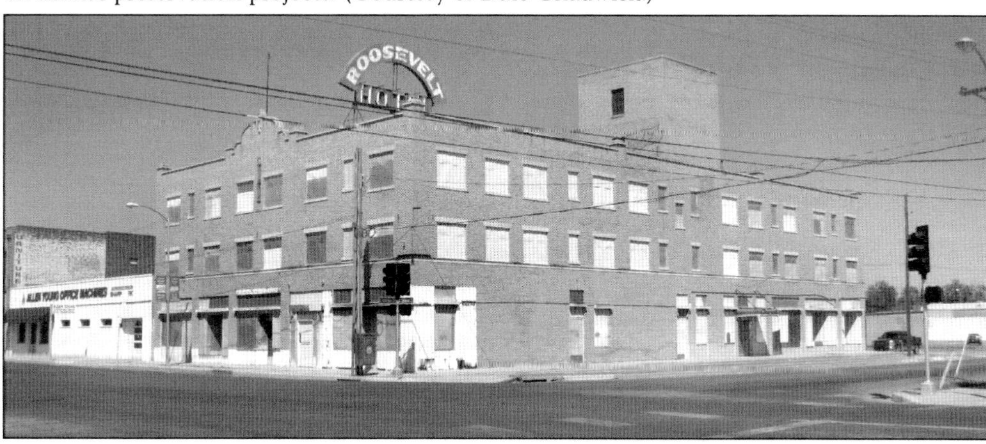

ROOSEVELT HOTEL. The Rainbow Hotel, built in 1929, was located at 50 North Chadbourne Street. The hotel was billed as a simple lodging place for travelers and businessmen. It closed during the Depression, but under the new name Roosevelt Hotel, it reopened after some remodeling. The owner closed the place on July 5, 1995. Shannon Hospital purchased the building for storage. Concern grew that the building might be demolished, thus replacing a historic building with a vacant corner lot. In July 2012, Shannon Hospital agreed to give the building to Downtown San Angelo, Inc., to find a buyer and preserve the building. (WTC.)

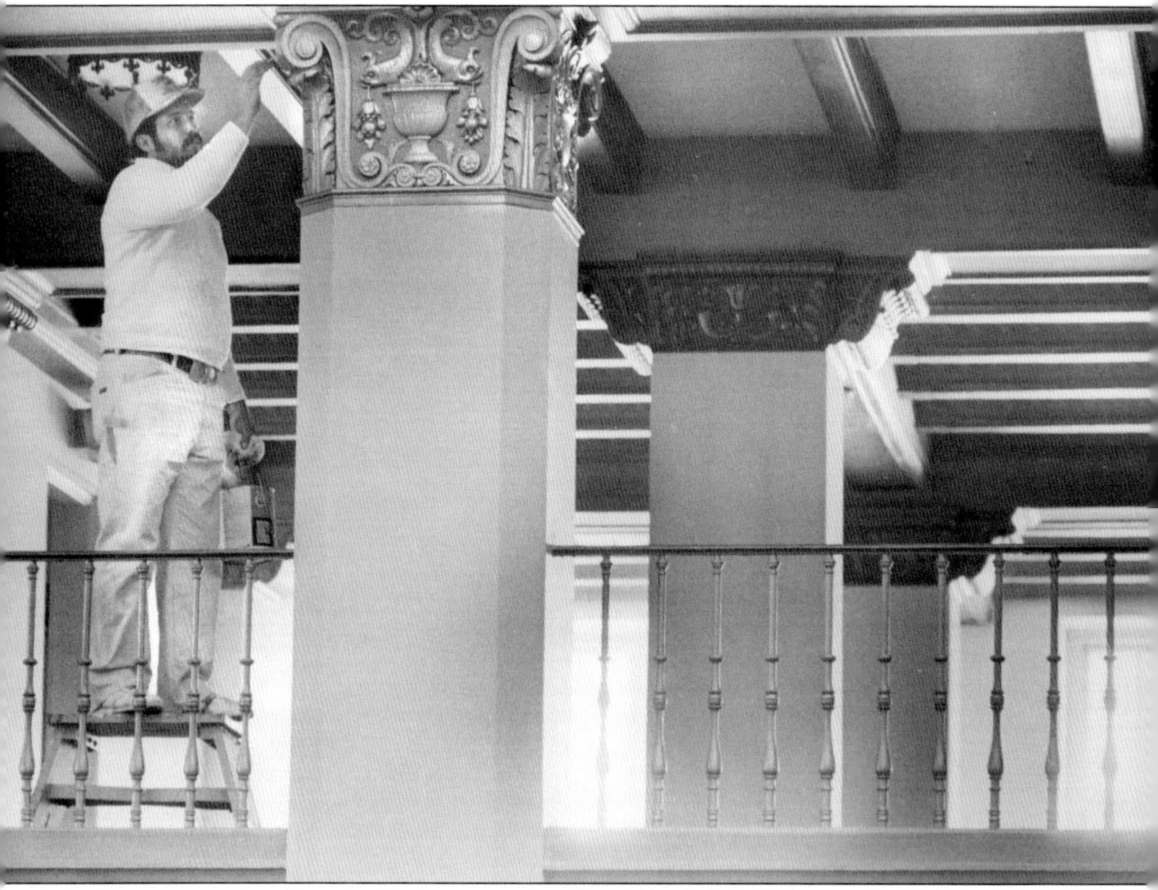

Restoration of Cactus Hotel. Conrad Hilton's fourth hotel, the 14-story Cactus Hotel was constructed in 1929, with extravagant decorations and ballroom. Work in the 1980s resulted in the ballroom and lobby being restored. However, in the early 1990s, its contents were sold at a public auction. Lee Pfluger assumed responsibility for the building in 1992. He felt this building could be one of the catalysts that would bring the historic downtown back to life again. The Historic City Center Project, Inc., headed by Pfluger, now owns the Cactus Hotel. After nearly two decades, the process of restoring the building is close to completion. (WTC.)

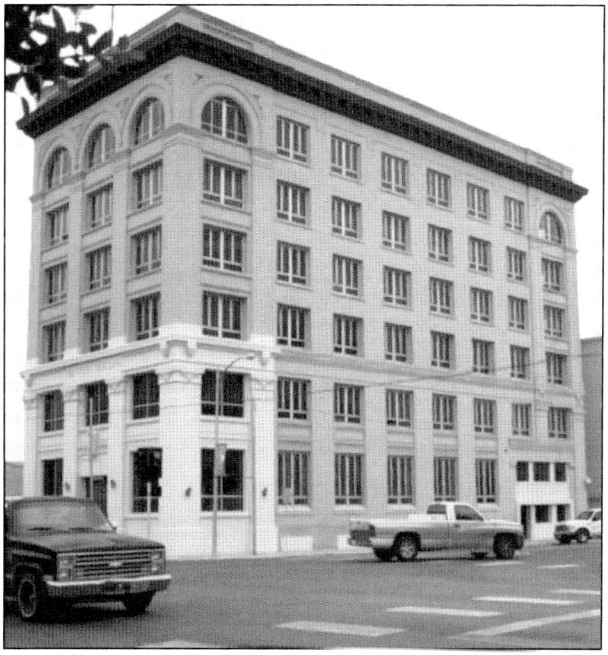

Trust Building. Originally called the Trust Building and known mainly from the name on the side of the building, Central National Bank dates to around 1900. Unfortunate remodeling in the 1960s to make the building look modern, at least at the street level, permanently damaged the stone surrounding the entrance and resulted in the replacement of all the windows. Kirby Hartman had been looking at the vacant building for 15 years and was able to purchase it in 1998. He restored the damaged granite, returning it to the original appearance in form but not material. This six-story building is located at South Chadbourne Street and Beauregard Avenue. (WTC.)

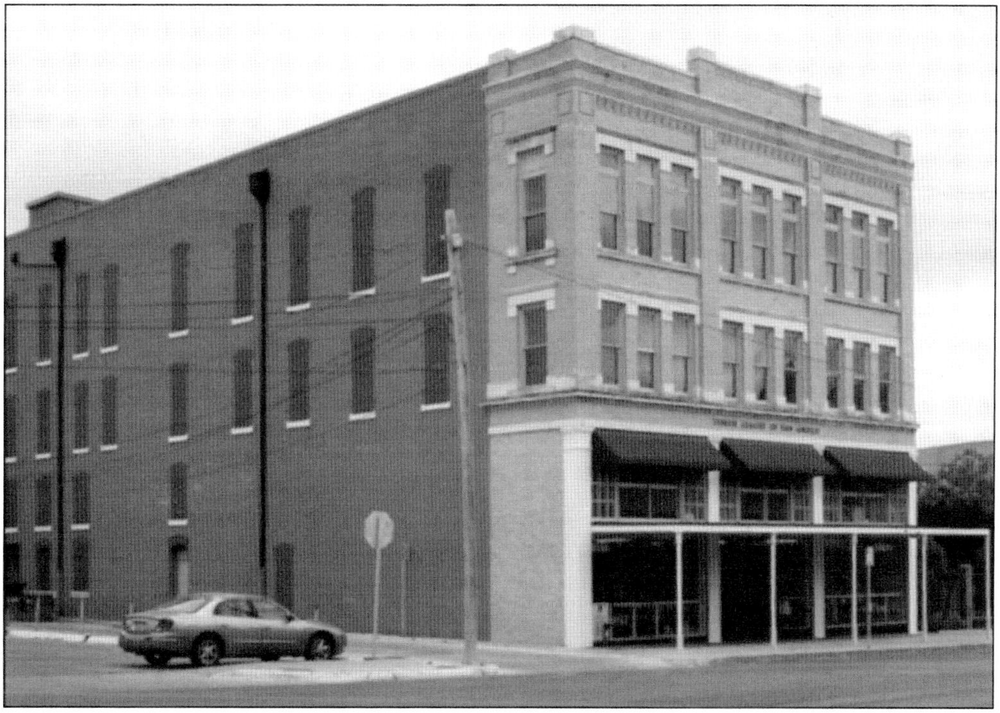

Junior League Building. The junior league took on the challenge in 1999 of restoring the W.E. Newton Building, later known as the Robert Massie Furniture Store, located at 12 East Twohig Avenue. The first phase of the project included work on the basement and the first and second floors of the building, originally designed by Oscar Ruffini to be used for the Sacks Thrift Store and offices. The league has been involved over the years in many historic preservation projects in San Angelo, and this project proved its continued commitment. (WTC.)

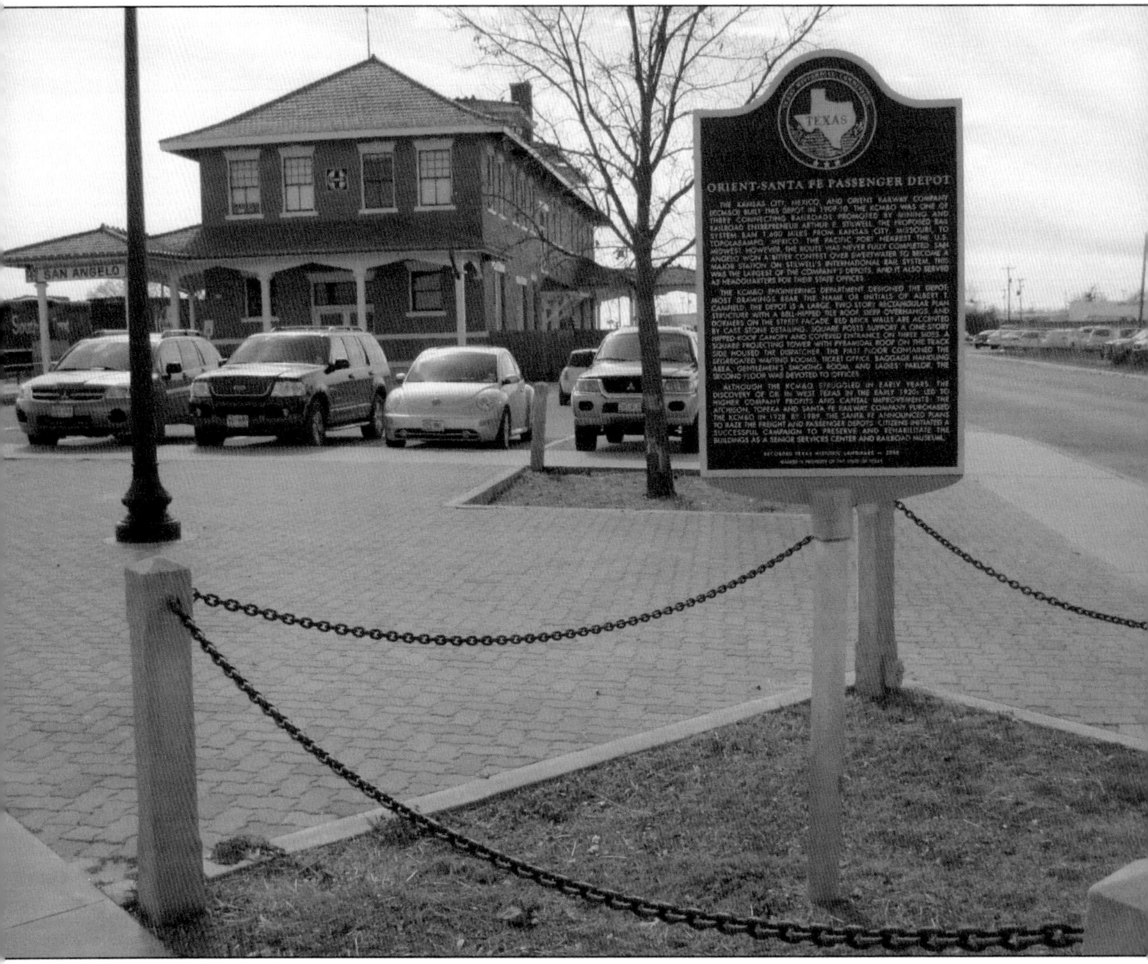

ORIENT–SANTA FE DEPOT. The Kansas City, Mexico & Orient Railroad depot was built in 1909. The rival line's station, the Santa Fe depot, was demolished in 1947, and the Orient roundhouse was also gone. The passenger and freight depots were saved by concerned citizens. A group of citizens joined together to save the buildings from demolition, and formed a nonprofit preservation organization, the Historic Orient–Santa Fe Depot, Inc., in partnership with the City of San Angelo. The passenger depot was initially restored as a transportation center but is presently used as a railroad museum. The city restored the exterior of the freight depot, located across the street from the passenger depot. It serves today as the offices of the San Angelo Parks and Recreation Department and community's senior citizen center. (Photograph by author.)

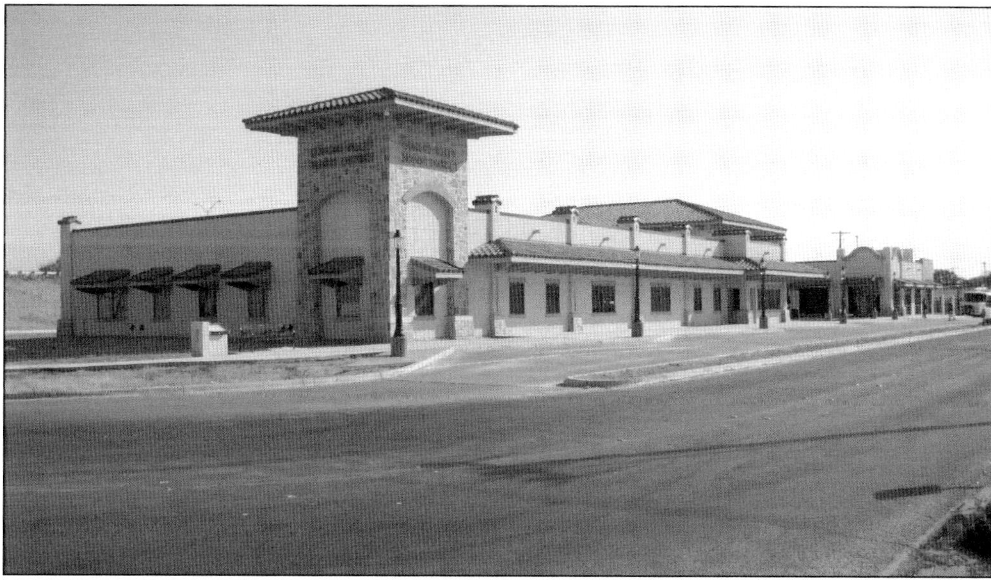

New Transportation Center. The new San Angelo Transportation Center is located across the street from the site of the historic Santa Fe depot on Chadbourne Street. The center was officially dedicated in May 2012. It was designed by Schwarz-Hanson, architects, of Fort Worth, and its look is similar to that of the historic depot demolished in 1947. Transit-oriented development is an important element to the success of the downtown and to the transportation of people around the community without the aid of cars. (Photograph by author.)

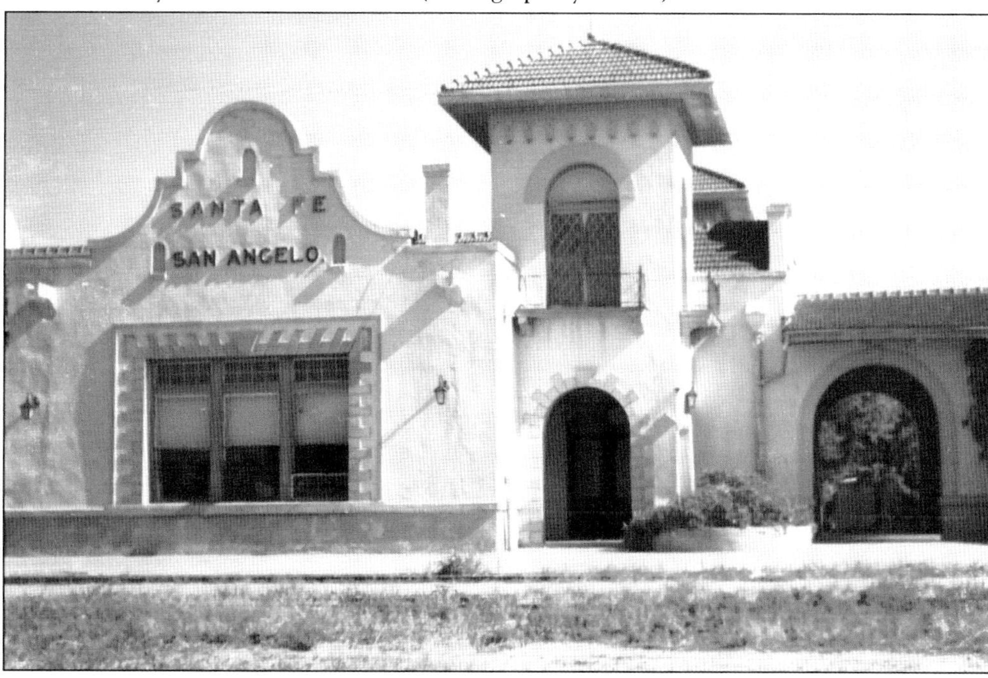

Catholic Outreach Service. On the site of the Santa Fe depot, the Catholic Outreach Service and Thrift Shop constructed a building with a facade that makes reference to the historic structure (pictured). Many communities lost their passenger depots as transportation patterns moved to individual cars. (Photograph by author.)

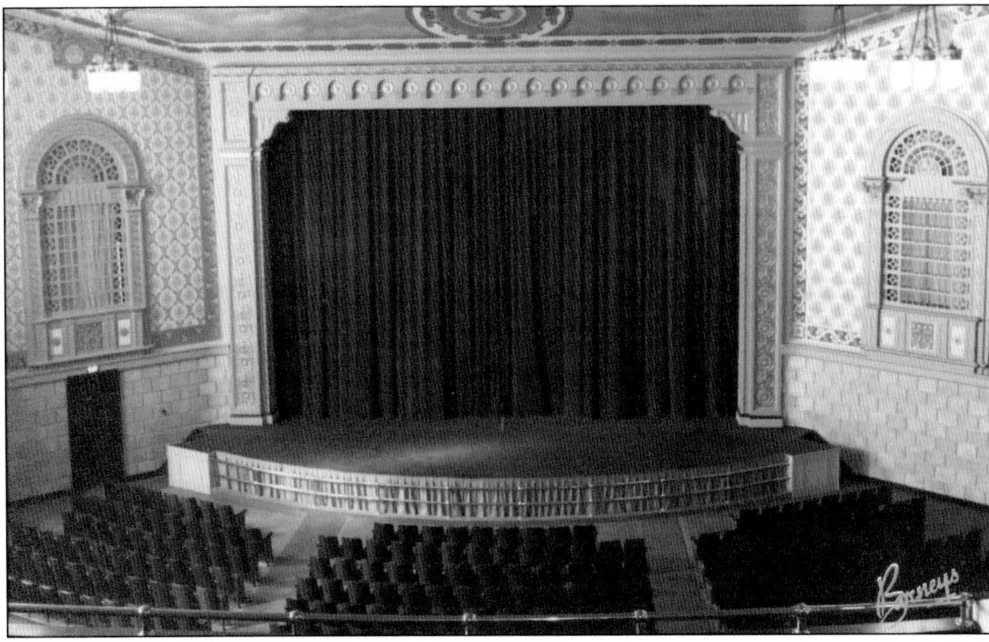

City Hall Auditorium. The San Angelo City Hall and Auditorium was designed in 1929 by Trost & Trost, an El Paso architectural firm. This picture was taken in 1984 after completing work on the auditorium. In 2009, city employees were moved to temporary offices to allow for rehabilitation/restoration work to commence on the city hall. The systems (electrical, plumbing, and heating and air-conditioning) needed replacement. Inappropriate modifications over the years were removed returning to its original 1929 appearance. The grand reopening occurred on October 18, 2012. (Courtesy of Barney's Studio.)

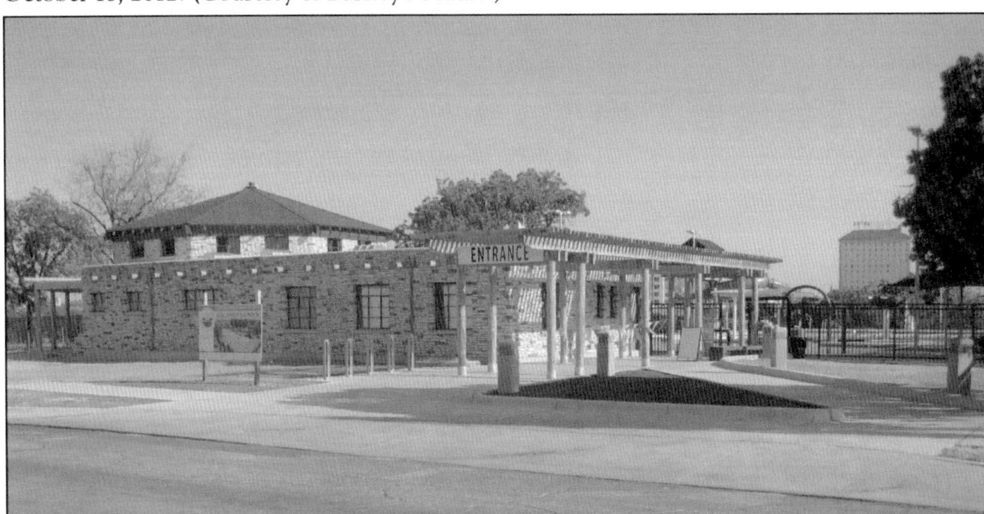

San Angelo Municipal Swimming Pool. After the first pool was washed away in a flood, the San Angelo Municipal Swimming Pool was a Works Progress Administration (WPA) project. Many people in town fondly remember spending summer days at this facility. In 2011, the City of San Angelo Recreation Division undertook a $3 million renovation of the municipal swimming pool and the exterior restoration of the historic pool building. The project was completed in time to be used during the summer of 2012. (Photograph by author.)

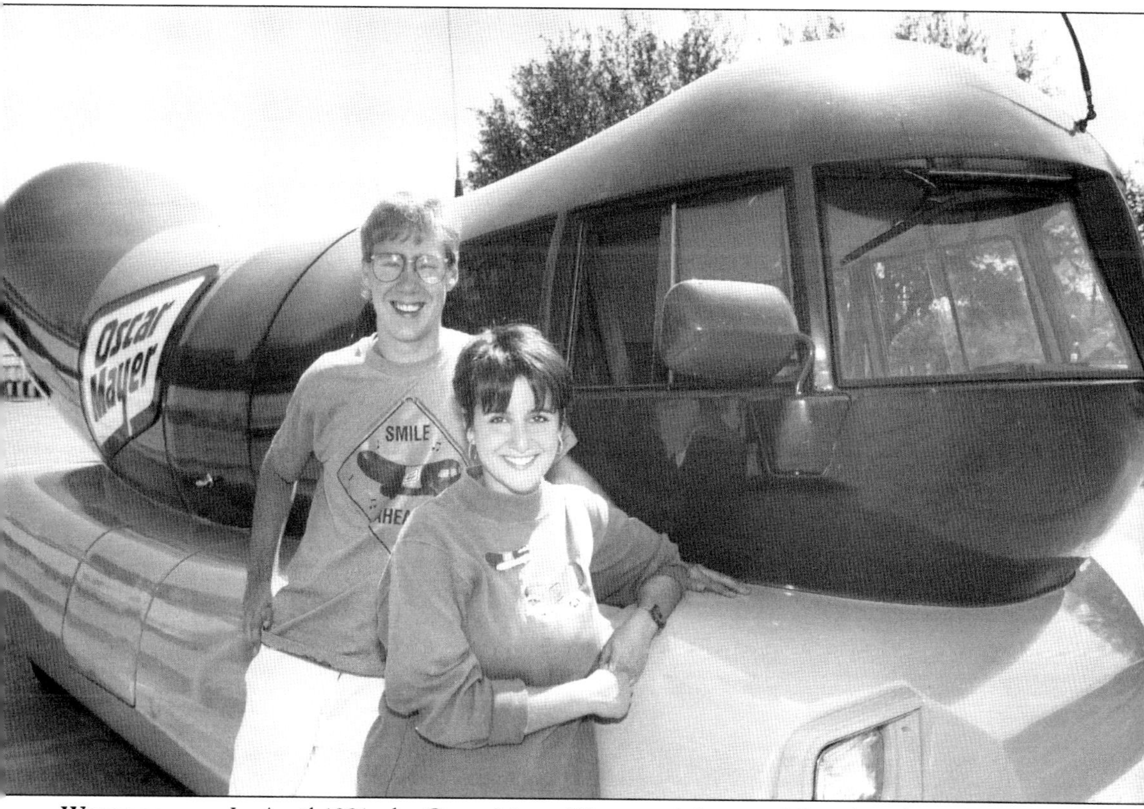

WIENERMOBILE. In April 1991, the Oscar Mayer Wienermobile visited San Angelo, and Russell Coy and Isabelle Ferrera posed in front of the vehicle. The first Wienermobile evolved from a design developed by Carl Mayer in 1936, and many different versions have been constructed over the years. In 1988, the company began the Hotdogger program, which allowed graduating college seniors to apply to drive the vehicles for one year. (WTC.)

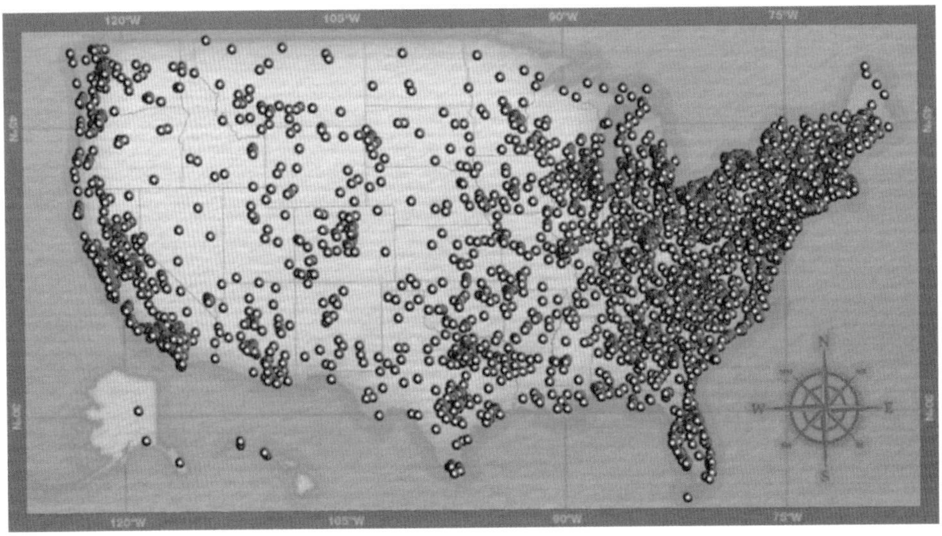